THE WOMAN IN THE VIOLENCE

# THE **WOMAN**
## IN THE
# **VIOLENCE**

Gender, Poverty,
and Resistance
in Peru

M. Cristina Alcalde

Vanderbilt
University
Press
NASHVILLE

© 2010 by Vanderbilt University Press
Nashville, Tennessee 37235
All rights reserved
First printing 2010

This book is printed on acid-free paper
made from 30% post-consumer recycled content.
Manufactured in the United States of America

Book design and typesetting by Judy Gilats

Library of Congress Cataloging-in-Publication Data
Alcalde, M. Cristina
The woman in the violence : gender, poverty,
and resistance in Peru / M. Cristina Alcalde.
        p. cm.
Includes bibliographical references and index.
ISBN 978-0-8265-1729-6 (cloth : alk. paper)
1. Women—Violence against—Peru—Lima.
2. Poor women—Peru—Lima.  I. Title.
HV6250.4.W65A499 2010
362.82'92098525—dc22
2010004902

*Para Joe y para nuestros hijos, Santiago y Emilio,*
*y para mis padres, Pilar y Xavier, con amor,*
*gratitud, y esperanza*

# Contents

# Acknowledgments

MY DEEPEST GRATITUDE goes to the women whose stories appear in this book, for sharing parts of their lives with me and providing me with the opportunity and trust to examine their experiences. Each of the women I met in Lima taught me something important about survival during especially difficult moments in her life, and I am forever grateful for that. I am also grateful to the shelter workers and other service providers who took the time to explain how things worked and discuss their experiences with me. The Centro de la Mujer Peruana Flora Tristán and the Peru section of the Liga Internacional de Mujeres pro Paz y Libertad (LIMPAL Perú) played a vital role in allowing me to conduct this research by providing me with the opportunity to affiliate with them and assisting me during my research.[1] I am especially grateful to Ana Güezmes at Flora Tristán for meeting with me during a preliminary research trip and discussing with me the possibility of focusing on domestic violence in Lima. I am also very grateful to Miryan Quispe at LIMPAL Perú for her early and ongoing assistance and support, and for her friendship.

Summer travel grants from Indiana University's Center for Latin American and Caribbean Studies and Department of Anthropology provided me with the time and funding to conduct preliminary research. A Fulbright Institute of International Education (IIE) grant and a summer Foreign Language and Areas Studies (FLAS) award supported me during the bulk of my field research in Lima, and a John Edwards Fellowship from Indiana University and a grant in women's studies from the Woodrow Wilson National Fellowship Foundation supported my writing. At Indiana University, Gracia Clark, Rick Wilk, Anya Royce, Arlene Diaz, and Helen Gremillion provided important feedback at different stages of the initial writing process. I am especially grateful to Gracia Clark and Rick Wilk for their encouragement. I am also grateful to Anne Pyburn and Jeff Gould for their early support of my projects and career.

When I returned to the United States from Peru, after almost two years away, the baby playgroup get-togethers with Emily Frank, Olga Kalentzidou, and Laura Campbell proved invaluable in helping me to develop my skills simultaneously as a new mom and a new writer grappling with many of the ideas in this book.

At Southwestern University, many people made it possible for me to work on earlier drafts of this book. I could not have found a more collegial and supportive environment in the Sociology and Anthropology Department. I am especially grateful to Melissa Johnson for her collegiality, support, and constant reminders to just say no when she knew I was preparing to take on too many projects. Her passion, friendship, and intellect are inspiring, and our conversations about research, family, and balancing the personal with the academic are always a pleasure. I am also very grateful to Maria Lowe—I could not have asked for a better chair and colleague my first year in the academic world—and to Sandi Nenga, for our regular chats as we began our careers at the same university. Eric Selbin also provided me with a warm welcome, and many stimulating conversations during my time at Southwestern. Jim Hunt, in his role as Provost, provided me with much-needed funding through summer travel grants to continue my research in Peru. My students at Southwestern inspired me to search continuously for ways to bring together my research and teaching. Laura Senio-Blair has been a constant source of support and friendship since we met, and our lives have paralleled each other's both in positive and challenging ways; even after we moved to different parts of the country, we and our families have continued to grow and remain close.

At the University of Kentucky, summer funding and time off from teaching during the 2008–2009 academic year made working on the revisions for this book possible. My Gender and Women's Studies colleagues—Susan Bordo, Joan Callahan, Deb Crooks, Patty Cooper, Srimati Basu, Lucinda Ramberg, Ellen Riggle, Jan Oaks, and Karen Tice—have all shown me incredible support and collegiality, and I am very grateful for that. Betty Pasley has also provided me with important assistance since my arrival at UK, as has Michelle del Toro, and my day-to-day tasks have been made more manageable because of their hard work. Susan Bordo offered me valuable comments early on in the book proposal process, and she and her family have accompanied us on many fun and relaxing evenings in the months during which I revised the book. Srimati Basu, Lucinda Ramberg, and Erin Koch provided me with important feedback on an earlier version of the Introduction, and with a very fun and tasty evening as we discussed it. I have also been fortunate to receive the support and guidance of colleagues such as Francie Chassen-Lopez and Sue Roberts: in spite of busy schedules and heavy workloads in their own departments, both have been generous with their time. I am also appreciative of Sarah Lyon's friendship. She and I have concurrently ventured into annual reviews, pregnancies, and balancing the caring for infants with the writing of books.

At Vanderbilt University Press, Eli Bortz's interest and enthusiasm encouraged me to develop this project further, and for that I am very grateful. I have also received insightful, stimulating, and very useful commentary from María Elena García and an anonymous reviewer. I appreciate the time and effort they put into this project. I would also like to thank Peg Duthie for her meticulous copyediting.

Last, but most importantly, I am forever grateful to my family who has supported and stood by me before, during, and after this project. My parents, Pilar and Xavier, made sure Joe and I had a home in Lima, and made not only my year of research but also the months I spent on bed rest after my research as comfortable as possible. They have been there for me in the United States, Peru, and everywhere in-between, and their love, interest, and involvement in my work and life have been constant and essential. I feel very fortunate to have them as parents. With her cooking and multitasking abilities, Margarita made coming home after a long day of interviews something to especially look forward to, and our conversations are something I always enjoyed. She is a central part of my Lima family. My siblings, Gonzalo and Gabriela, and I have been on many trips together between the United States and Peru, and even as our lives have led two of us to settle in the United States and one in Lima, our bond has helped sustain me both in times of field research and other moments in my life. Gabriela read and provided feedback on various parts of the manuscript throughout the years and I am grateful for that. The almost daily conversations I have with her and with our mother are constant reminders of the strength women are capable of and of the importance of love and friendship. My brother-in-law, Raymond, and nephews, Nico and Lucas, have been with me throughout various research and write-up stages, and have helped remind me of the importance of more fun and less stress. My parents-in-law, Paula and Dan, have been supportive of me and my research from very early on and have helped me in innumerable ways. Their love and support has been invaluable.

More than anyone else, my husband, Joe O'Neil, has been with me throughout the research process, and his companionship, love, and support have allowed me to pursue this and other projects that have made their way into our lives. Our older son, Santiago, was born in Lima after I completed the field research for this project and spent several months on bed rest. Developing my parenting skills as I sought to write this book was not without its challenges, but it is something I cannot imagine doing any other way now. Having Santiago's love, questions, hugs, kisses, and cuddles, as I sought to make sense of piles and piles of notes and interview transcriptions kept me grounded. Having him, and our life with him, reminds me of all the wonderful unpredictables in life and has helped me develop into the mother and scholar I am becoming today. Seven years later, as I prepare to send this manuscript to its publisher, I am within days of welcoming our second child, Emilio, into this world. I look forward to the love, questions, hugs, kisses, and cuddles he too will bring. And I hope that for them and for my nephews, the world they grow up in will be a less violent and more just one in which boys and girls, and women and men, can live more peacefully and with more tolerance.

# Introduction

∎ IT WAS A WARM, SUNNY DAY in February 2001 when twenty-six-year-old Ana found out she was expecting her third child. One week later, when she knew none of her neighbors were around to stop her or call her husband, she escaped. She took her children and left without telling her husband that she had become pregnant again as a result of his raping her. When she arrived at the shelter farthest from her house, Ana looked pale and tired, feeling sick from the pregnancy. It had been a long and tiring trip.

Ana spent her mornings at the shelter carefully plotting where to look for work in the city, strategically identifying places she felt fairly certain her husband would not visit in his search for her and the children. Before her daily job search, she completed her chores and played with her two young daughters, who relentlessly asked when they would see *papi* again. This was her third stay at the shelter in two years. From experience, Ana knew her husband would beat her, rape her, and lock her up if she returned home. She also feared the abuse toward the girls would escalate. When she arrived at the shelter, Ana had been determined to leave her husband permanently. After staying at the shelter for two weeks, she returned home.

Twenty-nine-year-old Daisy and her four sons were the only residents at the shelter after Ana and her daughters left. I had not paid much attention to Daisy until then, because I had been focused on keeping Ana and her daughters company, and on assisting Ana with finding a job. It had been a frantic search. On the day Ana left, the phone at the shelter was not working. Earlier that day, I had heard from an acquaintance who had agreed to hire Ana part-time to clean her house; this person had also agreed that Ana could bring her daughters to the house when she went there to work so that she did not have to worry about childcare. By the time I arrived at the shelter with the news, it had been three hours since Ana left to return to her husband.

Each time I visited the shelter, I stayed for several hours to contribute to its daily functioning and to meet women interested in discussing their lives with me. That day, after learning that Ana had gone home, I felt unsure about whether I could speak to other women about their experiences. I could not get out of my head the thought of what had just happened and the images of what I feared Ana was experiencing.

Just then, Daisy sat next to me on the dilapidated bench in the back patio. I turned toward her to offer an automatic, thought-less greeting, and noticed her almost toothless smile—the smile of a young, tired woman on whose life poverty and violence had left a heavy imprint. As we sat in silence for the first couple of minutes, the strong smell of her sweat and the dirty clothes she had been wearing for days brought me out of my self-absorbed daze. Then, without any prompting on my part, she began to tell me about her life—at first slowly, and then very quickly, as if to make certain she fit everything in before her time ran out: Daisy had left her partner over a month before arriving at the shel-ter. Since that time, she had stayed at another shelter and been homeless for several days. If she did not find a job and a place to live soon, she and her children would again be homeless.

At the shelter, each woman had a distinct life trajectory, yet all of the women I met there shared the urgent need for a job. Daisy's words made it very clear to me that she desperately needed a job—any type of job—and I told her about the job that had been intended for Ana. Daisy started the part-time work a few days later. On the days she did not clean, she strapped her youngest son to her back and sold candy on the streets and on buses. She slowly began to save money to leave the shelter. The money she earned was far from enough to provide for her four sons and herself, but it was a start.

I met Ana and Daisy during my first month as a volunteer and researcher at the shelter. Eight years have passed since our initial meetings. It is now impossible for me to think of Daisy as the almost toothless woman who sat beside me at a moment when I most wanted to be left alone. She has rebuilt her life sev-eral times over since our first meeting, and she has been patient and generous in sharing her experiences with me through the years. Her life is a constant reminder of the complex realities in a bustling urban center like Lima. These are realities in which we are all implicated—realities that remind us that in life things seldom go as planned. Since meeting Ana, I have also met many more women who struggled to leave their partners and, after periods at shelters or other temporary housing, returned to their partners.

How did each of these women end up living with an abusive man? What conditions in their lives and in the broader environments in which they live made it possible for each woman to stay with her partner, and, in Ana's case, why did she go back to the man who abused her and her daughters? How were Ana and Daisy able to survive and protect themselves and their children from their partners' violence, and, in Daisy's case, from broader forms of violence after leaving her partner and the shelter? This book engages with this set of questions by situating at its center the life stories of poor women who experience multiple forms of violence, especially intimate partner violence. It brings to the forefront women's everyday experiences before, during, and after abusive relationships to explore structural, institutional, and interpersonal manifestations of violence as these intersect with women's identities as poor, nonwhite, rural migrants with little or no formal education living in Lima.

In examining women's experiences in Lima, however, this book does not purport to represent the lives of all poor, indigenous, or mestiza Peruvian women. I met women of white, indigenous, mestiza, and Afro-Peruvian descent from Peru's coastal, Amazonian, and highland regions in Lima. Most of the women I interviewed, however, were either born in rural communities in the highlands or in Lima from families originally from the highlands. In privileging the experiences of first-, second-, and third-generation migrants from the highlands, I did not deliberately exclude women from any background or region. Instead, this book reflects the population of women I encountered predominantly in Lima shelters—and, to a lesser extent, in reproductive health clinics, through women's nonprofit organizations, and via personal contacts—because these were the main spaces available through which to contact women in abusive relationships.

The glimpses I have provided of Ana and Daisy's experiences are only small pieces of lives that are remarkably normal, and remarkably brutal. Based on these pieces, we know very little about Ana and Daisy's multidimensional identities, the specific context

COLOMBIA

ECUADOR

AMAZON

Iquitos

Marañón

BRAZIL

Cajamarca

Marañón

Trujillo

Huallaga

Ucayali

PACIFIC

OCEAN

P E R U

LIMA

Ayacucho

Apurímac

Urubamba

Cuzco

BOL.

Lake Titicaca

Arequipa

0    100    200
miles

CHILE

Amazonian Jungle

Highlands

Coast

Map compiled by Donna Gilbreath, cartographer

*A map of Peru and its three popularly identified regions.*

in which their struggles take place, how others view and treat them, and how these women's very personal struggles intersect with impersonal social structures. It is only by learning more about Ana and Daisy's lives and the settings in which these lives unfold that their actions can be better understood. For example, in understanding what resources are available to Ana, Daisy, and other women seeking to leave abusive relationships in Lima, it is important to know that almost a decade before Ana and Daisy arrived at the shelter, Peru passed a family violence law and set up women's police stations to respond to women's complaints of violence. Shelters were opened in the 1980s and 1990s, but because they are not supported by the state, and because they suffer from chronic understaffing and lack of resources, they must restrict each woman's stay to a maximum of fifteen days in order to provide adequately for residents and meet the high demand for their services. Two weeks is not enough time to begin to recover from emotional and physical wounds, find a job and a place to live, save money, and file all the paperwork necessary to begin trial proceedings.

*Situating Women's Lives: Methods and Identities*

My field research and the writing of this book have been informed by four broad goals. The first goal is to dispel myths regarding women, particularly poor women, in abusive relationships in Peru. In debunking myths regarding poor, indigenous, and mestiza women in abusive relationships in Peru as passive and accepting of violence as a form of affection, I hope also to contribute more generally to challenging stereotypes applied to women in abusive relationships elsewhere. In local and global media coverage of domestic violence, women in domestic violence situations are commonly depicted as passive, or somehow miraculously able to leave abusive partners and start new lives without any assistance (Alat 2006; Alcalde 2009; Sokoloff and Dupont 2005:53).

My second goal is to address and help bridge the gap between activist practice and academic research on domestic violence. On the one hand, I identify tensions between academic research and activism. On the other hand, I suggest that for academics, engaging in on-the-ground advocacy with women in abusive re-

lationships and activists working on domestic violence issues—
and acknowledging our role in the creation and maintenance
of tensions between advocacy and academic research—leads
to a more holistic view of women's experiences and of the cultural, social, and political worlds in which individuals live and
research is conducted. In viewing the worlds in which wom-
en's lives unfold more holistically, academic research becomes
well-positioned to identify both the small and larger contexts
in which the racism, discrimination, and multiple forms of violence that inform women's lives take place. For scholars, engaging with activists and in advocacy allows us to learn from—as
well as provide support for—actions by and on behalf of women
in abusive relationships.

A third goal is to show multiple dimensions of women's lives.
In doing this, I move beyond the dominant exclusive focus on
episodes of physical violence in domestic violence literature to
provide a multifaceted picture of women and the violence they
experience. My title, *The Woman in the Violence*, is a play on
Emily Martin's *The Woman in the Body* (1987), a book that provides a cultural analysis of how scientific representations de-
tach women's bodily functions and biological processes from
women's experiences of these functions and processes. Similarly, studies of violence commonly make individual women invisible by focusing instead on acts or episodes of violence as if
these acts and episodes could be detached from the complicated
lives of individual women and the sociocultural worlds in which
these take place.

The fourth goal is to contribute to a theory of everyday resistance that speaks directly to the experiences of women in abusive
relationships. The theorizing of women's acts of resistance needs
to be made context-specific by being culturally sensitive and by
taking into consideration broader structures of gender, class, and
ethnicity as well as the material constraints within which women
strategize. In discussing everyday resistance, I move beyond the
simplistic dichotomy of staying versus leaving in relation to wom-
en's options in coping with abusive relationships.

By engaging with these four goals, this book contributes to
the continued opening of the anthropological imagination to the
widespread phenomenon of violence against women. In particular, my hope is that the book will illustrate how ethnographic

attention to the details of everyday life and feminist anthropology's concern for problematizing power relationships among
researcher and researched make anthropology particularly well-
positioned to contribute to knowledge on women's experiences
of violence outside as well within the home.

The main vehicle through which this book explores poor
women's lives are the stories of thirty-eight women in Lima. I
agree with Abu-Lughod that "focusing on individuals encourages familiarity rather than distance and helps to break down
'otherness' for it not only corresponds to the way we ordinarily
think about those close to us in our everyday world, but also actively facilitates identification with and sympathy toward others"
(1993:29). In inviting readers to explore women's lives in specific
situations and moments in Lima, my goal is to make familiar the
largely unfamiliar setting in which the women's lives unfold, and
to make visible the invisible and intersecting forms of violence
that women experience. I thus examine the "invisible cage" of
fear and intimidation that informs women's lives in ways that
move beyond the physical bruises on women's bodies (Adams
1995:57–58). I more broadly examine the structures of violence
and domination that perpetuate fear but which are difficult to see
due to misrepresentation, victim-blaming, and indifference by
those with more power (Adams 2000:54, 78).[1] I frame women's
intimate partner violence experiences in the context of women's
lifespans rather than as isolated phenomena. I also draw on the
experiences and lives of many women rather than on a single life
story to depict more accurately the variation in women's experiences, challenge images of homogeneity associated with women
in abusive relationships, and underscore the varied intersections
of gender, class, and race and racism in women's experiences of
violence within a single city.

Ana and Daisy are among the thirty-eight women and five
service providers I interviewed during my year of fieldwork in
Lima in 2001–2002. I stayed in touch with several women over
the next two years, but distance and safety considerations made
long-term contact very difficult or unviable. Women must be
careful not to leave traces of where they are going to avoid being found by abusive partners. Over the next several years, I
continued to conduct research on violence against women in
Lima during annual summer trips, but I lost touch with more

and more of the women I originally interviewed, even as I added interviews with other women. Eight years later, I continue to communicate regularly with one service provider, with Daisy and her sons, and with two other women. I visit the shelter at which I met Ana and Daisy during my annual trips to Lima.

With the exception of three group interviews, my interviews with the women were one-on-one and were based on an unstructured guide that allowed for additional sessions to elicit the women's life stories. During all of the interviews, I took notes, and in all but four cases I used a tape recorder. After women leave the shelters to rebuild their lives in this city of almost ten million people, little is known about them. The absence of follow-up programs, the scarcity of telephones (and money to use public telephones) in many of the neighborhoods to which women move, and the constant movement from one place to another before finding a permanent place of residence are all obstacles to finding out what happens after a woman leaves a shelter.

All of the women I interviewed had been involved in heterosexual relationships. Most of the women had filed or attempted to file at least one domestic violence complaint, and they were separated or in the process of attempting to separate from a husband or partner. Three women had never attempted to file charges against their partners. The average age of the participants was thirty-seven, and their ages ranged from nineteen to sixty-eight. Most of the women were born outside of Lima, and over half were born in rural communities in the highlands. Six of the women were native speakers of Quechua, the most widely spoken indigenous language in the Andes. Of the twenty women who provided information about their partners' level of education, two women had more schooling than their husbands, ten had the same number of years of schooling as their husbands, and eight had fewer years of schooling than their husbands. Of these eight women, two had never attended school. With the exception of two or three cases, there was no significant variation in the racial identity that would have been ascribed to the women and their partners by other Peruvians in public spheres in Lima: in the majority of cases, the women and their partners would have been identified as indigenous or mestizo. Of the participants involved in relationships, 29 percent were legally or religiously married and 71 percent were *convivientes* (common-law spouses).[2]

Analysis of court records of domestic violence cases, shelter records, and articles and editorials on women, violence, and gender roles in three popular Peruvian newspapers complemented these interviews.[3] I also volunteered at a shelter for the duration of the fieldwork as a form of reciprocity and to further research violence against women. Like other shelters in Lima, the shelter was significantly understaffed and relied primarily on the staff's volunteer work, creativity, and goodwill toward residents for its continued operation. I contacted the majority of the women I interviewed through three shelters and one community reproductive health clinic. I also contacted some women through women's organizations and personal acquaintances. The interviews at the clinic and through personal contacts allowed me to include women whose experiences often remain invisible to researchers because the women do not use institutions intended specifically for domestic violence, such as family violence sections in police stations and shelters.

Each interview lasted from one to four hours. Before beginning an interview, but after obtaining informed consent, I asked each person what name she would like me to use when referring to her experiences. In the majority of cases, the names the women chose are the ones that appear in these pages. In a few cases, I changed the names to avoid confusion, because several women requested the name "Maria" and did not offer alternative names at the time of the interview. The names that appear in this book are pseudonyms in all but three cases. In two of these cases, the women asked me to use their real names, and using their names will not endanger them, their families, or their communities. In the third case, the director of the shelter is a well-known public figure in her community. Changing her name would not conceal her identity as a shelter director and political figure. When I refer to her experiences as a woman in an abusive relationship, however, I use a pseudonym because the details pertaining to those experiences earlier in her life may not be as publicly known.

Regarding the interview process, Patai asks, "Of the frequent claim that the interview process, as conducted by feminists, is empowering in that it 'gives a voice' to those who might otherwise remain silent, one may well ask: is it empowerment or is it appropriation?" (1991:147). This question is particularly relevant to my research in Lima, where my middle-class status contrasts to the poverty experienced by the women I interviewed. While there is no easy answer to this question, I suggest that on many occasions, the interview process constituted both appropriation and empowerment. Although what I and the women I interviewed have gained from the research process is qualitatively and quantitatively different, I do not consider the interview and research process as a whole to be exploitative. It was only through negotiated appropriation of the women's information that I was able to analyze the information, and to work with the women to make the information more widely available to others and contribute to a better understanding of women's experiences. I needed the information the women shared with me for my research, but I also believe many women felt empowered during the interview process.

"Empowerment" is commonly used in development and feminist scholarship, yet it is rarely defined in much detail. Existing definitions of "empowerment" include "the process by which those who have been denied the ability to make strategic life choices acquire such an ability" (Kabeer 1999:437) and giving "voice to those who might otherwise remain silent" (Patai 1991:147). "Empowerment" has also been defined as Freire's (1973) consciousness-raising among disenfranchised individuals whereby individuals and groups develop political efficacy and collectively work toward broader change (see Reidner 2004). According to these definitions, "empowerment" implies some sort of reflection, agency, and action.

In discussing the interview and research process, I employ the term "empowerment" to refer to the women's increased sense of control, knowledge, and feelings of safety during the interview process or as a result of it. The women wanted to speak, and in most cases I was one of an extremely small group of people they had spoken with about their abuse. Several women had not previously been able to discuss their experiences of violence in a safe setting, or to have their experiences validated by someone who listened to them without limiting what they said to fit predetermined questions (as women may be asked to do when filing domestic violence complaints). The women expressed satisfaction at being listened to, and the process of listening to women whose experiences and surroundings had prevented them from having their feelings validated by others was a positive aspect of the interview process. The interviewees decided and controlled what to tell me, and in this sense, within the space of the interviews, held some power to shape their own voices.

I also understood empowerment to be a possible result of knowledge gained through providing lists of resources appropriate to each woman's circumstances, such as shelters, police stations, psychologists, nonprofit organizations, and clinics, because these resources could further support a woman's desired outcome in filing a claim or temporarily leaving: protecting herself and her children from an abusive partner. A safe space for discussion and knowledge of available resources did not, however, necessarily lead to a woman's permanent escape from situations of intimate violence.

Material aspects of the research and of my relationships with its participants included covering the costs of the women's transportation to and from the interview sites and of work time lost as a result of participation in interviews, small gifts of food, clothes for children, and money for medicines and food. I also became more personally involved in four cases, and I continued to be in touch with those individuals for approximately three years after the completion of my initial fieldwork.

Because I was dealing with sensitive topics, and it was important to build trust and understanding, I did not interrupt the women when they discussed experiences unrelated to what I had originally anticipated as part of my research. Although I referred to a thematic guide that had been initially written and subsequently memorized during interviews, the actual themes discussed varied depending on the person. A person might not want to talk about her childhood, but a question or comment regarding her employment might trigger a flood of information about other significant aspects of her life I had not anticipated. In the end, it was precisely the flexibility of the interview process and of listening to someone's life story that allowed me to understand better the women's experiences in the context in which they had taken place.

On the one hand, my selection of which specific moments from the women's lives to analyze and my interpretations of the women's experiences significantly shape the voices heard and the themes illuminated through these pages, making it entirely possible that a woman who discussed her life with me may "talk . . . in a way she never talked before" (Behar 1993:19) in this book. In this sense, it is a shame that "once discourse becomes text, its openness as dialogue, together with its evocative and performative elements, are lost" (Salazar 1991:98), both in spite and because of my best efforts to transmit the women's experiences to readers in an understandable way that is also true to the women. It is thus important for me to recognize and claim responsibility for the fact that as the interviewer and transcriber, I am in a position of power and that this power includes "some form of invention, transformation" of the women's voices (Mallon 2002:18). On the other hand, it is equally important to recognize that the voices of the women who shared their lives with me are also heard in this book and shape it, because the women selected what I was and was not told and how each of the aspects of their lives they selected to discuss with me was presented to me.[4]

Within Western feminist ethnographic practices, giving voice to ordinary people and critically examining the power relations inherent in the research process has been a central concern (Behar 1993, 1996; Behar and Gordon 1996; Lamphere, Ragoné, and Zavella 1997; Visweswaran 1994). In Latin America, *testimonios*—narratives based on the lives of subaltern individuals and mediated through collaborations with individuals with more social power and status—became popular in the 1970s as a way to break silences, give voice to marginalized individuals or groups, speak to and envision a new future, and exalt the connection between the personal and the political (Sternbach 1991:92). A *testimonio* seeks to make abstract notions such as violence and poverty real to readers by showing the effects of these notions in the life of an individual, most often that of a woman. Yet, the goal of giving voice to the "voiceless" often results in the scholars' own interpretations and biases simultaneously "getting out of the way and getting in the way" (Lather and Smithies 1997:xiv) of representing others accurately.

This book draws on women's words and experiences to break silences about violence against women and illuminate connections between women's personal experiences and broader political, social, economic, and cultural contexts, yet it does not adapt to the testimonial genre. There exist at least two important differences between testimonial literature and this book. First, this book focuses on the lives and experiences of many women rather than the life of just one individual or family. It does this to depict accurately the variation in women's experiences, to challenge images of homogeneity in regard to women in domestic violence situations, and to highlight gender, class, and ethnicity dynamics in Lima. Second, while I emphasize women's experiences, I also believe those experiences are better understood when presented along with—and sometimes embedded in—analyses of wider historical, economic, ethnic, gender, and class dynamics. Rather than presenting the women's words as the readers' main source of information, I draw on multiple sources to present specific aspects of the women's experiences. *The Woman in the Violence* builds on previous work in testimonial literature, but it is more an analysis of women's experiences than primarily a description of these experiences.

Significantly, although this book does not adhere to the testimonial genre, some of the dilemmas inherent in attempting to represent the multidimensional lives of the women I interviewed can be better illustrated through a brief discussion of one of the controversies on the politics of representation that preceded my work and is relevant to it. Rigoberta Menchú's *testimonio* on the plight of the K'iche' Indians of Guatemala, collected over the course of several days in Paris by Elisabeth Burgos in 1983, has been the subject of one of the more recent, heated debates on the politics of representation and truth-telling within anthropology and Latin American studies.[5] In 1992, Menchú received the Nobel Peace Prize for her work in advocating for indigenous rights and against human rights abuses during the Guatemalan civil war (1960–1996). Six years later, the *New York Times* published a front-page story that alleged that parts of Menchú's *testimonio* were lies. The source for the story was U.S. anthropologist's David Stoll's book, *Rigoberta Menchú and the Story of All Poor Guatemalans* (1998), in which he accused Menchú of fabricating and misrepresenting parts of her life—a life Menchú proposes is representative of "a whole people" (Burgos 1983:1).[6]

There are three issues connected to the difficulty of "giving voice" to others by both the researcher and the researched that may be better understood through the Menchú controversy. The first issue is the role of the researcher in shaping and presenting the voices of others. In attempting to provide a space for Menchú's voice, Burgos provides very little information about her own role in shaping the narrative. Yet, in the prologue, we discover that Burgos corrected Menchú's grammar, omitted what she considered to be excessive repetition, and organized Menchú's narrative according to themes Burgos identified. What may first appear as Menchú's narrative in reality also bears the mark of Burgos even as Burgos purposely omits herself from the narrative. Similarly, in this book, I edit the women's words and organize the appearance of these words according to the book's themes. This book thus includes the women's voices and, undeniably, my own. In situating my voice and providing space for the discussion of how my identity shaped my relationships with women—especially in Chapters 1 and 6—I am guided by work in feminist anthropology that appeared, for the most part, after the Menchú-Stoll controversy and which recognizes the importance of self-reflexive accounts to examine one's positionality as an important factor in discussing how researched-researcher relationships are forged (Behar 1993; García 2000; Zavella 1997).[7]

Second, Menchú's *testimonio* underscores that marginalized peoples speak both through silences and words (Sommer 1994). Even as she narrates intimate details of her life and community, Menchú's deliberate silences demonstrate her agency in deciding what to reveal and what to keep hidden from Burgos and readers. She states, "We Indians have always hidden our identity and kept our secrets to ourselves" (Burgos 1983:20). Menchú's refusal to tell all is a reminder that marginalized peoples may also control what information outsiders have and do not have access to.

The women I interviewed also decided what information I, and therefore readers, could access, through their decisions to share or hide specific life experiences. For example, after an especially long and emotionally charged first interview, one woman asked if I could return to her house the following week so she could tell me more about her life. Upon my arrival at the house the following week, the woman decided she no longer wanted to speak with me about her life. In this, as in other cases, an initial agreement to speak did not guarantee continued participation in the project or that everything about a woman's life would be revealed. The women retained, throughout their relationships with me, the ability to limit my, and readers', access to their lives. Recognizing that the people whose lives we wish to represent have voices, therefore, necessitates acknowledgment that our portrayals of them will be necessarily partial and limited even as we focus on the multidimensionality of their identities, as I do here, and even after repeated interviews and relationships with the researcher that last for years, as was the case with several women I interviewed.

Third, Menchú's *testimonio* underscores the difficulty of representing others from the same group or community. Throughout her narrative, Menchú emphasizes that her experiences are those of her community and that she is speaking for her people. By contrast, among the women I interviewed in Lima, none claimed to speak for a broader community. The women believed other women had similar experiences of abuse but did not believe they could represent all poor women in abusive relationships or all women in abusive relationships from their communities of origin. More broadly, the women did not represent a specific indigenous group. In fact, migration to the capital had in many cases resulted in the loss of indigenous self-identification. Rather than seeking to represent others, the women I interviewed shared their experiences to raise consciousness about domestic violence among women of diverse backgrounds. Thus, the stories presented in this book should not be assumed to be representative of all indigenous women, of all indigenous migrant women, or of all poor women.

Across Latin America it is difficult to find a woman's published testimonial, including Menchú's, which does not mention domestic violence. This book acknowledges the importance of *testimonios* in bringing attention to questions of how to understand and represent women's multifaceted identities, particularly as these intersect with different forms of violence. Close readings of *testimonios* of Latin American women (for example, Alvarado 1987; Barrios de Chungara 1978; Behar 1993; Brown 1991; Burgos 1983; Mallon 2002; Tula 1994) and more specifically of Peruvian women (Denegri 2000; Miloslavich and Moyano 2000; Valderrama and Escalante 1986; Zamudio 1995) make clear that women's lives are shaped by factors that include but are not limited to gender. These factors, which include race, migration, cultural background, class, and kinship ties, have been absent from feminist analyses of domestic violence until recently.

Martin's *Battered Wives* (1976), in which men's violence against their wives is presented as a means of maintaining dominance within marriage, was one of the first published feminist analyses of violence against women. Building on this, as well as later work that emphasized the traditional feminist perspective that men's violence is a result of gender inequality in society (e.g., Yllö 1993), more recent feminist works have expanded their approach to domestic violence by examining how factors such as race, sexuality, immigration, cultural background, class, and kinship ties also affect women's experiences in abusive relationships (see Abraham 2000; Das Dasgupta 2007; Sokoloff and Pratt 2005; Van Vleet 2008). The ethnographic approach I take in this book draws on insights from women's life stories to contribute further to this more recent intersectional body of feminist literature.[8] *The Woman in the Violence* presents a grounded account of the multidimensionality of women's identities and experiences of violence by focusing on women's everyday lives both as witnessed by me and as narrated in women's life stories, complemented by my and others' observations of the spaces in which women live. This approach is further strengthened by an analysis of my relationships to the women whose lives I write about, thereby providing a holistic portrayal of the places and women in these pages.

It is through this grounded, intersectional, and reflexive approach to women's identities and experiences that the violence that permeates most if not all aspects of women's lives becomes visible. Yet, to define the women I interviewed solely as battered women or victims of violence provides an incomplete image of their lives, because it misses other significant identities that inform their experiences and which were both discussed by the women in their life stories and witnessed by me. Women are all too frequently treated by others in accordance to stereotypes and beliefs associated with the identities women claim or are attributed by their partners, employers, shelter workers, police officers, and other service providers. The women I interviewed are wives, mothers, daughters, sisters, workers, migrants, *dirigentes* (community leaders), and clients. These roles often conflict with one another. As wives, women want to fulfill what they perceive as their obligations to their partners. As mothers, they want to protect their children from their abusive partners. This often means going against their partners' wishes and demands. Similarly, as wives, some women must demonstrate submissiveness and dependence. As workers and *dirigentes*, they demonstrate leadership, assertiveness, and independence. Regardless of the role a woman seeks to satisfy at any given point, when her partner is violent toward her, all her roles become more difficult to fulfill.

Based on women's rich lives, I understand women's multifaceted identities as "both imposed and self-made, produced through the interplay of names and social roles foisted on us by dominant narratives" (Alcoff 2004:3) and that "a single subject can no longer be equated with a single individual" (Moore 1994:55). That identities are hybrid, relational, fluid, and situational (Glissant 1989) has been documented by researchers working in various regions of Latin America (de la Cadena 2000; Frye 1996; Gould 1990). I found, for example, that a woman who de-emphasizes ethnic markers such as language and dress to avoid being treated as an *india* (literally, an indigenous woman; however, the term is commonly used as an insult to denote inferiority and backwardness) in public urban areas may nonetheless be labeled *india* and treated according to the negative connotations of the word by her partner in the intimacy of her home.

### Approaching Violence against Women

Available country studies from around the world indicate that between 10 percent and 50 percent of women are abused by an intimate partner and that the perpetrators are almost exclusively men (WHO 2001). In spite of its prevalence, violence against women continues to be a hidden pandemic. It was not until the 1980s that violence against women was first discussed as a human rights violation, and not until the 1990s that it began to receive more focused attention from social scientists (Merry 2006:21; Pleck 2004:xix).

Domestic violence can include intimate partner violence, child abuse, and elder abuse, all of which occur in the context

of heterosexual as well as same-sex relationships. This book focuses on intimate partner violence among heterosexual couples
to reflect the experiences of the women I interviewed.[9] My general approach to women's experiences builds on and complements a Violence Against Women (VAW) approach and contributes to an ecological framework. VAW is one of two dominant
approaches in the study of domestic violence. The second dominant approach is the Family Violence (FV) approach. FV, the
earlier of the two approaches, is commonly associated with
the works of sociologists Straus and Gelles (1988, 1990). It is
characterized by viewing the home as a normatively safe place,
employing a quantitative approach and neutral tone, and, for
the most part, not taking gender into consideration.[10] VAW, associated with the work of Dobash and Dobash (1979, 1992), is
a feminist critique of the FV approach. It rejects the idea of the
home as a normatively safe place, emphasizes gender as well as
power in gender relations, and uses qualitative and quantitative
methods. It also addresses the importance of identifying women
as the primary targets of violence in the home, thereby challenging the appropriateness of a neutral tone.[11]

Explanations of domestic violence have long been debated,
and few approaches fully embrace the complex realities in which
intimate partner violence unfolds or note how cultural beliefs interact with structural and individual factors. Although cultures
constantly change, "culture" is too often singled out as the explanation for violence against women, especially when referring
to non-Western settings (Narayan 1997). The ecological perspective (Heise 1998) proposes that we recognize factors that
contribute to women's experiences of violence in at least four
overlapping dimensions in an individual's life: personal history,
microsystem, exosystem, and macrosystem. "Personal history"
refers to experiences that shape an individual's responses to
environmental factors, such as witnessing violence as a child.
"Microsystem" refers to the "immediate context in which the
abuse takes place" (264), such as familial relations and relationships with peers. "Exosystem" includes formal and informal
structures within the community that affect a person's ability
to respond to violence, including neighborhood resources and
social networks. The "macrosystem" is the broadest level and
represents societal and cultural norms and policies. While I do

not restrict myself to using the terms Heise suggests or neatly fitting ethnographic details into an ecological model, readers will find that my identification and discussion of elements in the broader cultural, social, economic, and political contexts that inform women's lives correlate with Heise's general proposal for approaching violence. Readers may also note that my emphasis on connecting lived personal experience to broader forms of structural power and violence follows the feminist tradition of linking the personal to the broader political, social, and economic context.

## Domestic Violence in Peru and Beyond

The term "domestic violence" originated in the early 1970s as a "code for physical and emotional brutality within intimate relations" (Ferraro 1996:77–78). Like other forms of domestic violence, intimate partner violence results from multiple contributing factors and takes various forms in different cultural settings as well as within the same cultural setting. For the purposes of this book, I use "intimate partner violence" and "domestic violence" interchangeably. Men's intimate violence against women includes physical, psychological, economic, and sexual violence. Physical violence may affect women through bruises and broken bones and through miscarriages due to severe blows and forced household labor. Psychological violence includes insults and humiliation and may affect self-esteem through insults about women's worth as women, wives, mothers, and members of a particular culture or ethnic group. Economic violence includes withholding household income from women as well as the destruction of women's property and it affects women ability to secure resources to adequately ensure their well-being and that of their children. Sexual violence threatens women through forced sex, a sense of loss of control over their bodies, and the risk of unwanted pregnancies and sexually transmitted diseases.

Intimate partner violence rates vary by Latin American country from 10 percent to 70 percent (Buvinic, Morrison, and Shifter 1999). Although intimate violence affects women of all socioeconomic backgrounds, "the presentation of 'good behaviour' in public often hides the violence that is taking place behind closed doors" (Seidler 2005:xiii) among the middle and upper classes, for whom wealth may purchase increased privacy. Most often only violence among poor people or, less frequently, in celebrity cases, is publicly scrutinized.[12]

In Peru's capital, 51 percent of women have experienced physical and sexual violence (Güezmes, Palomino, and Ramos 2002). Although I will focus only on women in Peru, and more specifically on poor women in Lima, it is worth noting that women of all backgrounds in other Latin American countries also experience intimate partner violence and that domestic violence is recognized as a problem throughout the region. In Chile, 25 percent of women have been victims of what is commonly known as *la violencia privada* (the private violence) (McWhirter 1999). In Mexico, up to 40 percent of women are abused by their partners (UNICEF 2001). In the 1990s, almost all Latin American countries established national women's offices to focus on eradicating violence against women. In 1993, Peru became the first Latin American country to pass laws specifically on domestic violence. By 2000, and largely as a result of pressure from women's groups, the majority of the countries in the region had passed domestic violence legislation (Jelin and Muñoz 2003).

Men's violence against women also crosses national, cultural, social, racial, and economic borders beyond Latin America, and affects approximately one in three women worldwide (Heise, Ellsberg, and Gottemoeller 1999). In spite of the prevalence of intimate partner violence against women cross-culturally and of efforts to denounce violence within specific communities, anthropologists have for a long time shied away from studying and at times even from acknowledging intimate partner violence. This silence regarding intimate partner violence against women in the anthropological record risks perpetuating simplistic notions of cultural relativism ("it's part of their culture") and may contribute to the secrecy surrounding men's violence against their intimate partners, as well as to the uncritical blaming of women for staying in abusive relationships.

Historically, anthropologists have tackled issues of ethics, advocacy, and violence. Anthropologists have focused on intergroup violence, human rights violations, and genocide in Latin America and elsewhere (see Gill 2004; Goldstein 2004; Goldstein 2003; Green 1994; Hinton 2002; Maalki 1995; Nordstrom and Robben 1995; Robben and Suarez-Orozco 2000; Scheper-

Hughes 1995; Scheper-Hughes and Bourgois 2004; Schmidt and Schroeder 2001; Sluka 1999; Theidon 2004: Tishkov 2004). We have been particularly attentive to the abuses of states against indigenous populations, land struggles and rights, autonomy and self-determination, and socioeconomic inequalities. Feminist anthropologists have examined gender inequality and human rights issues across cultures, "condemning acts of violence against women. They have opposed acts of aggression that occur not only on battlefields elsewhere or on the twilight frontiers of inner cities but also closer to home, on university campuses that can be hotbeds of perilous masculinities" (Aggarwal 2000:25). Unfortunately, we have not focused on violence *in* the home until recently, nor have we focused on how broader forms of violence impact women's experiences of intimate violence.

Although anthropologists often stay with families during fieldwork, very few analyze the existence of conflicts resulting in violence within families. Up to the late 1980s, "anthropologists had ignored or had glossed over with throwaway one-liners a topic of great importance" (Counts, Brown, and Campbell 1999:xvii). Anthropologists have provided several explanations for why domestic violence is ignored in final published accounts of fieldwork. One reason is that to expose the "dark side" of a culture is to exploit the hospitality offered by the host community. Second, and on a more pragmatic level, there is the fear that if an anthropologist publishes research on domestic violence, she or he will be denied permission to return to the field. Third, there is the concern that informants may be punished if others find out that they have spoken to an outsider about violence in the home. Fourth, there is the argument that by focusing on domestic violence, anthropologists would be imposing their own political agenda on other societies and that the results might be harmful to those societies (Counts, Brown, and Campbell 1999).

Reflecting on his long-term fieldwork among the poor in Peru, Mitchell concedes that "anthropologists are neither prosecutors nor judges," yet he goes on to note that cultural relativism does not, and should not, be used as an excuse by anthropologists to avoid making "informed ethical judgments" regarding the knowledge and behaviors we encounter during the research process (2006:166). Scheper-Hughes goes a step further by proposing that anthropologists embrace the role of witness because witnessing "positions the anthropologist inside human events as a responsive, reflexive, and morally committed being, one who will 'take sides' and make judgments" (1995:419). I have found that once I listen to stories of intimate partner violence and see the effects of violence on women's bodies and lives, it is impossible to avoid judging violence against women as harmful not only to women, but also to the children and men with whom they share their lives and ultimately to society as a whole. Were I to discuss the lives of the women I interviewed in Lima without providing in-depth analyses of the ways in which intimate violence permeates so many aspects of women's lives and is connected to broader forms of violence, I would present an incomplete and distorted portrayal of the women I met. Had I not volunteered at a shelter or become involved in the lives of several women who allowed me to take part in their lives, I would have been an observer, not a witness or an ethical researcher.

Beginning in the 1990s, anthropology's attitude toward domestic violence slowly shifted as a growing—yet very small—number of feminist anthropologists began to publish critical ethnographic studies identifying and examining men's violence against women in the communities in which they conducted fieldwork and from multiple perspectives (see Adelman 1997; Counts, Brown, and Campbell 1999; Gutmann 1996; Hautzinger 2007; Lazarus-Black 2007; McClusky 2001; Merry 2006; Plesset 2006; Snajdr 2005; Van Vleet 2008). The published ethnographies, however, tend to focus on domestic violence among people in distant places rather than within the anthropologist's own society. Given this pattern of looking away from our own societies to study violence, we must be careful to avoid assuming that the reason for studying violence in a specific, far-away place is that violence is especially prevalent there and, by contrast, insignificant and not worth studying in our own societies.

As Plesset notes, violence "exists in many different forms in many different parts of the world" (2006:4), including anthropologists' own societies and families. Hautzinger (2007) underscores the need to recognize the existence of violence in our own societies even as we learn about violence elsewhere by briefly discussing violence in her hometown of Denver, Colorado, in an ethnography of violence and women's police stations in Brazil. This book shifts the anthropological analysis of violence to my hometown of Lima. Yet, even as I focus on a familiar place, the dynamics of class, race, place, and educational status within Peruvian society, and my life and career outside of Peru, among other markers of difference, also complicate my approach to violence in Lima. I will return to this point in Chapters 1 and 6.

When anthropologists have focused on domestic violence, several problems have arisen. In spite of the many forms of violence (e.g., sexual, psychological, physical, and economic) that men perpetuate against women, studies have emphasized physical violence at the expense of acknowledging other forms of violence. At the level of practice, police in charge of receiving domestic violence claims demand to see signs of physical violence and may ignore women's attempts to place claims for other forms of violence. Physical violence may be the most visible form of violence, but it is by no means the only or most common one. Physical violence often occurs in combination with other forms of violence, such as threats and insults, forced sex, and denial of money with which to feed and clothe children.[13]

The women in Lima repeatedly said that all forms of violence affected them profoundly. When a woman's partner routinely threatens and insults her, he damages her self-esteem, and the effects of harsh words may take much longer to disappear than the marks left by physical blows. When he forces her to have sex, he violates her body and mind and risks transmitting diseases and impregnating her. When he prohibits her from working or going to school and refuses to give her money for their family's basic needs, he forces her into a state of dependence, prevents her from acquiring knowledge, and increases her and the children's risk of malnutrition and health problems.

In compiling narratives of state violence in the Southern Cone, Robben (1996) emphasizes that the ideal encounter between ethnographer and narrator is "built on empathy, trust, and openness" (75) and notes that "highly emotional issues that touch the basis of our common humanity" (81) may arise during interviews. Similarly, interviews with intimate violence survivors are ideally built on empathy, trust, and openness, and their narratives typically include highly emotional issues. Although I did not ask for descriptive details of violent episodes, many women provided graphic details of emotionally charged episodes of physical, sexual, and psychological violence.

As an overarching approach to a closer understanding of women's experiences as survivors, and as a way of getting to areas that touch our common humanity, I find anthropologist Linda Green's 1994 description of the routinization of fear and terror particularly insightful. Her approach, developed to discuss state violence in Guatemala, captures the feelings and circumstances women repeatedly described to me in discussing the routine presence of their partners' intimate violence in their lives in Lima. I purposely employ Green's approach to state violence to examine intimate violence as a way to emphasize the connections between different forms of violence and their similar effects on women's lives. In writing on peace in a feminist context, Enloe declares that "peace" refers to "women's achievement of control over their lives" (1987:538). This sort of peace is difficult to achieve both in times of war, as described by Green, and in times of peace, as exemplified by women's lives in Lima.

Acknowledging the difficulty of expressing fear and terror in words, Green suggests that "fear is an elusive concept; yet you know it when it has you in its grips. Fear, like pain, is overwhelmingly present to the person experiencing it, but it may be barely perceptible to anyone else and almost defies objectification" (1994:230). She then explains that for those who experience terror, "terror's power, its matter-of-factness, is exactly about doubting one's own perceptions of reality. The routinization of terror is what fuels its power. Such routinization allows people to live in a chronic state of fear with a façade of normalcy while that terror, at the same time, permeates and shreds the social fabric" (1994:231). The fact that the terror women experience is invisible to, or ignored by, outsiders makes the terror even more persistent for women victims of state violence in Guatemala and for women experiencing domestic violence in Peru.

Karen was one of the women I interviewed. Although she was only twenty-four years old, the following statement expresses her feelings after being abused by her partner for approximately four years: "When I was younger I was convinced and said that I would never allow my partner to hit me or to yell at me. . . . [now] I feel like a boring old woman. . . . I would like to walk and walk and never return and climb up the tallest hill and scream."

To outsiders, and even to her extended family, she and her partner had a good relationship. Karen and other women lived fear and terror through a "façade of normalcy" because they saw no way out; some rightly believed their partners' violence would escalate if their plans to escape were discovered. The women in Lima lived knowing that their husbands could attack and seriously hurt them at any moment. Some women drew parallels between their husbands' violent tempers and a bomb. Both could go off at any moment, regardless of the women's behavior. The comparison to a bomb that can go off at any moment is particularly noteworthy because for the women I interviewed, bombs constituted an everyday reality during the 1990s in Lima. The group Shining Path, discussed in more detail in the following chapter, planted bombs throughout Lima during this period, and it would be difficult to find a Peruvian living in the city at the time who did not personally hear one of the middle-of-the-night bomb explosions or see the aftermath of a bomb placed close to their neighborhood or place of work. Thus, for the women I interviewed, bombs associated with political violence were not an abstract idea but a reality that they also connected to the potentially lethal explosions of their partners' tempers. The routinization of terror that the women lived during periods of heightened political violence—as well as in their homes before, during, and after periods of political violence—prevented the women from fully enjoying their lives, expressing themselves, and enjoying their time with their children.

*Latin American Men, Peruvian Men, and Violence against Women*

In my research on the intersections of multiple forms of violence in women's lives, I did not include interviews with men.[14] In these pages, most of the references to men are about men who employ violence within intimate relationships, and these men's voices are heard mostly through the narratives of the women I interviewed. In spite of my focus on the women's experiences of men's violence, however, this book does not dispute that "though most killers are men, most men do not kill or even commit assault. Though an appalling number of men do rape, most men do not" (Connell 2000:22). Most men do not beat their wives or partners. However, most of the perpetrators of violence against women, and men, are men, and this has a significant impact on the lives of the women I interviewed.[15] Additionally, women experience a range of physical, psychological, sexual, and economic forms of violence that are generally less visible than homicide, physical battery, and rape, and these everyday forms of violence affect women's well-being in multiple ways. The women whose lives I discuss in the book resist not only battery and rape but also these other everyday forms of violence, suggesting that battery and rape should not be considered the only or most important markers of men's violence against women, and that most men need not to be batterers or rapists to be violent toward women.

Although this book does not focus on men, it recognizes the variability of men's behaviors cross-culturally as well as within cultures. Moore's point that "a single subject can no longer be equated with a single individual" (1994:55) applies to Peruvian men as much as it does to the Peruvian women whose lives this book examines. Thus, my references to men's use of violence should not imply that I advocate an understanding of these or any other men as unitary beings whose identities can be summarized through such labels as "batterer" or "abuser."

This section cautions readers against a one-sided and limited view of men, particularly poor Andean men, given that most of the book examines poor indigenous and mestiza women's experiences as informed by the attitudes and actions of poor Andean men who employ violence against them. In contextualizing the heterosexual relationships of the women I interviewed, I have found the literature on Latin American, and more specifically Peruvian, masculinities I describe in the following paragraphs very useful.

In Latin America, research on men and masculinities has significantly increased since the 1990s and has predominantly come from anthropology, sociology, and social psychology (Viveros 2003:29). Paz's 1950 interpretation of the dominant form of masculinity—the distrustful and distant macho who attempts to overcome internalized feelings of powerlessness through violence and whose identity has been largely shaped by the trauma of the Conquest—continues to be a popular understanding of Mexican as well as Latin American masculinity. More recently, however, scholars have developed approaches that consider both the historical context of a society and the many changes that have taken place over the past several hundred years, revealing a rich tapestry of diverse masculinities. In the case of Mexico, a study focusing on men's views on sexual and reproductive health brings men's diverse voices to a topic commonly reserved for women (Gutmann 2007). In Peru, a study examining men's experiences as perpetrators of violence and men's beliefs regarding nonviolence points to men's varied perspectives on violence as a characteristic of masculinity (Ramos 2006).

In recognizing diverse forms of masculinity and experiences in Latin American men's lives, Connell's 1987 differentiation between "hegemonic" and "subordinate" masculinities underscores the differential access men have to power according to their social position. The hegemonic Latin American construction of masculinity is one of dominance over women. This model facilitates discrimination against men who do not satisfy the ideal of the dominant, heterosexual man, as well as against women who challenge this form of masculinity (Movimiento Manuela Ramos 2003:19). Given this form of masculinity, "to deny the existence of a cult of 'exaggerated masculinity' in Latin America would be inappropriate, when there is so much evidence of male domination and/or mistreatment of women" precisely as a result of this hegemonic construction of masculinity (Chant and Craske 2003:16). At the same time, the practices and beliefs of men in diverse social positions and settings challenge the view of "a biologically fixed master pattern of masculinity" that is inherently violent (Connell 2000:22). When Mirandé asked Latino men in the United States to describe what it meant to be macho, the responses ranged from negative characteristics such as violence, irresponsibility, disrespectfulness, and selfishness to positive characteristics such as courage, responsibility, and respect (1997:78). In his description of a low-income community on the outskirts of Mexico City, Gutmann (1996) noted that masculinities vary according to class, age, region, ethnicity, and stage in life, and introduced us to men who hold and play with their children, are responsible, and view fatherhood as one of their most important lifetime commitments.

Research on masculinity in Peru similarly underscores variations according to "racial, ethnic, class, regional, institutional, and other categories" (Fuller 2003:136; see also Barrig 1982; Callirgos 1996; García Ríos and Tamayo 1990; Guzmán and Portocarrero 1992; Movimiento Manuela Ramos 2003; Nencel 2000; Ramos 2006; Ruiz-Bravo 2001). In referring to hegemonic masculinity in Peru, Peruvian anthropologist Portocarrero aptly reminds us that "since childhood we hear the idea that the worth of a man depends on his ability to impose himself through violence and that women exist to please and serve. This would be the reality and whomever would try to deny this would be a coward or a dummy or, in either case, a homosexual" (2007:220). Not surprisingly, Nencel (2000) found that the men she interviewed in Lima emphasized their power and assertiveness by describing their sexual encounters with women in terms of conquests and possessions. More recently, young men in rural areas stated in workshops that they "feel and see themselves [as] less 'machista' than men in previous generations" (Movimiento Manuela Ramos 2003:39).

In the Peruvian urban context, gender roles vary largely by class. Fuller (1996) finds that traditional gender roles are most strict in the upper and lower classes, and most malleable in the middle classes. However, in contrast to the lower classes, where physical strength is given great importance, in the upper classes physical strength is not considered to be as important as responsibility or work in defining what it means to be a man.

Based on interviews with men from the middle and lower classes, Fuller (2003) further identifies three different configurations of masculinity in the Peruvian context: the natural, the domestic, and the outside or public. Natural masculinity refers to men's genitalia, (hetero)sexuality, and physical strength, all three of which are understood by men and women as innate and foundational to being a man. The domestic construction of masculinity prioritizes family, marriage, and fatherhood. The outside or public form of masculinity emphasizes men's activities in the world outside the home and is associated with virility, politics, competition, rivalry, and seduction. Men may identify with different forms of masculinity at different stages of their lives. For example, a man may prioritize public forms of masculinity during his teenage years and domestic forms of masculinity after becoming a father. Significantly, across these varying constructions of masculinity, men from the lower and middle classes overwhelmingly emphasized that "control over the sexuality of the spouse and authority over her and over the whole family is a key component of masculine identity" (147)—a point that is further illustrated through the women's narratives in the following chapters.

For a man from the lower or middle class, the race of his partner may play an especially important role in the construction of his gendered identity, and this too is a point emphasized by women's narratives of intimate violence, particularly those discussed in Chapter 2. Portocarrero suggests that "Peruvians tend to reject all that is indigenous and to believe we are all the more valuable the more white and Western we appear" (2007:223). Fuller's interviews with middle and lower-class men (2003) allow us to take a step further into men's preferences for intimate partners to see how these structural preferences also function at the microlevel. According to Fuller's interviews, these men prefer women with lighter skin. Similarly, in defining masculine beauty, "for most of the men of the popular sector interviewed, a handsome man has white skin, blond hair, and blue eyes" (141). However, in comparing themselves to these whiter, more Western men, "the men from the popular sectors, and those with Indian or black ethnic or racial features, can claim to be more masculine than the men of the dominant racial or ethnic groups. Their attractiveness lies in their bodies, in the very essence of their masculinity, whereas the attractiveness of men of other races resides in their beauty, a quality symbolically associated with femininity" (141).

Beauty, then, is symbolized by lighter skin, and this is what Fuller suggests men from the lower classes desire in an intimate partner. Fuller introduces us to men who are more concerned with defining themselves as men through their physical strength than through their physical beauty. And, as the women I interviewed make clear, this emphasis on manhood through physical strength may facilitate violence against women. In workshops in rural areas, Movimiento Manuela Ramos found that men most frequently cited women's failure to fulfill domestic roles properly as the motivation behind the men's use of physical violence, and that the suspicion of infidelity could be sufficient to trigger abuse (2003:41).[16] Women's narratives further support these findings for Lima.

During my research, building trust and placing myself "inside human events as a responsive, reflexive, and morally committed being, one who will 'take sides' and make judgments" (Scheper-Hughes 1995:419) included working at shelters and with women who narrated, sometimes in excruciating detail, the violence they experienced at the hands of their partners. The powerful details drew me in emotionally to each woman's experiences and, together with my ongoing interactions with the women and their children, and my work at shelters, increased my empathy for her. Thus, it was not only beyond the scope of this study but also subjectively difficult for me to consider taking on the task of interviewing abusive men and being open to their narratives in the same ways I was open to the narratives of women during the same research period. At the same time, I never lost sight of the fact that the portraits of the men in the women's narratives were only part of individual identities that, like those of the women whose lives I was so generously allowed to examine, are multifaceted and complex. In this sense, this book serves as an important building block for future studies that will directly include men's experiences to provide a more integral understanding of men and women's lives as they intersect with violence.

## Intersectionality, Violence, and Resistance

In listening to women discuss their experiences of discrimination, family life, and public and intimate violence, many differences among women emerge. Age, length of time in a relationship, place of origin, native language, and educational background are among the differences in women's lives. Yet there are also common themes in women's lives, and this book emphasizes two of these interrelated themes in women's life stories: survival and resistance. This section introduces the principal theoretical frameworks that underpin my analysis of women's experiences of survival and resistance: intersectionality, the regionalization of race, institutional and structural violence, and everyday ambivalent resistance.

Crenshaw (1991) coined the term "intersectionality" to refer to the ways in which women's identities and experiences of oppression are founded on multiple intersecting markers of difference, such as gender, race, and class.[17] Similarly, hooks (1989) conceptualizes how systems of domination and ideologies of superior and inferior within these systems affect the lives of women of color in referring to what she describes as "interlocking systems of oppression." An intersectional approach allows us to address differences among women as we explore how the interrelationships between gender, family role, class, race, and ethnicity, among other social divisions, inform women's lives and are interpreted by others in ways that result in the oppression of particular women.

Daisy is not simply a mother one day, a wife another, an indigenous woman on a third day, and a battered woman on a fourth day. All of these identities intersect on an everyday basis in Daisy's life. These identities inform the choices available to Daisy and the decisions she makes and are embedded in the social divisions within which her life unfolds and which others call upon to oppress her. When Daisy is angrily told to go back home to the highlands by strangers on the streets in Lima, she knows she is being discriminated against, but it is not clear whether she is mistreated because of how others identify her based on her gender, her ethnicity, her poverty, her work (selling candy), or a combination of two or more of these. While the possibilities for different identity markers within a specific life cycle are almost endless, women's lives cannot be reduced to a laundry list of identities precisely because these identities are multiple, fluid, and changing. I focus on those identities that most often appear in women's narratives by describing how women experience specific intersecting identity markers in specific times and places rather than attempting to undertake the impossible task of documenting and including all of the identities in each woman's life.

The regionalization of race, and the resulting association of various negative connotations with women from the highland region, also serves as a backdrop for understanding the everyday experiences of many of the women I interviewed. On the one hand, "Indianness" is constituted of multiform, multispatial, multitemporal identities that should not be reduced to a single classification or to being localized in an absolute manner (Mires 1991). On the other hand, *indio* and *india* are commonly used as pejorative terms, and Indianness and deficient education have historically been associated with rural spaces in Andean nations. In the case of Peru, the nation is commonly understood to be made up of three regions: *la costa* (the coast), *la sierra* (the highlands), and *la selva* (the Amazonian jungle). The *sierra* and *selva* are imagined as poor, backward, and racially inferior precisely because Lima, and the coast in general, is perceived as more powerful and white. Whites and mestizos are associated with the *costa* and indigenous people with the *sierra* and *selva*. In referring to those who come from the *sierra*, where most of the women I interviewed traced their descent, the term *serrano* popularly denotes both place of family origin (*sierra*) and race (*indio*).

In Lima, self-identified whites may refer to indigenous people from the highlands as *serranos* regardless of how long they have lived in Lima. In other words, in Lima, where the women I interviewed live, *serrano* refers to perceived racial and ethnic distinctions as much as it does to geography. Negative characteristics such as backwardness, brutality, and ignorance are commonly attributed to indigenous people of the largely rural highlands. The experiences of women in this book illustrate how women may be perceived to embody the negative characteristics assigned to their region of origin in spite of the varied ways in which the women self-identify and the number of years they have lived in Lima, and the consequences for individual women of these associations between regions, races, and bodies.

Explaining away the suffering and misery of others by associating suffering with cultural difference is a form of essentialism, yet this essentializing often goes unquestioned (Farmer 2004) even as it transforms into racism. In Peru, the racist and sexist saying *"más me pegas, más te quiero"* (the more you beat me, the more I love you) is popularly used across socioeconomic urban classes to refer to *amor serrano* (highland love) and is facilitated by the regionalization of race and culture. The idea behind this saying is that physical, psychological, and sexual intimate partner violence against women from the *sierra* need not be addressed by state policies because these practices are based on customs and traditions. This saying implies that *serranas* enjoy violence because of their race and culture. According to this logic, women are complicit in their own suffering as members of a backward race and culture tied to a specific region, the *sierra*.

The regionalization of race also results in the concentration of power and resources in urban mestizo and white areas, thereby restricting access to basic services in rural indigenous areas. The unequal access to legal, educational, social, medical, and economic resources that the women I interviewed experienced are all examples of the structural violence that prevents women from living violence-free lives. Structural violence is indirect violence embedded in unjust societal structures that are hegemonic and taken for granted by those in power and that negatively affect those in marginalized spaces. In 2000, the maternal mortality rate in the highly industrialized and wealthy capital of Peru, Lima, was 52 per 100,000 live births, while in the more rural and poor Andean city of Puno, where fewer medical resources are available, the maternal mortality rate was 361 per 100,000 live births (Physicians for Human Rights 2007). Structural violence results in suffering inflicted by poverty, exclusion, and other forms of social injustice (Anglin 1998; Farmer 2004; Galtung 1969). It is often invisible because it is founded on the ideas and actions of many, rather than a single individual or institution, yet it is even more widespread than institutional violence. Institutional violence refers to how institutions we take for granted can also be sites of violence, specifically through the policies they enforce and how service providers within them interact with individuals seeking assistance. Chapter 5 discusses the institutional violence women experience in police stations, including specialized women's police stations.

Within the constraints of structural, institutional, and intimate violence, "women are not totally powerless. In fact, women have proven incredibly capable of exerting agency even within the most constrained social conditions" (Heise 1997:422). Yet women's routine contestation of intimate violence is rarely acknowledged, and staying or leaving continue to be the only two viable options women are popularly believed to have (Mahoney and Yngvesson 1992). Women in Lima are not merely victims of men's violence but also social and cultural agents who challenge men's actions and beliefs. An understanding of women's lives and experiences cannot only focus on the aspects that oppress them but must also include an analysis of women's attempts to transform aspects of their environments that harm them.

To recognize women's agency and strategies of resistance in the space between staying and leaving, I define "resistance" as including overt and covert strategies for contesting what the affected person perceives as unjust or harmful—strategies that range from the conscious performance of assigned cultural categories to hitting back to temporarily leaving. Through everyday resistance, women seek short-term solutions by contesting specific situations or behaviors while not necessarily challenging the broader structures that undergird abusive behaviors. As I discuss in Chapter 5, the most public forms of resistance are leaving and filing a domestic violence complaint. However, filing a domestic violence complaint is an especially difficult and discriminatory process and leaving is not always realistic. In this context, analyzing what women do or abstain from doing to survive or contest their partners' violence on an everyday basis offers valuable insight into women's power, experiences, needs, and desires.

In Lima, the forms of women's everyday resistance I examine are numerous and likely to continue to increase. They include not cooking; secretly using birth control; secretly undergoing sterilization; refusing to have sex; employing silence to curb a partner's power; hitting back; telling the husband's family about the abuse; verbally responding to the husband's ethnic slurs; temporarily leaving; secretly working; taking steps to prevent children from witnessing their father's violence; encouraging daughters to finish school and be financially independent so they will not have to depend on a potentially abusive man; secretly collecting copies of important documents and money in preparation for leaving; intervening in other homes when violence erupts and calling the police; and going to newspapers to denounce institutional abuse.

Women employ these strategies of resistance to survive violent episodes and contest their partners' power over them. Yet these forms of resistance and the beliefs that inform these actions may also reify sexist, classist, and racist practices that dominate Peruvian society and facilitate violence against women. Thus, while it is important to include aspects of women's experiences that are hopeful in writing about violence against women (Hautzinger 2007:31), I also dedicate a significant amount of space in this book to discussing the limits of women's resistance, to ground my analysis of women's experiences in their complicated social and cultural worlds.

If there are generalizations that I make regarding women's everyday resistance in Lima, they are that resistance is varied and ambivalent, and that women's strategies are often directly tied to their roles as mothers (I return to the latter point in Chapter 4). As Ortner has suggested in her review of research on resistance, "Individual acts of resistance, as well as large scale resistance movements, are often themselves conflicted, internally contradictory, and affectively ambivalent" (1996:287). Others have pointed to the inherent ambiguity in various forms of gendered resistance that, in using dominant frameworks to express disagreement, ultimately reinforce existing gendered power relations (Bordo 1993; Lewin 1993). In Lima, although women seek to resolve specific conflicts with their partners through resistance, not all women who resist disagree with overarching ideas regarding gender roles. When a husband hits his wife because she did not cook an acceptable meal, she may in fact agree that she should be cooking meals acceptable for him, but resist him because he did not provide her with enough money to purchase ingredients for such a meal. When another husband pressures his wife to have intercourse, she may in fact believe that he has the right to expect intercourse on demand, but resist him because she does not want to rear more children in poverty. That same woman may later acquiesce to her husband's demands for intercourse while at the same time resisting his efforts to control her body and reproduction by secretly undergoing sterilization or using another form of contraception.

In examining women's resistance within domestic violence situations, I suggest that accommodation of dominant values or behaviors, or of an abusive partner's demands, should not be viewed as the simple acceptance of dominant ideals or of the partner's power. A closer look reveals that accommodation and resistance may be nearly inseparable in some cases, as acts of resistance may include accommodation, and accommodation may include resistance. Thus, in some actions, "what appears to be accommodation is itself a form of resistance," and accommodation of some mainstream ideals may be a tool with which women resist broader forms of mainstream discrimination (Anyon 1983; Olmedo 2003:376) even as these actions reproduce yet other forms of oppression (MacLeod 1992, 1993), a point I discuss further in Chapters 2, 4, and 6.

In underscoring ambivalence and accommodation in women's acts of resistance, I seek to address and contribute to calls to de-romanticize resistance (Abu-Lughod 1990). On the one hand, in interpreting various forms of women's resistance as ambivalent, I make visible very creative and courageous forms of action that allow women to survive and defend themselves. On the other hand, I point out that resistance is not independent or outside of the power it seeks to change, and that it does not always mean getting rid of or transforming power completely (Abu-Lughod 1990:47, 53) or avoiding future violence. As Gordon (1996) emphasizes, resistance should not be equated with victory. The women I interviewed attempted to change the practical dynamics of men's domination to tolerable levels, sometimes through partial accommodation of men's expectations. At the same time, partly due to earlier gender socialization, many women continued to believe in the broader forms of power that permit the domination of women by men and men's violence against women, which are reinforced by schools, the media, government workers, families, and friends.

As Abu-Lughod (1990) points out, in ethnographic research, using power as a diagnostic of resistance can be difficult: how and where do we find the resistance to these forms of power? In my analysis of everyday forms of agency and resistance, I follow Abu-Lughod's suggestion to take the inverse of Foucault's "where there is power there is resistance" (1978) as a way to acknowledge and examine women's resistance. By identifying women's forms of resistance before the forms of power, I am better able to acknowledge the institutions and structures that facilitate violence against women and in which women's lives are embedded.

Scott's now-classic approach to resistance (1985) has been the subject of various debates, criticisms, and reevaluations (Hart 1991; Ortner 1996; Sivaramakrishnan 2005); I find parts of the original framework especially worth critically engaging with in my attempts to understand and de-romanticize women's experiences of violence and resistance in Lima. In his work on peasants in Malaysia, Scott argues that the poor are not duped or manipulated by the ideology of the rich. They see through the ideologies of the rich and, realizing that a revolution or other forms of rebellion would be bloody and dangerous, they opt for safer, subtle everyday forms of resistance such as foot dragging, gossiping, theft, and false compliance. This form of resistance "prevents the worst and promises something better" (1985:350).

Scott's emphasis on covert everyday forms of resistance may not be the best tool with which to analyze resistance as a whole in Latin America, given the various overt forms of collective resistance that have and continue to take place through social movements and armed revolutions in the region, but the utility of Scott's framework of resistance to the study of women's experiences within intimate relationships is worth exploring. Women in violent relationships must often feign complete compliance with their partners' demands on an everyday basis in the hopes of avoiding violence and surviving. Many women also rightly believe that leaving is extremely dangerous and could be bloody, and so employ everyday forms of resistance while they prepare and wait for a suitable moment to leave, or instead of it.

Scott's work on resistance focuses primarily on class as a structure of inequality. In the cases I discuss, we must also take into consideration gender, race, place, and the intimacy of the home as spaces of oppression. In emphasizing these structures in my discussion of resistance, Stokes's work on political ideologies and behaviors in a shantytown in Peru (1995) proves to be particularly relevant. Stokes problematizes Scott's findings by arguing that in some cases it is better to acknowledge both the persistence of hegemony and an emerging counter-hegemony in the minds of the poor than to assign "being duped" if not to the poor then to the rich. In the case of abusive relationships, an emphasis on ambivalent resistance allows us to move beyond the simple dichotomies of acceptance versus resistance and staying versus leaving to take into account both women's individual actions and the broader social context in which they take place.

Since the publication of Scott's work, cross-disciplinary studies have further explored and applied the concept of resistance to subjects as diverse as hairstyles (Kuumba and Ajanaku 1998), windsurfing (Wheaton and Tomlinson 1998), poetry (Abu-Lughod 1986), and spirit possession (Ong 1987). Over a decade ago, Brown decried the fact that "resistance and hegemony [have] come to monopolize the anthropological imagination" (1996:729) and that this has led not only to stimulating

critical analyses but also to the "indiscriminate use of resistance" (1996:730) within the discipline. Many studies call upon
the concept of resistance, but as Hollander and Einwohner note
in their cross-disciplinary review of resistance, it is also the case
that "many writers seem to invoke the concept of resistance
in their titles or introductions but then fail to define it or to
use it in any systematic way in the remainder of their writing"
(2004:534). Today, as in the past, there is widespread disagreement over what constitutes resistance.[18]

I share Brown's concern over the fetishizing of "resistance"
as a catch-all term, but as my discussion of resistance makes
clear, I also advocate the continued exploration of the concept
of resistance, and find it especially applicable to certain cases of
intimate partner violence. While leaving abusive relationships
may be possible for some women, societal pressures, lack of institutional support systems, and economic need make it impossible for many others to leave. We know very little about what
happens on an everyday basis when women stay, and it is in
this space that the study of resistance and ethnographic attention to the details of everyday life become especially significant.
In considering everyday forms of resistance, we better position
ourselves to see change where many believe there is no change
or desire for change, and to understand the complex ways in
which women's intimate lives intersect with broader social divisions and power structures.

*Book Organization*

This book travels to the more intimate spaces in which the lives
of poor indigenous and mestiza women unfold in order to understand these spaces and to examine the broader structures
that maintain and produce oppressive conditions. To examine
the experiences of women in situations of violence, *The Woman
in the Violence* is structured in three parts to correspond to
women's experiences before and during intimate abuse, while
attempting to leave, and after leaving abusive relationships.
The focus throughout the chapters remains on how violence
is constructed by and shapes the experiences of women in the
realm of the everyday, and on the links between intimate and
broader forms of violence.

Part I, "Violence and Everyday Resistance in Women's Lives," includes Chapters 1, 2, and 3. Chapter 1, "Life in the City: Lima, Its Possibilities, and Its Discontents," invites readers to explore the cultural, social, and political contexts in which women's lives unfold and the interconnections between different forms of violence in the capital. The chapter pays special attention to connections between political and intimate forms of violence, examining how the racism and inequality inherent in varying forms of violence permeate women's everyday lives. It also briefly discusses my own positionality and relationship to the women I interviewed—as a middle-class feminist anthropologist from Lima educated, working, and living in the United States—as a way to situate further my perspectives on the book's themes and within the Peruvian context.

Chapter 2, "Reproducing Structural Inequalities within Intimate Relationships," focuses on the regionalization of race to examine the reproduction of social divisions and discrimination based on gender, class, race, and place of origin within abusive relationships. It is guided by Virginia's life story, which includes a vast number of examples of how she has dealt with gender, race, and class-based discrimination inside and outside of her relationship. Discussions of the life stories of two other women, Racquel and Inés, further suggest that in the most intimate of spaces, the Indianness attributed to women by their partners may be a significant factor in the violence some women experience.

Chapter 3, "Women's Bodies, Sexuality, and Reproduction," examines one of the most contested and violent terrains within abusive relationships: women's bodies, as well as the meanings and practices attached to them. The chapter discusses marital rape and other forms of sexual violence. It also examines women's secret use of birth control and sterilization as strategies of resistance that allow women to protect their bodies and health against a backdrop of multiple oppressions and restricted access to resources. It brings to the forefront women's experiences and desires within intimate relationships in Lima in the context of sexual abuse.

Part II, "Leaving the Relationship," includes Chapters 4 and 5. Chapter 4, "Families, Children, and Mothering," discusses the varying roles a family can play in a woman's life and in her

ability to protect herself and her children from an abusive partner. It also examines the relationship between motherhood and
women's everyday resistance. The chapter is based on the life
story of twenty-six-year-old Jimena. It analyzes how a woman's
three families (family of origin, nuclear family with her partner,
and family by marriage) affect her decisions and her ability to
cope with and leave an abusive relationship, and women's dilemmas and conflicts as they balance their different roles as mothers, wives, daughters, and workers.

Chapter 5, "Resources (Un)Available: Institutional Aid and
Institutional Violence," discusses legal frameworks for domestic
violence and shifts the focus to institutions outside of the family
and to service providers within these institutions to explore how
these institutions both assist and injure women during women's
attempts to access needed services. This chapter approaches
women's struggles to access external resources as overt forms
of resistance to men's violence. Institutions that are explored include specialized women's police stations, conciliation hearings,
and shelters. This chapter suggests that women's interactions
with existing resources are part of a larger web of structural violence in which women's lives unfold in Peru, and that women's
interactions with the police may play a significant role in prolonging women's abuse.

Part III, "Rebuilding Lives," consists of Chapter 6, "The Everyday Experiences and Dangers of Starting Over," and "Con-
clusions: Representing the Woman in the Violence and Approaching Violence in Women's Lives." Chapter 6 examines how
articulations of gender, race, and class continue to influence the
lives of women and their children after the women leave abusive relationships. Daisy's life story, collected between 2001 and
2008, guides the chapter and provides a longitudinal view of
women's experiences after escaping abusive relationships and in
maneuvering Lima's multiple systems of oppression. Data from
an interview with Daisy's teenage son, Yonatan, provides a com-
plementary perspective on the intersections of different forms
of violence in the lives of families in which the mother and children were once abused. Issues discussed in the chapter include
the effects of poverty on the lives of women and their children;
women's fear of homelessness; gang violence; and difficulties
in securing employment before and after leaving an abusive re-

lationship. Daisy's experiences may be interpreted as a success story because of the obstacles she and her sons overcame. Her experiences also underscore the complicated nature of this sort of success story by examining the grave obstacles she and her children continue to face. The concluding chapter provides a space for further reflection on issues of representation and contributing factors to women's experiences of violence.

As a whole, *The Woman in the Violence* contextualizes women's experiences of intimate partner violence in Lima and examines intimate partner violence as a rich and understudied anthropological area of research. The book is an attempt to infuse the familiar yet abstract knowledge that domestic violence exists with concrete, critical examples and analyses of what women in abusive relationships experience, both within and outside the relationships. Attention to various forms of women's agency in Lima reveals multiple, creative ways in which women contest the everyday workings of patriarchal, racist, and classist structures within constrained circumstances, and contributes to our consciousness of women's almost invisible actions in the space between staying and leaving and in rebuilding their lives. Attention to women's everyday resistance also provides us with the opportunity to explore the broader structures within which women's lives unfold and which inform women's experiences of violence and resistance. These structures, whether initially familiar or unfamiliar to us, affect the women whose experiences inform these pages and implicate their partners, as well as other Peruvians who will never meet these women, and even readers in other parts of the globe.

# PART I

# Violence and Everyday Resistance in Women's Lives

# CHAPTER 1 Life in the City: Lima, Its Possibilities, and Its Discontents

LOCATED ON A DESERT COASTLINE that meets the Pacific Ocean, Lima is commonly described by visitors, guidebook writers, and residents as a gray city with fall and winter days characterized by smog and drizzle. Yet, the city is as alive with movement in the gray fall and winter months as in the sunny and hot days of spring and summer. Year-round, within seconds of leaving the airport, the sounds and sights of honking cars, zigzagging *micros* (microbuses used for public transportation), and people crossing the store-lined streets as cars zoom by inform visitors that they are entering a loud, bustling city with constant movement. On the streets, *ambulantes* (street vendors) young and old offer all sorts of items—from chewing gum to fruit to toilet brushes—to passengers in approaching cars.

As Peru's political, economic, and cultural center, Lima has the country's highest concentration of economic, political, social, and educational resources, and every year it attracts thousands of women and men searching for better jobs for themselves and a better education and future for their children. These migrants come from Peru's Andean, Amazonian, and coastal regions. The majority of the city's new residents settle in the city's *pueblos jovenes* (young towns, shantytowns), which form a growing belt around the city's older neighborhoods. From their homes on the outskirts of Lima, these newcomers travel to the city's wealthier neighborhoods in search of work to begin their journey to *superarse* (not simply to survive but to get ahead).[1] These women and men find new opportunities in Lima, but they also confront obstacles that prevent their upward mobility and sometimes even the fulfillment of their most basic needs.

In the daily grind of life in Lima, there are many contrasting stories that take place simultaneously. This chapter introduces the cultural, social, and political conditions of Lima's highly fragmented and spatially segregated environment to understand better the experiences of the women I interviewed. In the first section, I examine urbanization, rural-to-urban migration, and deep-seated racism as factors that have historically shaped and continue to influence everyday life in the city. In the second section, we turn our attention to specific moments of political violence through which the women lived, and to the connections between these forms of violence and intimate violence in women's lives. The third section examines how specific governmental policies contributed to or challenged women's experiences of structural and intimate violence before, during, and after periods of political violence. The final section situates the researcher in the Lima setting to provide a deeper understanding of the relationships and perspectives that inform my position in Lima's cultural, social, and political worlds and my interpretations of them. Together, these sections illustrate diverse experiences in the city and the myriad ways in which seemingly disparate his-

*A view of shantytowns in northern Lima. Photograph by the author.*

torical periods, forms of violence, and identities inform women's lives and my interpretations of women's experiences.

*The Makings of the Present: Urbanization, Migration, and the Politics of Race*

To understand better Lima's contemporary social, cultural, and political worlds, it is useful to look back briefly to the city's origins. Andean cities, including Lima, were founded by Europeans who envisioned cities as spaces "of progress, of learning, and of light," in contrast to the assumed backwardness of rural areas (Goldstein 2004:13). Since the founding of Lima by conquistador Francisco Pizarro in 1535, spatial location within the city, the urban-rural divide, and the devalorization of indigenous identities have shaped life in the city. Beginning with the colonial period, "proximity to the city center [was] henceforth . . . equated with proximity to financial and administrative power" and urban life became central to national identity (Spitta 2007:295). During the early colonial period, the most valuable land closest to Lima's central plaza belonged to the most prominent Spaniards. The farther from Lima's center and the more rural the setting, the more likely it was to be considered backward.

In the late nineteenth and early twentieth century, as Lima grew and more migrants arrived in the city, residents of the once-wealthy, physically deteriorating downtown area began to move away into newer neighborhoods. In 1991, downtown Lima was added to UNESCO's World Heritage List, and the balconies and several of the buildings that characterized the colonial period received face-lifts, making the central plaza area attractive as a tourist area, if not a residential one. Today, Lima's wealth is spread across a number of neighborhoods that include San Isidro, Miraflores, La Molina, and San Borja.

Surrounding these and other neighborhoods, as well as the central plaza, are a series of formal and informal settlements that began in the 1950s. Many of these developed as squatter settlements on unwanted desert land. In many cases, to create shantytowns, groups of migrants and poor Limeños took over pieces of vacant land and began building houses. These "invasions" were sometimes violently repressed by the police. Today, many of the older settlements have consolidated and now boast city services, property titles, and brick houses, while newer *pueblos jovenes* are characterized by more marginal locations, lower-end housing materials, quasi-legal or illegal housing, and a lower likelihood of city services. Although proximity to downtown is no longer a measure of social status, spatial location continues to be an important indicator of social status. Limeños in Peru and abroad routinely ask one another what district and neighborhood the other person's family is from when they initially meet as a way to ascertain each other's social position.

In the 1940s and 1950s, the rate of rural-to-urban migration to Lima began to increase rapidly as industrialization gained momentum and Lima's labor supply proved insufficient. Between 1940 and 1960, the city's population almost tripled. By 1991, almost half of Lima's residents came from someplace else in the country (Kokotovic 2007:124). Since the mid-twentieth century, women from the highlands have made up a large percentage of migrants, partly due to the demand for domestic servants to work in the homes of wealthier Peruvians in the capital. To live in Lima has long been a sign of modernity and urbanity, and the middle and upper classes have sought to distance themselves from newer migrants, whom they commonly view as culturally and racially inferior. Well into the 1960s, public schools taught working-class students, many of whom were the children of first-generation migrants, about the discipline of "urbanity." Carreño's *Manual de urbanidad y buenas maneras* (Manual of Urbanity and Good Manners), the most widely used manual on urban etiquette, taught students that "urbanity greatly respects those categories established by nature, by society and by God himself, and *therefore it obligates us to give preferential treatment to some people over others,* according to their age, *their social position,* their rank, their authority and their character" (cited in Stokes 1995:19; my emphasis). Migrants from the highlands and other parts of Peru went to Lima in search of a better future for themselves and their children, yet their ability to *superarse* was significantly limited by persistent hierarchical structures and ideologies based largely on geography and race. Like other forms of structural violence, these taken-for-granted hierarchies are almost invisible in everyday life, yet they result in some groups being denied access to upward mobility, positions of power, and even basic services.

By 1961, approximately half of the Peruvian population lived in urban areas. Today almost three-fourths lives in urban areas, and Lima is home to approximately one-third of Peru's 29 million inhabitants. The urban-rural divide continues to be imagined as the contrast between "civilization and barbarism, people with history and people without history, and modernity and premodernity" (Spitta 2007:295). In Lima, migrants from the highlands face widespread discrimination, as many Limeños view the highlands and almost all of Peru outside of Lima as the ignorant, socially, and economically deprived backwoods (Wallace 1984:58–59). It is common for employers to require that women who work as domestic servants in their homes wear uniforms, making the differentiation between those who have power and those who serve (typically, first- or second-generation migrants) all the more visible, even when the skin color and physical features are similar for everyone living and working under the same roof.

Lima grew and grew without any form of urban planning, and from 1961 to 1970 the population living in shantytowns quadrupled (Córdova Cayo 1996:26). After 1978, shantytowns became more numerous but offered progressively smaller lots to their residents (Driant 1991:183). Today, it is impossible for visitors to Lima not to notice the growing settlements sprawled on the dusty hills. What I refer to as shantytowns are known by various names in Peru, including *pueblo joven* (young town) and *asentamiento humano* (human settlement).[2]

Rodriguez (1994) has noted that women living in shantytowns "perform a triple role: reproductive, productive, and community management" (34). It is not easy to balance the various roles many poor urban women assume, and the boundaries between different roles and interests may become blurred in the process. Practical gender interests, such as food and shelter, and strategic gender interests, including the reshaping of gender relations, often converge in women's lives (34). In shantytowns, women are usually at the forefront of struggles involving basic services such as water, electricity, and sewers. They are also active as *dirigentes* (community leaders) who intervene in homes when violence erupts.

The vast majority of the women I interviewed lived in shantytowns. The image of the typical woman shantytown dweller held by members of the middle and upper classes has been one that centers on "dirty, promiscuous, ignorant women who don't think twice before becoming involved with the first man they meet, or with the second or third. Lots of husbands in a short life full of children from different men: sexual desire exaggerated by their lack of culture. Unnatural mothers who don't hesitate to throw their young children to the streets to beg or work, instead of sending them to school and feeding them a balanced diet" (Barrig 1982:15). As Barrig points out, these images stand in stark contrast to the realities of women's lives in Lima's newer settlements. Such popular depictions of shantytown residents fail to consider the broader structures that create the conditions in shantytowns. Rather than asking why, despite long hours of work by the adults in the family, children must also work to help a family meet its basic needs, those without personal experience of poverty may blame the poor—whom they typically exploit through notoriously low wages as domestic workers in their homes—for their situation.

While those in positions of power in Lima do not necessarily refer to themselves as *blancos* (white) today, they use euphemisms such as *educados* (educated) and *gente decente* (decent people). The ways in which powerful, urban minorities describe others, however, makes it apparent that they self-identify against rural indigenous identities outside of Lima and within the sprawling city's expanding borders. The preoccupation with the urban-rural and modern-backward divide shapes the relationship both between Lima and rural areas and between individuals in Lima. It even shapes relationships among intimate partners, as Chapter 2 explains.

As in other parts of Latin America, in Peru dominant power has traditionally been associated with the rejection of indigeneity. Soon after Peru's independence from Spain in 1821, it became evident that the Peruvian elite associated poor indigenous Peruvians with resistance to modernization and considered them impediments to national progress (Méndez 1996; Larson 2004:51, 145). Between 1836 and 1839, Peruvian nationalism as an inherent rejection of Indians held a prominent role in the struggle against the Peruvian-Bolivian Confederation. Among the elite in Lima and northern Peru, the underlying cause for the rejection of the Confederation was that Santa Cruz headed it. Although Santa Cruz had fought alongside San Martin for Peru's independence and his father was a Peruvian of Spanish descent, his mother was an Aymara Indian. Because his mother was Aymara, for the Peruvian elite Santa Cruz represented Indians and therefore that which should not represent the Peruvian nation.

The exclusion of indigenous people from the national imaginary would later be challenged through the indigenism movement of the 1920s. During this period, *indigenistas* such as Luis Valcárcel and José Carlos Mariátegui brought attention to the plight of indigenous groups in rural Peru, yet their depictions of indigenous people tended to be romanticized and simplistic. Mariátegui related the "Indian problem" to land and the economy, and largely ignored cultural factors (Marzal 1995). Valcárcel equated indigenous groups in the highlands with a largely static past, and generally denied change (see Valcárcel 1972).

Almost five decades later, President Juan Velasco (1968–1975) set out to use his power to challenge the continued race- and class-based discrimination in the country. Unlike other military regimes in Latin American countries during that period, Velasco's government allied itself to the poor rather than to the rich, and developed close relations with unions and shantytowns. One of Velasco's most well-known actions was a land reform to take land from wealthy landowners and redistribute it among the poor. Velasco also prohibited the term *indio* and substituted it with *campesino* (peasant) as a way to alleviate the country's class and ethnic divisions and tensions. Although the land reform had some success, in the end it did not meet its goals. Instead, it "exacerbated tensions between ethnic groups, particularly between highland peasants and lowland 'natives' on the one hand and the *criollo* [Lima] middle and upper classes on the other" (García 2005:75). Similarly, the change in terminology from *indio* to *campesino* did little to diminish racism. Today, the term *indio* continues to be used among the wealthy as well as among the poor in Lima to denote backwardness and inferiority. Additionally, other terms, such as *chuncho*, are also commonly employed to denote the assumed backwardness and uncivilized nature of indigenous Amazonian peoples.

At the end of the twentieth century, the renowned white Peruvian novelist and former presidential candidate Mario Vargas

Llosa suggested that for an indigenous person, cultural identity is "in the best of cases, a fiction. And, in the worst, a prison from which it is best to escape as soon as possible if one wants to be a free and modern man" (cited in Ossio 1994:17). Vargas Llosa's statement exemplifies the continued racist views of the elite. More broadly, Bossio points to the continued widespread discrimination Peruvians who do not fit the hegemonic class, ethnic, or sexual orientation encounter in Peru. A gay rights activist and member of the Movimiento Homosexual de Lima (MHOL), Bossio emphasizes that "the television programs with the highest ratings are those based on jokes that denigrate people based on sexual orientation, ethnic background, or physical challenges" (1995:479).[3]

In spite of the widespread discrimination experienced by rural-to-urban migrants (as well as others) in Lima, newcomers—particularly Andean migrants—stay and significantly influence the city's politics, economy, and cultural expressions. *Cholification*, comprised of "processes of indigenous mobility, urbanization, and migration" (Greene 2007:340; Matos Mar 1984; Nugent 1992), reflects the ongoing complex cultural-racial processes in Peru that complicate nonindigenous/indigenous and urban/rural binaries and defy simplistic definitions and rejection of indigeneity. The term *cholo* is commonly understood to refer to someone transitioning from being indigenous to becoming mestizo (Quijano 1980) as a result of migration, improved socioeconomic status, or language use. In contemporary Peru, the term *cholo* is routinely used as an insult to refer to a person's inferiority due to her or his indigenous roots. Recently, however, the term *cholo* has acquired positive connotations as more individuals proudly self-identify as *cholo*.

The presidency of Alejandro Toledo illustrates both positive and negative applications of the term *cholo*. Toledo grew up very poor in a Peruvian highland town and went to university in the United States as a result of fellowships and grants. Before returning to Peru to run for president, he worked as an economic adviser at the World Bank. During his presidential campaign, Toledo stressed his Andean background. His campaigning culminated in his election as president in 2001. During his presidency he proclaimed for himself, and was given by the public, a commonly used Peruvian racial-cultural identity:

El Cholo. To claim and be ascribed a *cholo* identity allowed Toledo to appeal to a broad Peruvian base as he made a clear and positive association between an Andean background and power and leadership. However, the term *cholo* also continued to have negative connotations, and he was referred to as a *cholo de mierda* (fucking *cholo*) before as well as during his presidency by many Limeños.[4]

Although most of the women I interviewed had experienced some form of discrimination precisely because they were identified as *cholas* or *indias* by others, their own use of the terms sometimes reinforced the terms' negative connotations. On one occasion, I visited a group of women in a recently established shantytown in northern Lima to discuss their experiences of intimate and social violence. We met in their community child-care facility and sat around an old cement table in the middle of a room with dirt floors and a straw ceiling that allowed the cold wind to come in. As we sipped hot tea, one woman described reacting to her husband's persistent physical and verbal abuse by yelling and throwing things at him, stating, "I don't know, the *indio* in me comes out, the *cholo* in me comes out, all my generations come out!" All of her neighbors laughed at the woman's statement, some nodding in agreement. In this case, *cholo* and *indio* are associated with wild, uncontrollable forces from within.

When I asked another woman if her family intervened when her husband beat her, she responded that her mother would yell at her husband, "You are a fucking *cholo*!" as a way to show disapproval of him. Her mother would also refer to him as a *cholo* when speaking about how she thought her daughter deserved a better husband. In this case, *cholo* is identified with an inherent inferiority.

Yet, even as some women employ the term *cholo* in negative ways, it is common for those same women to resent being referred to as *cholas* in negative ways by others. In describing her frustration at the constant discrimination she and her children faced from other Peruvians who saw themselves as innately superior to them, another woman declared that in Peru, "we are all *cholos*!" regardless of whether or not each person is willing to admit this.

Contemporary ambivalence toward one's indigenous roots

can be better understood not only in the context of the historical devaluation of Indianness, which I have referred to, but also
through acknowledgment of historically persistent struggles to
resist the devaluation of indigeneity and gain recognition, respect, and power by and on behalf of those who self-identify
as indigenous. In Peru today, some indigenous rebellions of
the past are well-known while more recent forms of indigenous
activism are ignored. In spite of uprisings such as the Túpac
Amaru Rebellion in the late eighteenth century, scholars commonly suggest that "Peru is notable among countries with large
indigenous populations for its lack of an indigenous movement
and organization" (Ewig 2006:651) when discussing the present.[5] Contrary to this assumption, García (2005) makes visible
contemporary forms of indigenous activism. García focuses on
Quechua parents who resist bilingual (Quechua-Spanish) language educational initiatives for their children because of the
parents' historical memory of past top-down initiatives by the
government and their knowledge that in contemporary Peru,
Quechua peoples are marginalized. She presents a complicated
story of "changing agendas and alliances in which Quechua parents can mobilize against pro-indigenous NGOs [non-govern-
mental organizations], and NGO goals can converge with those
of both the state and international development community"
(2005:3) to encourage us to look beyond most well-known forms
of rebellion associated with indigenous activism. Greene con-
curs, pointing out that there are "more subtle ways of being
indigenous in the Peruvian present. In coastal cities and towns
they become *cholos* and identify themselves through urban pro-
vincial 'clubs' or as part of the broadly inclusive category of the
'poor' (Degregori 1998; Nugent 1992). In urban Cuzco they become indigenous mestizos, adapting the ideology of mestizaje
such that it encompasses rather than erases indigenous roots (de
la Cadena 2000)" (2007:458). Indigenous mestizos rid indigenous identities of their negative connotations, such as illiteracy,
by becoming literate and adopting urban forms of dress, yet
they also value and maintain indigenous identity through such
practices as membership in indigenous dance groups. Indigenous mestizos thus ensure social mobility without giving up
their cultural heritage (de la Cadena 2000).

Although indigenous peoples in the Amazon have long been

ignored because of the privileging of Andean indigeneity in discussions of what constitutes Indianness, recently their activism has become visible through their internationally recognized struggles for environmental justice and conservation (Greene 2007:462). These explorations of what constitutes indigeneity and indigenous activism in Peru suggest that the forms of indigenous self-identification and discrimination that exist in contemporary Lima defy a simplistic Indian/non-Indian binary.

*Connecting Sites of Violence: Racism and the Everyday Violence of Inequality in Times of Political Violence and "Peace"*

By the 1990s, Peru had no official statistics on the ethnic composition of its population (Radcliffe and Westwood 1996:32). This, however, should not suggest that in the national imagination all Peruvians are the same. As the previous section makes clear, historical divisions between the highlands (where most of the women I interviewed are from) and the coast (with Lima as its center) have been grounded on geographic, racial, and ethnic stereotypes that result in real forms of discrimination and unequal access to resources. Today, approximately 45 percent of Peruvians are indigenous, another 35 percent mestizo (mixed European-indigenous ancestry), 15 percent of white European descent, and 5 percent of African and Asian ancestry. At the beginning of the twenty-first century, the overall poverty rate for Peru was 49 percent, yet the poverty rate within the indigenous population was 70 percent. Similarly, on average, non-indigenous individuals attain 8.1 years of schooling, while indigenous individuals attain 5.5 years (Saavedra, Torero, and Ñopo 2002).

Wealthy and white-mestizo Limeños may deny that racism informs everyday life in the city (Portocarrero 2007), but the experiences of those who are on the receiving end of racist treatment provide a different image of city life. The advice anthropologists have been offered by well-meaning Peruvian acquaintances also reveals a racist undercurrent in everyday life. During her field research on issues of dress and gender in the city of Arequipa and nearby rural indigenous communities, several acquaintances told Femenías she should not "waste" her time "trying to help 'those Indians,' because they are too lazy to work" (2005:12). Similarly, during her research on the effects of political violence of the 1980s and 1990s on the rural population of Ayacucho, Theidon heard from the director of an NGO that the indigenous people she wanted to interview "have already forgotten what happened. Look. We are capable of thinking in the abstract, that's why we have suffered so much. But they only think in a very concrete way: only their bread for the day and their animals. They don't think beyond that. That's why they haven't suffered like us; they are not capable [of it]" (2004:26). These not-so-subtle racist attitudes are the same that inform the popular saying *"más me pegas, más te quiero"* (the more you beat me, the more I love you) that places the blame for indigenous women's experiences of domestic violence on their culture and on the women themselves, as discussed in the Introduction. By calling upon cultural difference to explain away the violence indigenous people experience, these attitudes promote and maintain, at the very least, indifference.

The following paragraphs discuss the more common forms of political and everyday violence that inform the lives of poor indigenous and mestiza women I met in Lima and which are sometimes met with indifference by those in positions of power because of the previously discussed racism of everyday life. Although empirical research on the connections between public and domestic violence in different settings is still underdeveloped, existing studies "demonstrate that domestic and social violence form an integrated whole, closely intertwined and mutually reinforcing" (Buvinic, Morrison, and Shifter 1999:9; Enloe 2000; Glenn et al. 2002; Solomon 1988). Before examining the connections between different forms of violence—particularly political and intimate violence—that affect women's lives in Peru, it is useful to discuss a few of these studies.

In one study focusing on Lebanese women affected by the 2006 conflict between Hezbollah and Israel, Usta, Farver, and Zein (2008) find that domestic violence is likely to increase during periods of armed conflict. Looking at evidence from Croatia, Boric and Desnica (1996) suggest that domestic violence is least visible during times of war. Kelly (2000) discusses Canadian women's experiences of abuse at the hands of their soldier-husbands who recently returned from the Gulf War, noting that these men dressed in military uniform before beating their wives. Based on her long-term research in Zambia, Colson (1995) similarly suggests that times of war may lead to increased rates of violence against women in the home. These cross-cultural findings suggest that during periods of war, domestic violence against women increases, or is at least particularly brutal. Morrison, Buvinic, and Shifter suggest that "increased social violence generates more domestic violence by lowering inhibitions against the use of violence, by providing violent role models, and by subjecting individuals to additional stress" (1999:10), an explanation that fits well with the findings of these cross-cultural studies and with the conditions in Peru. In Peru, as in other countries, during times of war and other forms of public violence, little attention is given to violence in the home.

Between 1980 and 2000, political violence wreaked havoc on life in Peru and was felt especially intensely by Peruvians in the largely indigenous highlands. The Truth and Reconciliation Committee (2003) documents 69,280 deaths between 1980 and 2000. The distribution of deaths clearly shows that indigenous rural areas were the hardest hit: 79 percent of those killed lived in rural areas and 75 percent spoke Quechua or another indigenous language (Theidon 2004:19). The state and the radical Maoist-Leninist-Marxist group called Sendero Luminoso (Shining Path) were overwhelmingly responsible for these deaths.

Sendero Luminoso originated in the southern Andean department of Ayacucho, one of the most impoverished and indigenous areas in the country. Under the rallying cry of class struggle and anti-imperialism, Sendero espoused armed struggle as the only way to destroy the old order and create a new, more just Maoist society (Poole and Rénique 1992; Starn 1995). Because of its particularly bloody and violent form of revolution, Sendero has been compared more to Pol Pot's Khmer Rouge than to other Latin American revolutionary movements (such as Nicaragua's Sandinistas) (McClintock 2001:61).

For many of Lima's elite, the level of violence practiced by Sendero was interpreted in a racist manner, as the manifestation of barbaric indigenous cultures that prevented the country from moving forward (Kokotovic 2007:29). In reality, its ideologies and top leaders had little to do with indigenous cultural traditions and sometimes even reinforced some prevailing ideas on race. Sendero's leader, Abimael Guzmán, was a white-mestizo

philosophy professor at the Universidad Nacional de San Cris-
tóbal de Huamanga in Ayacucho until the mid-1970s. Guzmán
traced "his political lineage through Marx, Lenin, and Mao, not
Túpac Amaru II, Juan Santos Atahualpa, Manco Inca, or any of
the other Indian rebels in Peruvian history" (Starn 1995:407).
Similarly, he "always appeared in party propaganda in the
glasses and suit of a university professor, echoing the standard
Peruvian association of wisdom and leadership with the white,
the urban and the educated" (Starn 1995:407). Recruitment into
the group was both voluntary and coercive, and focused mostly
on rural areas that had been largely abandoned by the state.
Sendero was particularly appealing to young women and men
who felt stuck between their parents' indigenous and rural roots
and the white-mestizo city that rejected them.[6] Women made
up approximately 30 percent to 40 percent of the *senderistas*
(Shining Path militants) (Balbuena 2007; Kirk 1993), a point I
will return to momentarily.

   Largely ignored as a threat in its early years, Sendero worked
toward its goal to overthrow the Peruvian state by concentrating
its efforts on marginalized and largely forgotten (by the state)
rural areas throughout the 1980s. It targeted for assassination
community and union leaders, elected officials, development
workers, police, and church personnel. By the late 1980s, it was
prepared to attack urban centers. As car bombings, murders,
kidnappings, electric outages, and water shortages due to Sendero attacks became more common in Lima during 1990–1991,
the threat of Sendero's takeover of the country became increasingly real for Limeños. The capture of Abimael Guzmán and several other top leaders in 1992 in a safe house in a middle-class
neighborhood in Lima was followed by a significant decrease in
Sendero activity. Without Guzmán and several other top leaders,
the group could no longer hold the power it once did and some
of its factions fled to the jungle. Sendero attacks in Peru are rare
today but do occur: in 2002, just a few days before U.S. President George W. Bush was scheduled to arrive in Lima, Sendero
set off a car bomb outside the U.S. embassy in Lima, killing ten
people and wounding several others. This attack took place at
the end of my stay in Lima, and hit especially close to home for
me, as the hospital at which I had given birth a month before the
attack and to which my husband and I had taken our newborn

son for a check-up just a few days before the attack stood just a few blocks from the embassy.

The women I interviewed lived through the prolonged armed struggle between the state, Sendero, and peasant communities. During the period of rampant political violence, little attention was given to their or other women's experiences of violence in the home. None of the women I interviewed was a *senderista*, nor had any of them been tortured or the victims of the widespread gang rapes perpetrated predominantly by the armed forces against women in rural areas. For many, however, their lives had been permanently impacted through the loss of relatives, friends, and neighbors, as well as by the experience of generalized fear and trauma in their communities of origin and in marginalized neighborhoods in Lima at the height of the conflict.

For one woman, her experiences during the Sendero-state conflict led to her paid and volunteer work at a shelter for domestic violence victims. This woman's paid work at the shelter in her neighborhood was initially motivated by her desire to earn money during an especially dire economic period for her family. Through her volunteer work at the same shelter, she hoped that by helping women to end the violence in their lives, she would ease the pain she carried from losing her son. Her teenage son had disappeared and was later found dead by his family in their neighborhood, an area labeled a "red zone" (an area infiltrated by Sendero and in which the rule of law was suspended) at the height of the conflict. She does not know whether he was a victim of the army or Sendero.

The shelter residents and other women I spoke with also felt the connections between the public forms of violence in the 1980s and 1990s and intimate violence. Maria Rosa reported that in the early 1990s, her abusive husband said that if she ever left him he would ask his *terruco* (terrorist) brother to kill her and her entire family. Two other women received similar threats from their husbands. Although the women could not be certain that their brothers-in-law were indeed *senderistas*, the threats instilled fear in them and added yet another barrier to their ability to escape their abusive relationships. In a northern shantytown in Lima, during a focus group on women's experiences of violence, women community leaders vividly recounted their experiences during the time when their neighborhood was classified as a red zone. For these women, as for many other women I interviewed, the term *violencia* sparked memories of public and private violence. In the 1990s, neighbors disappeared, mutilated corpses of strangers appeared on the streets, residents were publicly executed for being suspected of having betrayed Sendero, and other residents felt compelled to report on their neighbors' activities. The women described how the army would also venture into these red zones, doing house-to-house searches and punishing those found with Sendero flyers— flyers that *senderistas* had in many cases pressured residents to keep in their homes under the threat of death. In speaking about the lack of options for rebuilding her life after being abandoned by her husband, Daisy discussed how, although she had no job and no property in Lima, she could not return to her home in the highlands because her family's land had been taken over by Sendero.

In Lima, multiple forms of violence permeated everyday life, and protecting children from these intersecting forms of violence proved challenging. For example, in 2001, one woman described the combination of violence in the home and violence in the community. At home, she had attempted to protect her children from their father's abuse. When she and her children left their home, however, she felt powerless to protect them. On the streets, they witnessed public executions carried out by Sendero and saw mutilated corpses on their way to school. As the woman shared her worries about her children, she stated that she believed witnessing a particularly brutal killing near her home had permanently traumatized her very reserved teenage son, who had witnessed this event when he was five years old.

Experiences of intimate, State, and Sendero violence were also intertwined in the lives of shelter directors. Almost a decade after the capture of Guzmán, one director suggested to me that although it is important to document what happened in the shelters during the time of heightened political violence, "it is also a dangerous subject to write about."[7] After Sendero began its operations in Lima, it became increasingly difficult to run domestic violence shelters safely. According to one shelter director, it was a dangerous period for neutrality, as *senderista* women attempted to infiltrate shelters to find out what was being discussed and to determine each shelter's position vis-à-vis

Sendero. Shelter directors were told to cease all public education campaigns and to actively support Sendero.

Shelter directors who were pressured to take sides and cease their community activities were not alone among women community activists being pressured and threatened by *senderistas*. *Senderistas* accused numerous grassroots organizations and women activists of collaboration with the government and of maintaining the status quo by providing the poor with needed resources. Women grassroots leaders were thus considered "enemies of the people" because their community work was not directly tied to Sendero Luminoso's armed struggle (Poole and Rénique 1992:2). Feminist NGOs were also considered enemies.[8] In 1992, Maria Elena Moyano, a thirty-two-year-old Afro-Peruvian feminist organizer and the deputy mayor of the Villa El Salvador district, defied Sendero by publicly condemning its terrorist methods and continuing her work to provide the people in her community with basic necessities. In February of that year, *senderistas* gunned down Moyano and dynamited her body in front of her two young sons and dozens of other people at a public event in Villa El Salvador.[9] Her funeral was attended by thousands, including dozens of women's organizations, shelter directors, and staff.

In scholarship on Sendero Luminoso, the fact that between 30 percent and 40 percent of its militants—including some of those who participated in Moyano's murder—were women and the belief that acts of violence committed by these women militants were equal to or more brutal than those of men militants have received some attention (Andreas 1985; Balbuena 2007; Kirk 1993). It is therefore important to contextualize women's involvement in Sendero's violence by pointing out that given the few opportunities poor indigenous and mestiza women have for upward mobility in a largely racist society, Sendero militancy provided a unique way for women to achieve political power. The women's participation made women's violence especially visible because it occurred in a traditionally masculine domain: armed struggle.

The women's participation in armed struggle in Peru, however, does not "alter the fact that the use of violence—interpersonal, state-sanctioned, and insurgent—remains a primarily masculine preserve" (Kelly 2000:46) in Peru and elsewhere. In other words, the participation of women at all levels of the Sendero hierarchy should not suggest that Peruvian women generally use violence in the same way or to the same extent as men. Indeed, at the level of the family, since the implementation of the Family Violence Law in the mid-1990s, the vast majority of domestic violence claims have been filed by women against their male partners (Güezmes, Palomino, and Ramos 2002). Although women are capable of violence against those they view as public enemies as well as against their partners, their use of violence should not be equated to men's more generalized use of violence in these domains. Based on research in the United States, Miller finds that when women use violence against their partners, the most common reasons are to defend themselves or their children (2005:120). My research reveals similar reasons for Peruvian women's use of violence against their partners.[10]

### Governmental Policies and Women's Everyday Struggles

In Lima, conversations about public forms of violence and politics are commonplace, and women's political views and involvement in politics routinely appeared in women's life stories. The political violence of the 1980s and 1990s occurred alongside the everyday violence of poverty and discrimination maintained through the policies and programs of a series of governments. In this section, I briefly discuss different governmental programs and policies in the 1980s and 1990s to examine how they affected poor women in Lima.

In 1985, Peruvians of diverse backgrounds elected white, middle-class, charismatic Alan García, the candidate of the center-left American Popular Revolutionary Alliance (APRA), as president. One of his government's populist platforms was to improve the lives of the urban poor, especially those in Lima's *pueblos jovenes*. Soon after coming to power, however, García gained a reputation for mismanagement and corruption. His economic policies resulted in massive hyperinflation. By 1989, inflation had reached 3,400 percent, and by 1990 it was close to 8,000 percent (Poole and Rénique 1992:4). Under these conditions, which were accompanied by a decrease in wages, it was impossible to know how much basic food items such as bread, rice, oil, eggs, or the then-popular Enci powdered milk would cost from one day the next. People lined up outside stores to buy basic foodstuffs before the next price hike, not knowing how much they would pay by the time they reached the counter. It became increasingly difficult for poor families, as well as for many middle-class families, to provide for their households. By the time García left the presidency and Alberto Fujimori took over as president in 1990, Peru's economy was in shambles.

In 2001, after eight years of exile, García returned to Lima to run for president again. In conversations with women in Lima's northern *pueblos jovenes,* I found that despite their memories of the devastating effects of García's failed economic policies, many women expressed a willingness to vote for him again. When I asked the women what about a second García presidency appealed to them, several of them referred to the Programa de Apoyo de Ingreso Temporal (PAIT) as something they would welcome back.[11] PAIT was a top-down program administered through a government agency between 1985 and 1987 that sought to alleviate the economic crisis by providing temporary work for the poor. The program offered participants paid work and allowed them to work fewer hours (an eight-hour workday) than they normally would in the marketplace for the same amount of money. Through participation in the program, 65 percent of participants improved their incomes (Vigier 1986, cited in Buvinic 1996).

PAIT was especially appealing for several of the women I interviewed because it had allowed them to get paid for community work in which they were already involved and to which they could bring their children, thus freeing them from the worries of childcare during the workday. Most of PAIT's participants had been women between the ages of twenty and forty (Buvinic 1996). It is unlikely that poor women outside of Lima would have such positive memories of the program, however, because it was a predominantly urban and Lima-based program. PAIT is emblematic of government programs that, although positive in the short term and for a specific portion of the population, fail to be transformative in a sustained way and for larger sections of the population. Although his presidential bid was unsuccessful in 2001, in 2006 García campaigned again, and this time he regained the presidency. He promised not to repeat the mistakes of his first presidency, claiming that he had learned from them and had become an experienced leader. By May 2008, his approval rating had fallen to 26 percent, amidst complaints of rising food costs and inadequate economic policies.[12]

In between García presidencies, three presidents governed Peru. Alberto Fujimori, the first Peruvian president of Japanese descent, governed from 1990 to 2000. Fujimori is largely credited with reducing the threat of Sendero Luminoso through the use of the armed forces and the capture of Abimael Guzmán in 1992. He is also known for his authoritarian rule following his *autogolpe* (self-coup) in 1992.[13] In the realm of women's rights, Fujimori's record is mixed. On the one hand, he was the only male president to speak at the United Nations Fourth World Conference on Women in Beijing, and he sought to form alliances with Peruvian feminists. Fujimori legalized sterilization in 1995, despite opposition from the Catholic Church, and made sterilization and reproductive health education free to all Peruvians through the creation of the National Program of Reproductive Health and Family Planning (1996–2000). For some of the women I interviewed, as will be discussed in Chapter 3, access to sterilization played an important role in allowing them control over their fertility and to resist their partners' demands for more children.

On the other hand, in practice the family planning program counted "the number of women sterilized as an indicator of successful poverty alleviation" (Ewig 2006:644), thus making it possible to "conclude that the government's policies had little to do with the empowerment of women despite its laws and rhetoric" (Boesten 2007:15-16). Racism also played a role in the implementation of the family planning program. As in the past, in the late twentieth and early twenty-first centuries, poor indigenous women in rural areas were considered to be a threat to the nation's progress because of their high fertility rates and were therefore targeted "through a system of quotas that provided little incentive for high quality care" (Ewig 2006:633) and resulted in hundreds of coerced sterilizations (Alcalde 1999; Boesten 2007; CLADEM 1998; Ewig 2006). In 1996, Giulia Tamayo León, a Peruvian lawyer with the Comité de América Latina y el Caribe para la Defensa de los Derechos de la Mujer (CLADEM), blew the whistle on abuses perpetrated by government health workers within the national family planning program. By the following year, national criticism of the program also came from the national ombudsman and from smaller Peruvian NGOs.[14] The program also received international attention from the U.N. Committee on Elimination of Discrimination against Women. By 1999, national and international scrutiny of the program and revelations of widespread abuses had resulted in the withdrawal of international funding and modifications to the family planning program (Boesten 2007; Ewig 2006).

The women I interviewed in Lima did not suffer from coerced sterilizations, but hearing of these cases, some of which resulted in deaths, instilled in many women a sense of growing distrust toward state-funded health services. Also under Fujimori, although the Family Violence Law was passed—as a result of pressure from women's and feminist organizations—the government failed to provide sufficient economic resources to the institutions responsible for assisting in domestic violence cases to ensure proper implementation of the law (ICRW 2003:9). Many of the women I met had heard of the Family Violence Law, but many also experienced firsthand the lack of institutional resources necessary to implement the law properly. The women knew that existing resources provided few alternatives to living with an abusive partner, a point further examined in Chapter 5.

More broadly, although Fujimori campaigned on a populist platform, he implemented harsh neoliberal economic policies that forced the poor to bear the brunt of the national recovery process immediately after beginning his presidency. Known as the "Fujishock," these economic measures were designed to fix the hyperinflation of the García years. When protests spread in the first year of his presidency, Fujimori used his strong ties to the military to quell the protests through the massive use of force. In 2000, amidst clear evidence of corruption, Fujimori used an official trip abroad as an excuse to leave Peru. He did not return and instead took refuge in Japan. In his absence, Congress declared him morally unfit to serve as president. Valentin Paniagua stepped in as interim president to organize the elections to be held in 2001.

Alejandro Toledo, the first *cholo* president of Peru, won the 2001 election and served until 2006. Promising to improve the lives of Peru's largely disenfranchised indigenous population, Toledo received significant support from Peruvians throughout

the country. During his presidency, the economy grew and inflation remained low, yet early on in his term personal scandals
and accusations of corruption also plagued this president. At
one point in 2004, his approval ratings were in the teens amidst
accusations of corruption and complaints that he was not doing
enough to improve the lives of the poor.[15]

Given the failures of each of these governments to provide
long-term solutions for alleviating poverty, the task of securing
a family's daily survival has fallen largely on women, especially
mothers. *Comedores populares* (neighborhood communal kitchens), *Vaso de Leche* (glass of milk) committees, and *clubes de
madres* (mothers' clubs) are all grassroots forms of organizing
in which women I interviewed actively participated in the 1980s
and 1990s, and in which they continue to participate to meet
their families' basic needs and sustain their communities.[16] As
the economic situation worsened, *comedores populares* filled
an important need and the demand for them increased, going
from one hundred kitchens in 1980 to eight hundred in 1986
to over seven thousand following the "Fujishock" (Henríquez
1996:148). Even after the economic situation improved nationally, these forms of grassroots organizing have continued to exist because of the persistent absence of formal institutional and
structural resources to secure the welfare of poor and working-
class people. In 2001, a *comedor popular* near one of the shelters
I regularly visited charged one sol (about thirty U.S. cents) for a
meal that included soup, a main dish (such as lentils and rice),
and tea (typically chamomile). A woman who could not afford
to purchase meals for her family could sometimes work in the
*comedor* and receive enough food for her entire family in return
for her labor.

For the women who participated in these organizations, to
be a *dirigente* "is as important as to be a professional for women
from the impoverished middle class" (Henríquez 1996:152). I
interviewed four women *dirigentes* in Lima's shantytowns about
their personal and community experiences of violence. One *dirigente* explained that when there were extreme episodes of domestic violence in her neighborhood, children would sometimes
run to her house to ask for her assistance since she was respected
in the community due to her role. She was known as much for
intervening in domestic disputes as for fighting for electricity,

water, and other basic necessities for her neighborhood. She spoke of her pride in her role as *dirigente* while at the same time acknowledging that her public leadership role caused tensions within her home, because her husband resented that she spent so much time away from the house and because he disapproved of her interventions in neighbors' domestic disputes. In spite of Sendero's continuous opposition to and murder of women *dirigentes* in the 1990s, women continued to take on these leadership roles for the sake of their families and communities. Years after Sendero ceased to threaten their lives on a daily basis, being a *dirigente* is still an important source of pride and work for women in the midst of intersecting forms of violence.

## Situating the Researcher in Lima, Peru

In explaining why he includes a discussion of his identity and life in a book on nationalist violence in Sri Lanka, Daniel (1996) explains that his reflexive account is necessary "not because I like being autobiographical but because I have chosen to write on a subject upon which who I am has a bearing of more than passing significance" (9). In addition to being a naturalized U.S. citizen, Daniel is Sri Lankan, having spent the first twenty years of his life in that country, and his parents belong to the ethnic groups about which he writes. Although he neither participated in nor was directly victimized by the violence he describes, his attachments to and personal knowledge of Sri Lanka and its history provide a unique vantage point and influence the interpretations he presents in the book.

Similarly, in discussing her fieldwork in Peru and among Peruvian immigrants in the United States, García (2000) explains that her identity as a Peruvian-American held more than passing significance for the Peruvians and U.S. scholars with whom she discussed her fieldwork. In Peru, her "informants' discovery of the fact that my grandfather was Andean" led them to expect that her research would be especially beneficial to their communities and that she would engage in their causes to a greater extent than foreign researchers (92). Peru's regionalization of race and power further influenced how those she worked with viewed her, as she was also perceived as a "'white' Limeña who lived in the U.S.—a categorization that in Peru is synonymous to political, social, and economic access" by local bureaucrats who assumed she had access to powerful resources (2000:92). Similarly, during my own fieldwork, I was frequently viewed as an outsider to the worlds of domestic violence activism I studied and became involved in. At the same time, my identity as a Limeña led those I interacted with to expect me to become engaged in their causes to a greater extent than foreign researchers, to be already familiar with unspoken rules of behavior expected of me because of my family attachments to Lima, and to have access to powerful resources (see Alcalde 2007).

In this section, I discuss both my identity and some of the forms of engagement that were expected of me and in which I engaged during my fieldwork, because they inevitably influenced what I saw and did and the interpretations I present. To exclude myself completely from the presentation of my research findings would result in a distorted picture of my interactions with the women and of the ideas and situations that inform my interpretations of the women's experiences. This detached position would afford me more distance from the women's lives than I experienced.

My selection of Lima and the intersection of multiple forms of violence in women's lives as areas of study arose from both personal and academic interests. My initial interest in intimate partner violence against women began during an exploratory research trip to Lima while in graduate school in the United States during the late 1990s. Having finished a master's degree in Latin American Studies, I decided to pursue a doctorate in anthropology. I wanted to continue my focus on Latin America and use anthropology's tools to focus on my own society and the multiple intersecting cultural and social worlds within it. I wanted the topic to be relevant to women's lives in Peru. I was also particularly intrigued by the prospect of examining forms of violence that did not revolve around Sendero Luminoso, because the group had already received significant attention from Peruvianist scholars in Peru and abroad (for example, Degregori 1990; Kirk 1993; Palmer 1992; Poole and Rénique 1992; Starn 1995, 1999; Stern 1998).

After meeting with members of two of Peru's nonprofit women's organizations—the Centro de la Mujer Peruana Flora Tristán and Movimiento Manuela Ramos—and reading some of the works published by these organizations (for example, Merino 1997; Movimiento Manuela Ramos 1998; Nencel 2000; Yon 1998), I became convinced that intimate partner violence against women—a topic about which I knew little at the time—was a particularly relevant issue that needed more scholarly attention in Peru.[17] In the eight years that have passed since the start of my fieldwork in Lima, women's organizations have conducted a significant amount of research on domestic violence and the domestic violence law has been modified. At the same time, the issue continues to suffer from insufficient government funding and academic attention, and women continue to face discrimination and violence within and outside of the home. In short, there is more attention to domestic violence today than there was just a few years ago, but it is by no means sufficient.

Defining one's identity and spelling out one's position within a society is a difficult endeavor, especially in a project that foregrounds the fluidity of identities in individual lives. In conducting fieldwork in Peru, and more specifically in Lima, I join a growing group of anthropologists who conduct fieldwork in their countries or communities of origin and in their native languages (Abu-Lughod 1993; Agar 1996; Bacigalupo 2007; D'Alisera 1999; de la Cadena 2000; García 2005; Ginsburg 1989; Kondo 1990; Lewin 1993; Myerhoff 1978; Narayan 1993; Oboler 2005; Visweswaran 1994). Like many "native anthropologists," I recognize that just as shared experiences and solidarity based solely on gender cannot be assumed (Mohanty 1991; Nelson 1996), "simply by being of the country/culture/group/family, one is not automatically guaranteed infinite and nonterminable knowledge of the culture" (Panourgiá 1994:46). In an internally heterogeneous environment like Lima, differences based on location, class, education, and race all play roles in shaping everyday interactions between residents, and between researchers and participants.

I was born in Lima to Peruvian parents. In the early 1980s, my father received a Fulbright fellowship for graduate study in the United States, and as a result of this, our family joined the thousands of Peruvians who left Peru as the political violence increased. Determined not to allow their children to become too "Americanized" and lose their Peruvian roots, my parents insisted that Spanish be the only language we spoke at home and with each other, and that we spent the (U.S.) summer in Lima every year. In the late 1980s and in the early 1990s, my family returned to Lima for entire academic years on two occasions, giving my siblings and me the opportunity to re-adapt to the Lima school system we had left behind years earlier. I returned to Lima for fieldwork in 2001 after living mostly abroad for more than half my life. While my father's studies in the United States had been made possible by a Fulbright award for Peruvian citizens, my research in Lima was facilitated by a similar Fulbright award, but for U.S. citizens. Yet, as Daniel's experiences in Sri Lanka and the United States likewise illustrate, identity and identification with specific peoples, histories, and places are not limited to citizenship. I re-entered Peru as a U.S. citizen who was an outsider in many ways, yet in other ways, I was also already an insider in Lima.

In 2001, when I began my research in Lima, I entered the field as a young, middle-class, heterosexual, married student whose baggage included my identities in both Peru and the United States. In the United States, my Peruvian origin, relatively dark skin, physical features, and use of Spanish mark me as (a nonwhite) Latina. In Peru, my middle-class background, education, and relatively light skin mark me as white. In Lima, I introduced myself to research participants as a Peruvian studying and living abroad. Peruvian migration to the United States and elsewhere has become increasingly common in the last three decades, and today a large percentage of the population in Lima have a close relative planning to emigrate or already living abroad. Because Peruvian undergraduate and graduate students conduct interviews, write theses, and participate in internships as part of their education, participants understood my desire to study violence in women's lives as an integral part of my identity as a student.

During meetings with research participants, initial brief exchanges of comments and criticisms expressive of our mutual interest in the state of affairs in Peru at the time allowed for similarities in our concerns and differences in our lives in Lima to emerge. Metropolitan Lima is a city of close to ten million people and forty-three municipal districts. There are several different neighborhoods within each densely populated district. From my family's house to the opposite side of the city, a trip

I made regularly in order to interview one of the participants, it takes approximately two hours each way by *micro,* or forty minutes each way by a more expensive taxi. In a city this size, it is not unusual for residents to spend their lives without ever visiting some of its areas. In this context, shared national and cultural affiliation opened doors for me, but race, class, the spatialization of the city, and my status as an academic in a world of activism complicated my roles and made them unstable.

Sometimes the resources to which I had access as a member of a middle-class family in Lima and as a U.S. Fulbright awardee facilitated my engagement in women's lives. The ways in which I was able to engage and advocate for the women, however, were limited and temporary. As discussed in the Introduction, the women at the shelters I visited all shared the need for a job. Because my extended family lives in Lima, on several occasions (some more successful than others) I was able to utilize my kin networks as I attempted to locate employment opportunities for women and to market products made and sold by shelter residents. I also asked my cohort of Fulbrighters for assistance in identifying employment possibilities for women, and I have given talks on domestic violence in Lima in the United States because I was able to examine the topic as a result of Fulbright funding.[18] None of these, however, solved the women's problems in protecting themselves and their children from violence in sustained ways, nor did the other forms of engagement in which I took part that I discuss later in this book. Similarly, while conducting research on and writing about women's experiences raises awareness, I do not consider my writing to be a form of advocacy that will necessarily have long and lasting effects on the communities in which I studied. I do hope, however, that in limited ways, the combination of writing and on-the-ground advocacy I engage in has some impact on our long-term awareness of women's experiences as well as on women's well-being.

In terms of engagement with politics, the year I began fieldwork (2001) was a particularly important year for Peruvian politics and a particularly difficult year to maintain a neutral political stance. As an election year, the stakes were high for the women's organizations, shelters, and individuals with whom I interacted on a regular basis. The three main contenders for president—Alan García, Lourdes Flores, and Alejandro Toledo—

held rallies throughout Peru. Among the shelters with which I worked, Toledo had the most support, while among the individual *dirigentes* I visited in shantytowns in the northern part of the city, Alan García held the lead.

In spite of my attempts to cite my position as a researcher and my obligation as a Fulbright awardee not to take political sides, it was difficult to avoid becoming involved in the political issues to which the people I worked with and sought to gain trust from were dedicating so much of their time and effort. The individuals expected me to become involved in politics, just as they expected me to move beyond the role of researcher and into the role of advocate in the course of working with, and in, a shelter. I occasionally found myself being recruited to help organize political events, some of which were initially presented to me under the guise of nonpartisan events about women's issues. In one event, the job I had been assigned, as a member of the shelter, was to sign people in and place "reserved" signs on the "special" seats that were to be occupied by Eliane Karp—Toledo's wife—and her entourage. I never totally shook my discomfort about participating in these sorts of rallies as a researcher who on a personal level did not yet wish to commit to one political party or another. However, I understood that my non-involvement in these events would have signaled an equally or even stronger political stance against the issues people with whom I worked cared about deeply. In the end, participation in these sorts of events and conversations with other participants in these events provided me with important glimpses of what each political party had to offer in the realm of human rights and domestic violence issues and of how women connected their personal experiences to broader political issues. Thus, my research included and led to forms of engagement that have ranged from writing to participation in political rallies to searches for individual jobs for women to long-term relationships with individual women and their families.

This chapter has examined social, political, and cultural dynamics in the city; the moments and processes that have informed women's experiences of political and everyday violence; and the positions and identities of the researcher presenting and interpreting the women's experiences. The following chapters build on this information to focus on women's experiences of violence that are invisible to many inside and outside of the context of Lima. Referring to minority women who stay in domestic violence shelters in the United States, Crenshaw suggests that "the physical assault that leads women to these shelters is merely the most immediate manifestation of the subordination they experience" (1991:95). Similarly, in Lima, we must explore varying forms of violence—political, institutional, the everyday violence of poverty, and intimate partner violence—to move from "ethnographically visible" violence (Farmer 2004) to less visible but perhaps more widespread forms of violence, and to the strategies women employ to cope with these different forms of violence.

# CHAPTER 2 ❧ Reproducing Structural Inequalities within Intimate Relationships

❧ WEISMANTEL NOTES THAT ALTHOUGH "in the Andes, people are notoriously unwilling to use racial terms of any kind as self-descriptors" (2001:xxxiv), racism abounds. Similarly, although racism within intimate relationships is rarely discussed, race and racism can play a significant role in abuse within intimate relationships. This chapter focuses on women's intimate relationships to examine how the biases founded on the regionalization of race that women deal with in public venues also impact their lives in intimate spaces. I discuss the multiple, complicated systems of subordination that first-generation Andean migrant women experience within abusive relationships in Peru's capital and emphasize that while their gender is a significant source of subordination, it is far from the only or perhaps even the most significant identity marker that shapes their violence. In the most intimate of spaces, the ascription of Indianness and the amount of education attributed to them by their partners are also major factors in the violence experienced.

During my time in Lima, my interviews and informal conversations with service providers included psychologists, shelter staff, officers at the main women's police station, and health care staff. During these interviews and conversations, I asked about the causes of men's violence against their partners. Carmen, a community activist and the director of a reproductive health clinic, explained that when men didn't work, they turned to alcohol and became abusive. According to Carmen, their use of violence against women was largely a result of their lack of formal education and alcohol consumption.

The view that alcohol is one of the main causal agents for men's violence also appears in academic and clinical analyses of domestic violence (see Canessa 2005b:146; Canessa 2007;

74

Straus and Kantor 1987). Although the women I interviewed are not representative of all Peruvian women, or of all women in abusive relationships, it is worth noting that the majority stated that their husbands beat them while sober. Some women even described how their husbands became more calm and affectionate toward them when drunk. For these men, alcohol did not bring out so-called natural violent impulses, but more hidden, less accepted forms of masculinity, including affection and tranquility. Maria, thirty-five years old and a mother of eight, laughed when I asked her if her husband became violent when he drank, stating that her husband "gets drunk once in a while but he actually becomes gentle when he gets drunk."

Sara is a psychologist and directs support groups for women in abusive relationships in a middle-class neighborhood. She believes gender inequality within society to be the main cause of men's violence against women. This view is one traditionally found in feminist literature on violence against women (see Dobash and Dobash 1979, 1992; Yllö 1993). The women I interviewed discussed their husbands' abusive behavior in ways that underscored the gender inequality that shaped their relationships. However, the gender inequality the women referred to, often as "machismo," did not fully explain their experiences of violence.

To understand what other factors informed the women's experiences of abuse, I looked to broader Andean studies. What I found is that it is nearly impossible to read an Andean study of women's experiences without coming across anecdotes of domestic violence (Babb 1989; Boesten 2006; Femenías 2005; Gavilano Llosa and Gonzalez de Olarte 1999; Harris 1994; Harvey 1994; Paulson 1996; Rivera Cusicanqui 1996; Seligmann 2004; Weismantel 2001). Femenías (2005) notes that domestic violence occurs all too often, while Weismantel tells us that men's violence leaves "women battered, blinded, miscarrying, or even dead" (2001:163). Recent public health research on domestic violence in Peru underscores the pervasiveness of intimate partner violence, and points to a variety of contributing factors—in addition to gender inequality—at the personal, community, and societal levels (Güezmes, Palomino, and Ramos 2002).

A close reading of available research on Andean women's lives suggests specific directions for including—but also moving beyond—a primary focus on gender in the study of Andean women's experiences of domestic violence. Weismantel states that in Ecuador, domestic violence among women in Zumbagua increased after men began to migrate to and from Quito on a weekly basis (2001:163). Paulson (1996) views the increase in domestic violence in Bolivia within ethnic Mizqueña families as correlated with increased migration and the acquisition of urban behaviors. Among Aymara migrants in La Paz and El Alto, Rivera Cusicanqui (1996) finds that women who are second-generation migrants exhibit more vulnerability to domestic violence than first-generation migrants, in part due to an increase in exogamous relationships and a decrease in kinship networks. In sum, these studies suggest that although domestic violence occurs both in rural and urban areas, migration and the adoption of urban patterns of behaviors by one or both partners may increase a woman's vulnerability to domestic violence.

To examine the reproduction of structural inequalities based on race, place, and education within the intimate relationships of migrants in Lima, this chapter draws primarily on the experiences of Virginia, Racquel, and Inés. As noted by Alcoff, "one's placement in social categories of identity has an enormous impact on one's life" (2004:3). In the cases I discuss, the men's perceptions of their intimate partners as racially and culturally inferior drew on the popular division of Peru into three regions: *costa*, *sierra*, and *selva*. According to the accounts given by Virginia, Racquel, and Inés, their partners believed they each embodied the indigeneity, backwardness, and ignorance commonly associated with the *sierra*, and the extent of the embodiment affected the women's vulnerability to violence.

Just as in the national imagination "all geographic regions are not created equal" (Greene 2007:460; Orlove 1993), in intimate relationships some women are imagined to be inferior to others depending on their place of origin. Growing up in Lima, I learned about the regionalization of race early in school. By the time I finished first grade (if not earlier), I could identify Lima as the most modern, progressive, educated, and powerful city on the coast, and in Peru, and naturally contrast it with the less developed, poorer, and more indigenous *sierra* and *selva*. This racist reading of the Peruvian map is a common lesson for Peruvian students and has been historically maintained through official maps and documents dating back to the nineteenth century that link geography to race (Orlove 1993). According to this reading, the *sierra* and *selva* are poor, backward, and racially inferior precisely because Lima is powerful and white(r). As discussed in the Introduction, the regional dimension of race in Peru is such that the coast is usually associated with white-mestizoness, while *indios* come from the *selva* or *sierra*. For the women I interviewed, these broader categories of identity permeated the most intimate spaces of their lives.

In contrast to the identities Virginia's, Racquel's, and Inés's partners ascribed to them, the identities these women claimed were generally deracialized and accentuated the positive aspects of their lives, reminding us that "a single subject can no longer be equated with a single individual" (Moore 1994:55). In their narratives, the women commonly described themselves as *mujeres trabajadoras* (working women) and emphasized the number of years they had lived in Lima when I asked about their places of origin. Among the thirty-eight women I interviewed, only one woman described herself as an *india, chola,* or *serrana*. In spite of this, the identities commonly ascribed to them in public spaces, within state institutions (as discussed in Chapter 5), and by their partners were those of *india, chola,* and *serrana*. All of these identity categories served to mark the women as nonwhite and are commonly associated with a rural background that connotes poverty, deficient education, ignorance, marginality, and inferiority vis-à-vis whiter, more educated, and more mainstream and urbane Limeñas. As Mitchell noted during his long-term fieldwork in Peru, in creating an ethnic hierarchy, "education and competence in Spanish were (and are) the most important determinants of social position," yet "location and clothing are also important in defining the social hierarchy" (2006:53). For Virginia, it was precisely her identity as a *serrana* and the fact that she had never attended school that her first and second *convivientes* called upon to justify their abuse. Her experiences during her first and second *convivencias* underscore the significant roles of racial identity and education in experiences of public and intimate abuse and discrimination.

*Virginia*

Virginia's situation is illustrative of the precarious economic situations faced by many of the women I interviewed. Virginia, a woman in her mid-forties, has six children and moved to Lima from a small Andean community as a young girl. She is thin, has dark skin and long black hair, and speaks Spanish with a strong Quechua accent and Quechua sentence structure.[1] Virginia has filed several domestic violence complaints against her second *conviviente*, Jesús. She continues to share a house with him and their two sons, ages twelve and eight, because neither she nor he can afford to move out. Although she and he lead separate lives, she fears he will take all their property and belongings if they separate. For now, until she is better able to understand how their property would be divided, Virginia resists Jesús's efforts to begin the long and potentially costly formal separation procedure.

Virginia works as a domestic servant from eight in the morning until eight at night and has Wednesdays and Sundays off. The trip from her home to her employer's house takes about an hour. In 2001, her monthly salary (US$28.50) was slightly less than one-third the minimum wage. Her employer gave her an additional ten *soles* (US$2.80) per week for transportation, yet Virginia spent fifteen *soles* (US$4.30) per week on transportation. The money she earned was not enough to cover her family's food or school expenses. Virginia did not know about laws protecting domestic workers when I met her, but even if she had been familiar with these laws and demanded that her employer respect them, it is unlikely that her employer would have increased her salary.[2] Virginia needs her job and does not want to risk losing it, and her employer knows this.

Although Virginia has continuously asked for a raise, stating that what she earns is not enough to feed her sons (she does not eat at home on the days she works), her employer has refused to give her a raise. Virginia's employer argues that she cannot give Virginia a raise because of Virginia's handicap. Virginia has what she describes as a hernia, which prevents her from heavy lifting. Medical visits and prescriptions cost money, even in establishments for the poor, and whatever money Virginia acquires from work or as a gift, she uses to buy food and clothing for her children, not on her health problems.

In 2005, I called Virginia during my annual summer trip to Lima. She was one of the few women I interviewed who had a telephone. It had been a year since we last spoke, yet she immediately recognized my voice, and we set up a time to meet. During our meeting, Virginia explained that she had continued to work for the same family she worked for in 2001, and that her salary was the same as it had been in 2001. In 2005, the going rate for a full day of cleaning was between twenty and twenty-five *soles* (approximately between US$7 and US$8) per day, yet Virginia was making less than 10 *soles* (approximately US$3) a day. Chaney and García Castro's finding that domestic servants are "among the most oppressed and neglected sectors of the working class" (1989:4) is still true today. In addition to the low pay, long working hours, and widespread discrimination Virginia faced, domestic workers may also experience sexual harassment and abuse within the households in which they work.[3]

To get ahead and provide for her children, Virginia searched for better-paying jobs elsewhere as a domestic servant. Each time we met, I brought the "Help Wanted" ads from different newspapers. Unfortunately, the majority of the ads asked for live-in domestic servants. A live-in domestic servant earns more than Virginia does and does not have to pay for room and board. However, as a live-in domestic servant, she would have to be available at all times and have little, if any, time for herself and her family. Virginia has held other jobs in the past, including selling beer on the streets and preparing lunch for construction workers, but with two sons to provide for, she feels she cannot risk losing her steady though inadequate income.

*Meeting Virginia*

I had contacted Virginia in 2001 through a nonprofit women's organization from which she had sought information regarding her options for dealing with an abusive *conviviente*. The organization had given her information about my research and asked her if she would be interested in speaking with me. She had agreed to speak with me; someone from the organization then called me and gave me her phone number.

During my first phone conversation with Virginia, I had tried to determine if an initial meeting at her house was possible. As my contact in the women's organization had told me, Virginia "knows Spanish more or less." Due to communication problems, I had not been able to find out whether or not her *conviviente* lived in the house. By our second conversation, however, we understood each other much better. For her and my own safety, I asked her to meet me far from her home. After I gave her directions to our meeting place, she asked me to repeat them to her twelve-year-old son. Virginia is among the approximately 12 percent of Peruvians who can neither read nor write.

We agreed to meet near one of two benches near a large water fountain in a park. I arrived almost half an hour early. Within a few seconds of my arrival, a woman who had been walking nearby approached me and asked, "*Señorita*, excuse me, is this a water fountain?" It was Virginia. As soon as I introduced myself as the person she had spoken with on the phone, she began telling me her life story, all at once, and at a very fast pace. I led her to one of the benches so we could sit together as she continued to tell me about her life. About half an hour passed until I was able to say a word. It was early and not too warm yet, and there was hardly anyone around. We spent the next two hours together.

As Virginia later told me, I was the only person with whom she could speak about her problems. She didn't think other women should go through what she had experienced and this fueled her desire to tell me—and others through me—about her life. Although she did not speak to her family or acquaintances about the abuse she lived, she believed other women had similar experiences. During our meetings, I gave her information about different resources she could use to solve some of the problems she faced, and, when needed, I wrote letters on her behalf that she dictated to me. She provided me with information I discuss throughout this book, especially in this chapter, and with many valuable memories and lessons about life in Lima.

*Childhood Memories*

Virginia felt unlucky from an early age. Until she moved to Lima at age eleven, she had lived in a small rural community in Andahuaylas. Her father had died when she was one and a half years old and her mother had remarried a few years later. Virginia described her life from that point on as one of suffering. At age seven, her mother and stepfather had placed her in charge of putting the family's two cows to pasture. On days when it was so cold she found it difficult to get up early to take the cows to graze, her stepfather had beaten her. When it rained, the cows had refused to obey her and Virginia would cry, knowing she would be beaten at home if she did not take the cows where she was supposed to take them. She let loose a sad laugh as she remembered that as a child, not even the cows had paid attention to her.

It was during her childhood that Virginia learned about men's violence, through her stepfather's violence: "My stepfather beat my mother a lot. I remember all that. I saw it. He would throw my mother to the ground, then another hit, and would pull her by her hair like that. And since I was little, I cried and I cried. I didn't know what to do. I would go around in circles, crying, 'Mommy, help.' My poor mother, he beat her hard her whole life." Virginia remembered that her stepfather also regularly beat her and her siblings, and he teased them by talking to them about food as he ate while prohibiting them from touching or eating the food.

## Abusive Relationships

Virginia has been in two abusive *convivencias*. She was with her first *conviviente* from the time she was fourteen until she was twenty-two. During one of our meetings, she described just how closely related her migration to Lima, her first *convivencia*, and the end of her childhood were.

> VIRGINIA: From Andahuaylas I came here [to Lima] as a young girl. My older sister brought me when I was eleven years old. My older sister brought me because I suffered there [in Andahuaylas] because I had no father, only my stepfather. So my sister brought me here. My older sister was already married and she brought me here.
>
> CRISTINA: Your sister—
>
> VIRGINIA: Yes, my sister. I came here when I was eleven years old and when I was thirteen, fourteen years old she gave me to the man. [Even though I was] crying, she gave me to him.
>
> CRISTINA: When you were fourteen years old?

VIRGINIA: Yes, when I was fourteen she gave me to the man. And when she gave me to that man, we lived there [near my sister] for almost ten years. And from then, that man, it was the same thing [he abandoned me].

CRISTINA: And was there any violence in that relationship? Did he insult you or beat you?

VIRGINIA: Back then yes, that one, yes. He would punch me here on my leg, he would beat me like that.

CRISTINA: Was he like that from the beginning? From the time you were fourteen years old?

VIRGINIA: Yes, I was fourteen years old and it was violence. Because I didn't want to have anything to do with men. I cried a lot. A whole month, I cried. No, I couldn't get used to living with the man. I was afraid of the man. . . . That's why the man would say (that man was six years older than I was), he would say to me, since I cried, I was afraid of the man, he would say, "Maybe you should go live with your sister and I'll bring you here on a weekly basis. Go live with your sister." He took me to my sister's. Again, my sister forced me to come back [to him].

When Virginia was eleven years old, her older sister called for her from Lima because Virginia wanted to get away from her stepfather. With a family of her own to provide for and scarce resources, however, Virginia's sister had little time or money with which to help Virginia. As described by Virginia, her sister wanted Virginia to begin her own married life and stop depending on her. When she turned fourteen, her sister gave her away to a man who was interested in her as a wife. Virginia cried and refused to stay with the man, who was six years older than her and whom she hardly knew, but each time Virginia escaped from him, her sister would force her to return to him. According to Virginia, he began to beat her almost immediately because she refused to have sex with him: "I didn't want to have anything to do with men."

During her first *convivencia*, Virginia was forbidden from working outside the home and was financially dependent on her *conviviente*. Her *conviviente* wore Western clothing and came and went from the house freely. Virginia dressed in her community's traditional clothing and stayed home. In staying home, Virginia exemplified the gendered division between the house and the street in many women's lives in Lima. However, this division between home and street was not one she had been expected to respect in her childhood. Growing up in a poor household in a small rural community in the Andes, Virginia had spent most of her childhood outdoors in the fields taking care of the family's few animals and staying away from home as much as possible because of the abusive stepfather.

According to Virginia, her *conviviente* prohibited her from taking courses to learn to read or write, and she felt lonely in Lima. After almost ten years of abuse and two months before the birth of their fourth child, Virginia's *conviviente* abandoned her for another woman. When Virginia asked him why he was leaving her, he told her it was because the other woman was *limpia* (clean). The other woman was a single woman from Lima with some years of schooling. Although Virginia had been a virgin when she began to live with him at the young age of fourteen, the years of living together, her household duties, and the children she had borne may have made her appear less attractive than other women to him. The traditional clothing she wore marked her as indigenous, and therefore could have made her appear especially dirty and unattractive in his eyes. While she maintained her community's clothing of *polleras* (multilayered skirts) and wore her hair in two long braids, as many indigenous women do, he had become increasingly urbanized, acculturated to life in Lima, and distant from Virginia. It was not her gender identity but her ethnicity, rural background, dress, language, and lack of education that marked her as the inverse of a single, urban Limeña.

In discussing Virginia's case, it is useful to note that within some Andean regions, researchers have found that indigenous women are considered to be more indigenous than men either by members of those communities or by others in the country. De la Cadena analyzes how in Peru, within an indigenous community very close to Cuzco, differentiation is facilitated by equating gender to ethnicity to geography. In Chitapampa, men move to urban areas in search of work and women stay in the community (de la Cadena 1991). As a result of the men's migration to more modern, urban areas and the women's continuous residence in rural, poorer spaces, the women define themselves as indigenous whereas the men define themselves and are defined by their wives as *mistis* (mestizos). Canessa (2005a,

2005b) similarly observes that in Bolivia, within the small rural community of Pocobaya, monolingual Aymara women are understood to embody Indianness more than the men from the community.

Also focusing on Bolivia, but on the larger urban setting of La Paz, Stephenson finds that the clothing worn by indigenous women marks them as especially Indian, and therefore as unclean. This is especially relevant to understanding the connection between "dirty-ness" and racism that partly informed Virginia's abandonment by her *conviviente*. For the indigenous women of La Paz, it is their clothing that "is considered to be, by definition, unclean" by the middle and upper classes, and "*cholas* who don the *pollera* and *manta* [shawl] visibly depict racial and cultural difference and therefore are perceived as the embodiment of disorder" and uncleanliness (Stephenson 1999:6). Similarly, Virginia's use of her community's traditional clothing and hairstyle may have marked her as "dirty" in comparison to a single, mestiza Limeña. According to Virginia, her *conviviente* had insisted that she continue to wear her community's clothing in Lima because he feared that other men might find her attractive if she wore Western clothing, and that could encourage her to have affairs. According to Virginia's explanation of her *conviviente*'s demands, their intimate relationship had mirrored broader trends of equating women's use of indigenous clothing with uncleanliness and inferiority—two characteristics that could make her less attractive to men.[4]

Crain (1996) describes how, in Ecuador, Quimseña women are involved in the "sale of the self." Their identity and gender, which are viewed as authentically indigenous by the upper classes, are used to attract tourists to hotels where Quimseñas work. The Quimseñas' gender is conflated with authentic Indianness, yet the Quimseño men's gender is not. This conflation of Indianness with women's bodies throughout the Andes results in the widespread perception of women's bodies as "sites for the reproduction of Indian homes and families" (Canessa 2005a:16). Because "Indian homes and families" are precisely the elements believed to prevent the nation's progress in the national imagination, indigenous women are popularly viewed as especially dangerous and undesirable in their condition as bearers of an unwanted, or at least inferior, identity.

There are no studies on whether or not women are considered to be more indigenous than men within Virginia's community. However, I bring up the existence of other communities in which this is the case, and the widespread phenomenon within Andean nations of viewing indigenous women's bodies as more Indian than men's, because Virginia's first *convivencia* replicated the reproduction of racial and gendered hierarchies by associating the woman with indigenous spaces and the man with mestizo ones. In Virginia's relationship, it was she, not her *conviviente,* who had been pressured to maintain markers of her place of origin by dressing in a stereotypically (to others) indigenous way.

After her *conviviente* left her, Virginia stopped wearing the clothes typical of her community. More importantly, although Virginia felt strongly connected to her community, she did not want others to identify her as *serrana* or *india* any longer because, as she explained, she believed people discriminated against her because of her appearance. She was painfully aware of the prejudices terms such as *serrana* and *india* evoke in Lima—and in some intimate relationships as well. During her second *convivencia*, Virginia has worn only Western clothing.

Virginia's racial identity, as perceived by her first *conviviente*, played a central role in her experiences of discrimination, violence, and abandonment. I interpret her refusal to continue to "look" *serrana* as an immediate reaction and form of resistance to the low social status and generalized inferiority commonly assigned to women from poor, rural areas in the *sierra* in Lima. By breaking away from her first *conviviente*'s demands that she keep her hair in two braids and maintain her community's dress, Virginia's actions seek to contest the discrimination and prejudice she confronts not only on the streets but also within her home.

Virginia's actions suggest that accommodation and resistance may be nearly inseparable, as acts of resistance may include accommodation, and accommodation may include resistance (Anyon 1983; MacLeod 1992, 1993). At first glance, Virginia's change from her community's traditional dress to Western clothing signals accommodation to dominant conceptions of what constitutes undesirable and inferior dress versus desirable and modern forms of dress. However, her actions also convey a more complex story.

Virginia feels strongly connected to her community of origin and visits her elderly mother there almost annually. In spite of the violence that marked her childhood there, she speaks of her community of origin with affection, telling me that her older sister moved from Lima back to her community several years ago and that she too would like to return there some day.[5] Virginia has remained in Lima, however, because she fears that if she leaves the home she shares with her second *conviviente*, neither she nor her sons will be able to claim it in the future. According to Virginia, when Jesús becomes angry, he asks her, "Why don't you go back to Andahuaylas?!" and she responds, "This house will not be for you or for me. The first floor will be for one son, the second floor for the other."

To ensure that her sons will have access to the house when they grow up, Virginia is determined to stay in Lima and in the house as long as her *conviviente* is there. Her decision to stay in the house in spite of her desire to return to her community is a strategic one aimed at protecting her sons' property—to provide them with as many resources as possible to *superarse* in Lima. Similarly, Virginia's decision to wear Western clothes is a strategic move aimed at allowing her sons and herself to *superarse* by contesting the discrimination Virginia confronts because of how others perceive her based on the clothes she wears. In Cuzco, wealthier indigenous mestizos rid indigenous identities of their negative connotations by, among other things, adopting urban forms of dress (de la Cadena 2000). Virginia also seeks to contest others' initial perception of her as inferior by wearing Western clothing. Both in the cases of indigenous mestizos in Cuzco and of Virginia in Lima, changing one's outward appearance is a form of public accommodation to ensure social mobility but does not signal forgetting or giving up one's cultural heritage. In Virginia's case, she resists complete accommodation by valuing her connections—and possible return—to her community.[6]

During her second *convivencia*, Virginia's lack of formal education has played a key role in the power asymmetry within the relationship. Virginia and her *conviviente* own two small and precariously built houses, one in Andahuaylas and one in Lima. Throughout the *convivencia*, he has kept all the papers pertaining to their properties. Initially, Virginia did not challenge this arrangement because it seemed natural to her because he was the man and could read and write—he had studied through fifth grade. Several years later, when she attempted to separate from him, her *conviviente* denied Virginia access to the property titles. Fearful that her name may not be on the titles and that she and her children will lose everything if she goes through with a separation, Virginia continues to share a house with her *conviviente* and he continues to regularly verbally, and occasionally sexually, abuse her.

Virginia has continued to associate indigenous identity markers with discrimination during her second relationship. During these years, she has refused to speak Quechua to her two youngest sons. She has also encouraged them to value and attend school. She wants her sons to be modern and urban so that they can be successful in Lima and not suffer the discrimination she has experienced because of how others have identified her, as indigenous and uneducated. In erasing these two aspects of their ascribed identity—a nonwhite *serrana* identity and a deficient education—she hopes to protect her sons from discrimination and violence in Lima. For migrants, letting go of their native Quechua and speaking only in Spanish to one's children can be a strategy to help the children *superarse* in Lima. Other ways in which migrants can try to de-emphasize negative connotations associated with indigenous ethnicity include taking on urban forms of consumerism and pursuing higher education (Fuller 2001:364; de la Cadena 2000). Virginia can not participate in urban consumerism and does not have access to education, but she hopes her children will.

*Racquel*

Virginia is not the only woman whose experiences of violence in the home underscore that "race lies just below the surface in Peru" (Seligmann 2004:148). Racquel's case further illustrates the effects of the regionalization of race on migrant women trapped in abusive relationships. When Racquel was eleven years old, she and her mother migrated to Lima from a small community in Huambalpa, Ayacucho, to escape Racquel's abusive father. It was in Lima that Racquel met her husband. She married him in 1986, at the age of twenty-three. Racquel had attended school until third grade. Her husband was born in Lima and had dropped out of school after his second year of high school. Soon after they married, she and her husband moved in with her in-laws.

When I met Racquel in 2001, she was thirty-eight years old and was staying with four of her five children at a shelter. I regularly joined her and other women and children at the lunch table at the shelter. On several occasions, Racquel and I would walk to her room after lunch to talk, while her children played in the courtyard. Although Racquel, her husband, and their children had stopped living with her in-laws long before Racquel and I met, the years she lived with her in-laws are essential for understanding Racquel's experiences, as they relate to her ascribed racial identity and to the regionalization of race within intimate relationships.

Racquel remembers that soon after she and her husband moved in with her in-laws, her mother- and father-in-law repeatedly asked her husband, "Why, if you are a Limeño, why would you marry a *serrana*?" In other words, why had he married an ignorant, uneducated, poor, backward, and dark woman rather than someone more modern, with more years of schooling, and from Lima. Racquel felt despised and hated by her in-laws. Although her husband initially defended Racquel when her in-laws criticized her for being *serrana*, his defense soon turned into insults directed at her, and later into physical and sexual abuse.

While Racquel's in-laws identified her as *serrana*, Racquel self-identified as "more Limeña than *serrana*" and described her children as Limeños. By the time Racquel met her husband, she had lived in Lima for over a decade—almost half of her life. When I asked Racquel if she missed Huambalpa, she explained that after living in Lima for almost three decades, she no longer felt that she could live in a small rural community. The one time that she and her children visited her community, her children missed Lima so much that she now felt very anxious about the idea of being away from Lima for too long.

Given the identity imposed on Racquel by her in-laws and husband and Racquel's own self-identification, what is particularly noteworthy in this case is that, in Racquel's words, "My parents-in-law were from there, from my town!" and her husband was a second-generation migrant. As she told me this,

Racquel opened her eyes wide and shook her right hand in the air to make sure I realized this was an especially important bit of information. Whereas I did not interview Racquel's in-laws or husband—since an attempt on my part to contact them would have jeopardized Racquel and her children's safety—I interpret Racquel's in-laws' and husband's attitudes through her rendition of events. I find Wade's statement about the process of *blanquea-miento* (whitening) among some Afro-Colombians in Colombia particularly relevant to an understanding of the process whereby Racquel's in-laws could reject Racquel on the grounds that she is *serrana*. According to Wade, *"blanqueamiento* . . . may mean that blacks themselves come to adopt disdainful attitudes towards blacks and black culture, while being unable to fully escape categorization as blacks themselves" (1993:298).

As is the case for some Afro-Colombians in Colombia, some migrants from the *sierra* reject other migrants from the *sierra* because of their *"serrano-*ness," even though in practice they may also be labeled *serranos* by others. Racquel and her in-laws would both be perceived as *cholos* or *serranos*, not whites, by other Limeños. At the same time, the fact that the process of urbanization and acculturation allowed Racquel's in-laws to identify themselves in opposition to Racquel supports the view of identities as fluid and relational and adds a new dimension to the regionalization of race. In associating space with racial identity (and more broadly with social status) for themselves, it is not so much where one comes from but where one is now that is significant for Racquel's in-laws. From this perspective, for Racquel's father- and mother-in-law, integrating Racquel into the family signified a return to a lower status.

In regard to social status in Peru, Seligmann states that "being 'cultured' and 'educated' depend on with whom one socializes, how one behaves, the clothes one wears, the food one eats, where one lives, and one's occupation"(2004:148). By migrating to Lima, Racquel's in-laws had become upwardly mobile and their family more educated and less *serrana*. They had distanced themselves from rural areas and from people associated with them, and adopted an urban lifestyle. They had provided their children with educational opportunities unavailable in their community of origin, and at least one of their sons (Racquel's husband) had a stable and reputable job in the town hall. One interpretation of their rejection of Racquel is that with her mere presence, her in-laws felt that the characteristics (backwardness, ignorance, rural lifestyle) from which they had struggled to disassociate themselves now threatened to lower the family's status. In this case, the identification of Racquel as a woman is not sufficient to explain the abuse against her. What the in-laws resented was not that their son had gotten married, but that he had brought a woman of lower social and cultural status—a *serrana*—into the family.

According to Racquel, her husband demanded that she not work outside the home because he believed a woman's place was in the home and not "on the streets seducing men." On several occasions, he used a razor to scrape off polish Racquel had put on her nails and to rip her clothes, telling her that she looked like a whore and beating her to prevent her from leaving the house. Nonetheless, Racquel managed to leave the house on several occasions to secretly work cleaning homes. She used the money she earned for her children's expenses. If her husband noticed she had money and asked how she got it, Racquel responded that her cousin had lent it to her. In Racquel's case, her experiences and her husband's violence were informed by her gender identity, but the lens of gender fails to capture the complete picture of how the attitude of her husband's parents facilitated—or at the very least reinforced—her husband's devalorization and abuse of her.

*Inés*

The third case is that of Inés, a light-skinned forty-six-year-old woman with three children who worked as a math teacher during the early years of her marriage. We met in 2001 through a psychologist at a nonprofit women's organization. Although she had never stayed at a shelter, Inés's life story echoed many of the themes of men's jealousy, violence, and resistance in the life stories of shelter residents. After our initial meeting at the psychologist's office, Inés invited me to her house to continue discussing her experiences. Inés lived in an established working-class neighborhood twenty minutes away by taxi from where I lived.

Inés owns a small, sparsely decorated one-story house with

three rooms and a back patio. The white paint on the walls, which hold two large paintings, is peeling throughout the house. The family has transformed the garage into a small neighborhood *bodega* (grocery store) that specializes in soft drinks, a wide variety of crackers and candy, bread, oil, and eggs. The earnings from the store constitute the family's main source of income. Inés and her children take turns staffing the store. As I entered the house, it was impossible to ignore the strong smell of kerosene coming from the kitchen. Her eldest son, nineteen years old at the time, had just returned home from school and was busy cooking. As Inés invited me to join them for a meal, her son came out of the kitchen to greet me. He held two big plates piled high with rice, lentils, and a fried egg on top and placed one of the plates in front of me. The food smelled delicious. Inés and her family were relatively better off than most of the other women I interviewed, yet they still struggled to cover the bills each month. The generosity with which Inés and her son greeted me, however, was typical of all my visits to women's homes. Whether it was Kool-Aid, a soft drink, crackers, a cup of tea, or, in this case, an entire meal, the women who invited me to their homes typically offered me something to eat.

As we sat in her home, the peaceful home environment she had created for herself and her children stood in contrast to her descriptions of the violence in her past. Although Inés had separated from her husband years earlier, she and her children continued to seek therapy to cope with lasting emotional wounds. Originally from a rural area of Huancavelica, Inés had lived in Lima most of her life and spoke only Spanish. During her childhood and as a teenager, her parents had emphasized femininity and the importance of modesty to prepare her for the role she was to assume later in life as a wife. As we sipped our soft drinks, Inés described the values and roles her parents instilled in her as a child:

> We always lived with discipline inside my home. [My mother] never let us go out. She always told us that young women should stay inside their homes, washing, cooking, embroidering, and knitting. We were happy inside our home cooking, washing, doing the little things. I wasn't the type of girl who went to parties, had boyfriends . . . I was a girl who practically my whole life has

been from my school to my house and from my house to my
school. And when I started working, from my work to my house,
and from my house to my work.

Inés's limited movement outside her house emphasized her
primary identity as a woman. She avoided the street because her
parents had taught her that it was a space of "virility . . . and is
a dimension of the outside world that is disorderly and opposed
to the domestic realms" (Fuller 2003:137).

Inés's primary identification is as a woman, yet education
and ethnicity shaped her life more than the previous description of her childhood suggests. Her parents wanted Inés to
discontinue her studies after finishing high school so that she
would stay home and cultivate her feminine qualities to prepare
for marriage. In spite of her parents' opposition, however, Inés
postponed thoughts of marriage until she finished high school,
received additional training, and eventually became a math
teacher. Inés married in her early thirties, later than most of the
women of her generation as well as than her parents had hoped.
Until she married, her education had been a central component
of her identity. In contrast to what her parents had taught her,
Inés encourages both her sons and daughter to pursue their
studies beyond high school and teaches her children more egalitarian gender roles. At home, her sons and daughter contribute
to their home's and the *bodega*'s maintenance through cooking
and cleaning, in relatively equal amounts.

It was through her work as a teacher that Inés met her husband, also a teacher. He had lived in Lima all of his life. He began
to abuse her physically, psychologically, and sexually on a regular
basis soon after they began to live together. Inés described one
of innumerable violent episodes with the following words: "So
then he threw the food at me and he says, 'Maybe the people
from your land will eat this food. I do not eat this food. I am in
Lima, not in your land.' So then he threw the food at me again, at
my face, letting it all fall to the ground. Everything was a mess."
Inés's husband demanded that she provide food for him whenever he wanted throughout their sixteen years of marriage. The
demands corresponded to the traditional gender roles Inés had
learned from her parents. In the episode I just cited, Inés had
fulfilled the duties expected from her based on gender roles.

Inés's husband threw the food at her not because she failed to fulfill her wifely duties adequately, but because the food she cooked was not good enough for a Limeño. By telling Inés that the food may be good enough for "her people" but not for him, he asserted his superiority over her based not only on gender but also on identity as determined by place of birth. He emphasized his wife's connections to rural areas, and therefore to an inferior status.[7] Following Alcoff, I bring up Inés's case to illustrate how, in the case of women who are abused, the imposed identities and the negative connotations others attach to those identities do not always depend on skin color (Inés has light skin) or coincide with an individual's definition of herself.

## Gendered Expectations

The three cases I have described illustrate the ways in which ascribed racial identity and educational level (in the first two cases) shape women's experiences of violence within intimate relationships. Yet even as these aspects of the women's identities play key roles in their experiences of violence, as mentioned earlier, they are in addition to gender inequality as an important factor in women's experiences of violence rather than a replacement for it.

Within *convivencias* and marriages, disagreements regarding gender roles and obligations frequently preceded men's violence. On separate occasions, Lorena and Natalia discussed the more common competing notions of gender roles within intimate relationships:

CRISTINA: And what do you think he expected from you, from the woman he married?

LORENA: Well, to have her subjugated like a slave. Something like that, no? Something like he wanted to have someone exclusively for himself to give him anything he might want, but not a wife with whom to share ideas, share responsibilities.

---

CRISTINA: Have your convivientes helped you with the housework?

NATALIA: He didn't help me, *señorita*. Even though I went out to work, I arrived and found my house the same. Didn't do anything because he said that the man shouldn't wash clothes. His mother hadn't taught him that, that was for the woman.

Some women—and Lorena is representative of this group—viewed marriage as a partnership, with the man and woman as equals and sharing work within and outside of the home. Other women—and Natalia is representative of this group—agreed with men that a woman should serve and obey her husband, but added that this was only the case as long as the man fulfilled his duties by providing food and shelter for the family. At the time of our interview, Natalia was the sole breadwinner for her household. Her husband stayed home during the day but continued to expect Natalia to cook, clean, and care for him and their children in addition to working outside of the home. Like many of the women I interviewed, Natalia viewed her husband's expectations of her as aberrant because he failed to fulfill his role. While several women agreed that a wife has specific obligations to her husband, they also pointed out that a husband has specific obligations and that marriage can only work if both individuals fulfill their duties.

According to Fuller (2001), two dominant—and contradictory—cultural expectations of how a Peruvian man should behave are that "from the point of view of the virile man, a man should prove that he is strong, sexually active and heterosexual; from the point of view of the domestic man he should be responsible, to be a father is his greatest achievement and that which gives meaning to his life project" (322). The two men with whom Virginia became involved in serious relationships were more concerned with developing what according to Fuller would be their virility than with cultivating their domesticity. In emphasizing virility, Virginia's *convivientes* had extramarital affairs while demanding that Virginia remain faithful. According to Virginia, they wanted Virginia to have children and prevented her from using birth control, yet neither one took responsibility for providing for her and their children.[8]

Virginia believes that the man of the house should support his wife and children financially and that the woman should clean and cook for her husband and children. In Virginia's account, the men she lived with neither provided her with money for the household nor helped around the house, yet they demanded that she obey them. Virginia recalls that when she refused to have intercourse with her second *conviviente*, he would yell, "When are we getting a divorce then?" Because her *conviviente* did not live up to his end of the marriage contract, Virginia is convinced "he is good for nothing" and does not feel obligated to have sex with him.

After beatings, Virginia feels "afraid of the man. I can't breathe, my chest hurts . . . my body is paralyzed." On one occasion when she went to the police station to file a domestic violence complaint, the officers asked to see her *verdes* (literally, greens; bruises) before she could file a complaint. Because she did not go immediately after a beating, her bruises were no longer visible and the police told her to go home. Virginia is hesitant to return to the police station because of this experience and because she fears her neighbors might see where she is going and tell her *conviviente*. She feels trapped.

*Surviving and the Limits of Resistance*

All of the women I interviewed had ways of contesting what they viewed as extremely unjust treatment and thereby challenged varying forms of discrimination and violence. The women's actions of resistance within abusive relationships include changing or maintaining their appearance as a marker of ethnic identity (as in Virginia's case); teaching their children more egalitarian gender roles (as in Inés's case); and working outside the home, against their husbands' wishes (as in Racquel's case). They also include hitting back, as discussed later in this section. These seemingly "small acts" of resistance allow women to survive and make violent and discriminatory situations more bearable and less dangerous for themselves and their children, making these small, everyday acts powerful. Yet, if we are to understand the contexts in which the women live and act, it is better to acknowledge both the existence of their courageous actions and the limited effects these may have in the long term than to romanticize the actions by believing these actions on their own can permanently end the women's experiences of violence.

In Virginia's case, she identified domestic violence as the worst thing a woman could experience. Virginia also believed women should not use violence. At the same time, she encouraged her sons' use of physical force against their father to stop his abuse of her.[9] At twelve and eight years old, the boys had already learned and internalized that as men, they had more power than women and that their mother, as a woman, needed their protection.[10] What resulted in the short-term relief from violence against her thus also reinforced gendered uses of violence, and more specifically men's use of violence.

To cope with, change, and prevent abusive behavior, all of the women I interviewed developed strategies of resistance—what I describe as ambivalent everyday resistance. In Virginia's case, as previously stated, after her first *conviviente* left her, she stopped speaking Quechua to her children and began to wear her hair and clothes in more typically urban ways to de-emphasize her ethnicity. Although shedding external identifiers of indigenous identity and accommodation to mainstream norms did not directly challenge her *conviviente*'s power within the relationship, it was a strategy Virginia used to protect herself and her sons from and contest future violence based on how others perceived her and her sons. However, by distancing herself from an indigenous identity, her actions reproduced the dominant devaluation of non-urban, indigenous identities.

*Hitting Back*

Some of the women I interviewed described getting angry at their partners and hitting them as a form of self-defense. Little research exists on women and anger. In her interviews with women in abusive relationships, Griffiths (2000) describes two levels of anger: anger as an emotion and anger as a trigger to action. What concerns me here is anger as a trigger to action. In challenging cultural ideas of femininity that emphasize calmness, submission, and nonviolence, by hitting back some women reassert control over their lives and challenge men's violence against them. Of course, not all women are in situations in which they can hit back or in which hitting back could benefit them. In this sense, although physical force is not usually a successful way to stop violence permanently, it is important to acknowledge that some women have found asserting their physical strength within an abusive relationship to be empowering and effective in diminishing and even ending abuse.

Straus (1993) has argued that "it is the responsibility of husbands as well as wives to refrain from physical attacks (including retaliation), at home and elsewhere, no matter what the provocation" (80). Straus fails to discuss what other options are available to women who have been turned away by institutions charged with helping them. He fails to consider what women can do to survive and resist their husbands' violence when they are economically dependent on their husbands, when they have children whom they cannot support on their own, or when they realistically fear that attempting to leave may result in lethal violence against them. Straus bases his argument on the hypothesis that "assaults" by wives escalate men's violence against women. He suggests that "ending physical assaults *by* wives needs to be added to efforts to prevent assaults *on* wives" (Straus 1993:80; emphasis in original). What he calls "assaults," however, includes slaps and scratches, which women I interviewed employ as forms of self-defense.

Gordon's discussion of women's assertive behaviors within abusive situations challenges Straus's understanding of women's use of violence: "Wife-beating usually arises out of specific domestic conflicts, in which women were by no means always passive, angelically patient, and self-sacrificing. To analyze these conflicts, and women's role in them, does not mean blaming the victim, a common distortion in the literature on wife-beating. That women are assertive in domestic power struggles is not a bad thing; women's suppression of their own needs and opinions is by far the greater danger" (1988:252). The women in Lima viewed violence as a masculine trait but occasionally appropriated physical and verbal violence as tools to survive and resist their partners' abuse. The women delegitimized men's exclusive use of violence by asserting their own capacity to employ violence.

For Jacinta, whose husband continues to abuse her verbally after twenty-four years of marriage, getting angry the first time he attempted to beat her soon after they married led to her hitting back, which she believes is the reason why he has not attempted to beat her since then. Surprised that he hit her, she reacted by throwing "all the things that were nearby" at him, hitting him, and yelling at him. Jacinta showed her husband that she too was capable of violence as a way to contest his power. Similarly, Maria used violence against her husband after years of abuse to show that she too could use violence:

CRISTINA: And have you ever defended yourself by hitting him?
MARIA: Yes.
CRISTINA: Yes?
MARIA: One time I even planted a knife on him. . . . I grabbed it because it was already too much. There were insults on top of beatings. I grabbed the knife and I stabbed him here [armpit]. Then
afterwards he grabbed me and I got over it some.
CRISTINA: And was that the first time you'd reacted by hitting back,
or had you reacted that way before?
MARIA: No, that was the first time. Other times when he beat me,
before, I have scratched him. [*raises her voice*] Because I'm not
going to allow him [to beat me].

In hitting back, Maria contested her husband's power by showing him that violence is not an exclusive male privilege. Her
scratches and her use of a knife against her husband were acts
of self-defense in the context of her husband's long-term abuse
of her.

Representing women's actions simply as assaults, as some
family violence scholars do (Straus and Gelles 1990), therefore
fails to differentiate between the aggressor's violence as part of
a prolonged and escalating series of violent acts and a woman's
response to a specific assault. By transgressing gender lines, the
women I interviewed challenged the structural foundations of
men's use of violence: the culturally determined ideas of femininity that emphasize serenity, submission, and nonviolence,
and the ideas of masculinity that emphasize dominance, physical strength, and aggression.

Yet even in these women's cases, the short- and long-term effects of their physical resistance points to the limits of women's
resistance. Sexual, verbal, and economic violence are just as
prevalent as, if not more prevalent than, physical violence—and
wounds from insults and humiliating events may take longer
to heal than physical wounds. Jacinta's and Maria's strategies
worked to end physical but not verbal violence. Other studies
of Latin American women have found that during periods when
physical and sexual violence decreases (for example, during
pregnancy), the severity of verbal violence increases significantly (Warwick 1997).

*Identities and Violence in Intimate Relationships*

Some discussions of race and ethnicity in the Andes have focused on small communities in which a shared and distinctive cultural background, presented as ethnicity, can be identified (Abercrombie 1998; Allen 1988; Doughty 1968; Isbell 1978; Weismantel 1998), while others have focused on large-scale, more heterogeneous urban areas in which race intersects with class and cultural background to produce a variety of more fluid, gendered, and racialized subject positions (Henríquez 1996; Oboler 2005; Portocarrero 2007; Stephenson 1999). Both in writings on small, rural communities and larger-scale urban areas, the role of race, ethnicity, and racism within abusive relationships is rarely mentioned (but see Canessa 2005b). With few exceptions, the women I interviewed do not claim an indigenous racial identity. As many women in the Andes, the women I interviewed avoid racial and ethnic labels in describing themselves in Lima. In their intimate relationships, however, their rural origins, phenotype, and way of speaking and dressing may mark them as poor *indias, cholas,* and *serranas.*

The lens of gender is greatly enhanced when we also pay careful attention to less visible but perhaps equally contested aspects of women's identities. I have discussed the ascription of specific identities associated with indigeneity, lack of formal education, and rurality to underscore the many ways in which women experience inequality and violence within abusive relationships. Even in cases in which women reject the identities imposed on them and self-identify as more urban than rural (as in Racquel's case), they may continue to be vulnerable to racism and discrimination in the intimacy of their homes. In Virginia's case, language, dress, and lack of formal education became markers of an inferior status. For Virginia and other women, in this continuous process of imposing prejudicial identities on others, being identified as a poor, indigenous, and uneducated woman from a small rural community can have dire effects within an intimate relationship. While a woman may define herself in positive ways, she may also become painfully aware that the identity her partner ascribes to her may be constructed to justify his abuse.

# APTER 3 ▓ Women's Bodies, Sexuality, and Reproduction

▓ WHEN I ASKED FORTY-SIX-YEAR-OLD Inés if there was something that her husband had done to her that hurt her the most, Inés replied, "What hurt me the most was the disrespect towards my body." During interviews and conversations, the women's discussions of sexual abuse most often came up in descriptions of specific episodes of violence and during questions about gender roles. The men's sexual abuse made the women acutely aware of how knowledge regarding, and control over, women's bodies could be a source of power. According to the women, the men made them feel "like a mop," "like trash," and "like a whore" through their violence. The women were thus hurt by the men's sexual violence and by the lasting emotional wounds that resulted from this violence. This chapter examines one of the most contested—and violent—terrains within abusive relationships: women's bodies and the meanings and practices attached to them.

My interviews with the women provide information about their understanding of the images and expectations men held of women in regard to their bodies, sexuality, and ability to conceive. They also provide a window into women's strategies for resisting men's attempts to control their bodies, which can include refusing to acquiesce to their husbands' demands for sex; empowering daughters by teaching them about women's bodies and sexuality in ways that discourage women's dependence on men; secretly using birth control; and secretly undergoing sterilization.

Women take great risks to control the consequences of sexual abuse (such as unwanted pregnancies) when ending sexual violence is not a viable option. The women I interviewed understood that their complaints of sexual abuse are not normally heard by the police, and that during forced sex, it would be very dangerous to resist men's demands—as in the case of Inés, whose husband threatened her with a knife as he raped her. In these circumstances, women must often feign complete compliance to their partners' demands in order to survive. According to Scott (1985), resistance "prevents the worst and promises something better" (350), creating spaces of resistance in very constrained circumstances. Although women's resistance within abusive relationships does not get rid of or transform broader forms of gendered and racialized structural violence (Anglin 1998; Farmer 2004; Galtung 1969) that facilitate marital rape and other forms of violence, the scope of women's agency is significant because it allows women to protect their bodies and health precisely in the context of multiple oppressions and restricted access to resources in the most intimate of spaces.

*Marital Rape*

The women I interviewed described their experiences of sexual violence in the following ways:

> Sometimes I didn't want to be with him, and by force [he forced me to have sex with him].
> *Laura, thirty-six years old, mother of three, separated*

> He would beat me in front of my son. He beat me hard. He left my whole body bruised. And the following day he would want to have sex with me . . . sexually he forced me.
> *Daniela, thirty-eight years old, mother of five, in shelter*

> Sometimes he wanted to be with me and after using me he threw me off the bed and I had to sleep on the sofa. I mean, he was an animal.
> *Ester, forty-six years old, mother of three, separated*

In the late 1990s, Human Rights Watch (2000) found that police officers in Peru were reluctant to recognize psychological violence as a "real" form of violence in spite of the Family Violence Law's inclusion of psychological violence. Today, it is sexual violence that is not recognized as a form of intimate partner violence. More specifically, marital rape is not yet accepted as "real rape" by many Peruvians, including those in charge of enforcing the Family Violence Law, in spite of its legal definition as a form of family violence.

Marital rape is likely the most common form of rape in times of relative peace, yet it has been largely overlooked in the literature on rape and domestic violence (Bennice and Resick 2003). The Peruvian Truth and Reconciliation Committee (2003) found that during the years of internal war between the state and Sendero Luminoso, between 1980 and 2000, indigenous women were targeted for mass rape.[1] Today, most sexual violence takes place within intimate relationships. According to a recent study in Lima, 17 percent of women who were physically abused by their partners were forced to have sex by that partner either during or after the physical abuse (Güezmes, Palomino, and Ramos 2002:84). Among the women I interviewed in shelters, at reproductive health clinics, and in other venues, all had been forced to have sex by their partners at some point in their relationships.[2] All but two of the women became pregnant as a result of forced sex.

The connections between marriage and rape have, until recently, been legitimized through laws. Until 1997, when it was changed, Article 178 presented rape as an acceptable path to marriage. The law stated that a rapist could escape criminal prosecution by marrying the woman he raped. In cases of gang rape, all the rapists involved avoided prosecution as long as one of them married the woman. There are documented cases in which women were pressured to marry the men who raped them to save their family's honor (Merino 1997). According to a report by Human Rights Watch (2000), even after the law was repealed, police, communities, and women's families in rural areas continued to push for marriage between women and their rapists as a way to save the honor of the women's families. These practices suggest that rape has been treated as a violation of family honor more so than as the violation of a woman's rights and bodily integrity. The rape-marriage law and the practices connected to it even after it was repealed send the message that sex crimes are easily absolved by an offer of marriage. Even more troubling is the implication that although the use of force and coercion to obtain sex outside of marriage should be punished, rape within marriage and rape that leads to marriage is to be tolerated.

In a recent study on masculinity, violence, and nonviolence in Lima, Ramos finds that abusive men expect women to obey them without complaining about or questioning men's authority over the home and over women's bodies. Men also expect women to maintain the order imposed by the man in the household. Men may view sexual activity within and outside of marriage as a requisite to being real men and may therefore force sex on their partners even when they (the men) do not necessarily want to have sex (Ramos 2006). The women I interviewed reported being accused of infidelity if they refused to have sex with their partners. Several women stated that refusal to have sex was followed by forced sex. According to the interviewees, their partners accused them of infidelity even when there was little or no evidence of this. In all of the cases in my research, the women denied having been unfaithful to their husbands.

The women resented and objected to the men's forceful demands for sex and to the men's use of violence to obtain sex. Yet, significantly, only Inés used the term *violar* (to rape) to describe her experiences of forced and coerced sex within marriage.[3] In interpreting the women's understanding of their own experiences of forced sex, it is useful to consider the gender roles and obligations into which the women I interviewed had been socialized. Women have historically challenged the Marianist ideals of womanhood that subordinate women to men and limit their movements to the home (Lavrin 1989; Weismantel 2001; Miloslavich and Moyano 2000), yet dominant cultural mandates continue to encourage women to define themselves in relation to others rather than as autonomous individuals. Social relationships to children, parents, and partners commonly include women's service, and a woman's self-worth may be defined by how well these services are fulfilled. In relation to the men in their families, women are expected to be submissive, obedient, and self-sacrificing (Yanaylle 1996). Women are expected to fulfill their husbands' needs without consideration to their own sexual desires. These expectations of submissiveness and obedience to one's husband resonate within Peruvian society and directly influence women's hesitance to name nonconsensual sexual acts as rape.

The hesitance to publicly name forced sex as rape does not, however, signify the absence of agency and resistance during sexual abuse. On the one hand, through their actions, women reject men's sexual violence within marriage, and laws provide sanctions against marital rape. On the other hand, the broader cultural ideologies that dictate women's obedience and fulfillment of men's (sexual) needs within marriage silence women, and the attitudes and actions of the police as well as the women's partners reinforce these ideologies and further silence women. To contribute to a more holistic and nuanced understanding of women's experiences of sexual violence, we must examine but also move beyond the question of whether or not women view forced sex as part of their marital duties. We can examine the more intimate workings of women's experiences of sexual violence to understand how women create spaces of contestation to men's sexual violence.

Far from being dependent, passive, pathological, or masochistic, women who survive assaults assert independence, initiative and creativity as they resist violence in the most intimate aspects of their lives. The women's refusal to acquiesce to their husbands' demands for sex, their secret use of birth control and sterilization, and their conversations with daughters about sexuality challenge men's claims to ownership of and control over their bodies.

### Reproduction, Reproductive Rights, and Contraception

In Peru, family planning options and access to resources for reproductive health are limited. Between 2001 and 2003, President Toledo named two individuals who openly denounced reproductive rights as valid rights to consecutive terms as Ministers of Health, thereby seriously hampering progress in the area of reproductive and sexual rights. These men, Luis Solari and Fernando Carbone, allied themselves to ultraconservative groups in Peru and in the United States and prohibited the distribution of emergency contraception in public health clinics. In part, the men called upon the abuses committed under the state-funded sterilization campaign (briefly discussed in Chapter 1) in the mid 1990s as justification for further limiting the distribution and use of contraceptives. Today, access to contraceptive methods continues to be limited (Vallenas 2007:298–99). Thirty-six percent of women between the ages of fifteen and forty-nine use modern contraceptive methods. Among those women, 9 percent have undergone sterilization, making the procedure the most popular single form of modern contraception in Peru (Alcántara de Samaniego 1999).

What women do and do not do to assert control over their bodies to a great extent depends on their position vis-à-vis health care resources, economic resources, support networks, and employment opportunities (Gagnon and Parker 1995:14).[4] In connection to health care resources, abortion is illegal in Peru, and "conscience clauses" allow doctors to deny women services deemed offensive, such as care after a self-induced abortion. In connection to economic resources, Virginia believed she had the right to deny her husband sex after he stopped financially contributing to the household in spite of his continued employment. For years, Virginia had felt obligated to submit to her husband's sexual demands because he contributed the largest amount of money to the household, and because her salary as a domestic worker did not cover household expenses. Even after she stopped having sex with him, she continued to share a house with him, and to be vulnerable to his verbal and physical abuse. Virginia did not have the economic resources to move out. In contrast, for Inés, her decision to leave, although very difficult, was facilitated by a support network of friends with whom she could stay and by her job as a teacher, which initially provided her with money with which to continue to provide for her children after she moved away from the man who had sexually, physically, and verbally abused her.

Regardless of a woman's resources for leaving, during the relationship the man's behavior greatly affected how she expressed her sexuality and how she felt toward her body—and these feelings did not necessarily cease once she left her partner. Within intimate relationships, women also employed their bodies to assert their desires for autonomy, strength, and power, and to claim a limited sphere of power. Given women's limited resources within and outside of the home, how women employed their bodies to resist violence and assert their autonomy is all the more remarkable.

In a chapter on domestic violence in a community in Cuzco, Harvey describes how some men marked women's bodies through their insecurities and desire for power: "A woman once told me that she had been severely beaten by her husband and, when I pushed her to tell me why, she said that the wife always

suffers, that he had beaten her for all the faults of his other lov-
ers, even calling them by name as he did so. This woman's body
thus became the register of her spouse's previous relationships,
relationships in which he was unable to objectify his control in
this way" (1994:75). In the case Harvey describes, the woman's
body was punished for the faults the man perceived in "woman"
as a generalized category, thereby objectifying the woman-as-
wife in a way that denied her an individual identity. The women
I interviewed narrated numerous episodes in which, in addition
to becoming a "register for her spouse's previous relationships,"
their bodies became registers for the limits of men's power and
registers for their own autonomy. I now turn to some of their
efforts to limit men's power and control over women and their
bodies.

*Transforming Sex and Sexuality for the Next Generation*

The women repeatedly lamented how little information and advice their mothers had offered them about their bodies, sex,
and reproduction. Some had learned about their bodies through
experiences of childhood and adult abuse, others by attending talks by community health workers and women's organizations as adults, and others through a combination of these and
other sources. By openly talking with their daughters and sons
about their bodies, or more subtly acknowledging and agree-
ing with what their children learned about men's and women's
bodies and sexuality at school, the women challenged inter-
generational silence regarding bodies and sexuality. Whereas
their own mothers had believed that their daughters' ignorance
allowed them to remain innocent, the women as mothers now
knew that their ignorance had cost them too much emotionally
and physically.

The women wanted their daughters to understand what it
means to begin menstruating, how women become pregnant,
how having a child at an early age can greatly diminish a poor
woman's chances of having a successful career and being independent, and that men's violence did not have to be part of an
intimate relationship. In their interviews, the women repeatedly
contrasted their own ignorance with their daughters' knowledge
about sex. For example, while topics such as how babies are

made and born were difficult for Maria to discuss with her children, she was proud that her children know about these topics. A generational change in attitudes is exemplified through Maria's open discussion of how her children have learned about sex and sexuality from school, friends, and television:

> MARIA: She never advised us, my mother. She didn't even tell us how to take care of ourselves. Nothing.
> CRISTINA: Nothing? And do you talk with your eldest daughter about these things?
> MARIA: I talk to them about their periods. They already know about that [sex]. Just the other day she said to me, "Mom, I know that babies aren't born through the belly. You're a liar," she said to me! [*laughing*] My son has said to me, he's ten years old, the other one also said, "[The baby] isn't born through there, it's born through here" [*pointing down*]. And now they know that if girls don't take care of themselves, they end up pregnant. They know. That's why they [school teachers] explain all that to them [students] now.

Maria's experience learning about sex and sexuality had been very different. She had had her first child at age fourteen because, as she described, her mother never explained that the forceful "games" her boyfriend pushed on her could lead to pregnancy.

A talkative and energetic thirty-five-year-old *dirigente* in her community, Maria spent much of her time caring for her six children whose ages ranged from fourteen to six. Before having those six children with her current partner, she had had two children with her first husband. Both had died as toddlers.[5] Although Maria's current husband did not want her to work, Maria became very active in her neighborhood and secretly worked for money whenever she was able to in order to help pay for her children's education.[6] She did not want her children to miss the opportunities she had missed because she had become pregnant as a teenager, and she felt proud that she could contribute money to their education through her work and that her children would grow up to be educated and knowledgeable men and women.

As Ginsburg and Rapp emphasize, reproduction "provides a terrain for imagining new cultural futures and transformations, through personal struggle, generational mobility, social movements" (1995:2). By openly speaking with their daughters about sexuality, women allow their daughters increased freedom and knowledge about sexuality and thereby potentially contribute to the transformation of their daughters' future from one of sexual oppression and repression to one of increased choice and independence. Otilia, forty-six years old and a mother of four, challenged what her children learned from their father's insults and abuse toward women. She spoke with her children about how wrong it was to abuse women and insult others, and she taught her daughters that "it is not necessary to live with a man, and if we do have a man, he should love us with or without our defects."

### Pregnancy

Although differences of opinion regarding the timing of births and number of children existed among the women and men, one point on which all the women agreed with their partners was that marriage and cohabitation went hand in hand with having children. The women's value as wives was to a great extent dependent on their ability to conceive and carry pregnancies. Pregnancy, however, was often met with hostility and the escalation or onset of violence by the same men who had pressured the women to become pregnant. The men's annoyance and jealousy toward the women's physical and emotional changes during pregnancy, and toward the women's growing attention to newborn babies, often preceded violence.

In a study in Mexico, Castro, Peek-Asa, and Ruiz (2003) found that although physical and sexual violence decreased during pregnancy, the severity of verbal and emotional violence increased significantly. During my interviews, all the women made reference to verbal violence during their pregnancies. Because they are pressured to become pregnant and then abused while pregnant, abused women's experiences of pregnancy can be very different from those of other women. On the one hand, pregnancy constitutes a central part of the definition of being a good wife and of womanhood for many women. On the other hand, pregnancy provides a new terrain on which men can make women vulnerable, by aiming their violence at what women have been taught to cherish most: motherhood. Pregnancy held both the promise of a more gentle and loyal husband and the threat of more violence and less control over one's body and life.

The first study on abuse among pregnant women in Lima (Perales et al. 2009) found that 22 percent of women are abused at some point during their pregnancies (244).[7] During pregnancy, abuse carries risks both to the fetus and woman. Abused pregnant women are at "greater risk of miscarriage, abruptio placentae, preterm delivery, perinatal mortality, intrauterine growth restriction, fetal or infant loss, and low birth weight" in addition to being at higher risk of "chronic stress or fear . . . loss of appetite; gastrointestinal disorders; cardiac problems . . . [and] viral infections" (239). Some of the women I interviewed who had been abused during their pregnancies mentioned suffering miscarriages as a result of beatings; others mentioned a heightened sense of fear and feelings of powerlessness as a result of being attacked during pregnancy.

Of all the women interviewed, only one woman discussed difficulties in becoming pregnant. Like other women, Otilia felt pressured to become pregnant after moving in with her partner. She had felt inadequate because she was not able to become pregnant during the first three years of the relationship:

> OTILIA: He would tell me I was dumb, that I didn't get pregnant, that what was I doing—
> CRISTINA: It was mostly—
> OTILIA: My mother-in-law was the one that talked the most. She was the one who meddled. She said that why was I not getting pregnant, but I couldn't get pregnant. And I didn't even use any birth control.

Otilia was willing to try many things in order to become pregnant and please her husband. After following an herbalist's instructions, which included having two tablespoons of honey every morning, Otilia became pregnant and gave birth to her first daughter. Just a few months after giving birth, she became pregnant with her second daughter. According to Otilia, her husband and her mother-in-law were pleased that she could have children, yet her husband's violence did not cease when she became pregnant. As she explained in regard to her desire to become pregnant, "I thought, such was my ignorance, *señorita*, I thought that by having babies, I wanted to have babies, right? And right then it was to tie him to me. But it did not turn out that way. That was a grave error on my part. And late did I realize, *señorita*, that it was not that way. I thought that by having more babies, I tied him [to me]. I realized [that it was not that way] late." As she realized that fulfilling the expectation to become pregnant did not lead to a better intimate relationship, Otilia faced increased verbal violence. The women I interviewed described a wide range of violent behaviors they experienced from their husbands during pregnancies. These behaviors ranged from constant insults such as "ugly" and "stupid" to physical violence, including kicks to the belly and other behaviors that could result in miscarriages.

*Birth Control*

Given the risks and benefits associated with pregnancy, women sought to increase their control over if and when they became pregnant. One of the themes that repeatedly came up in their stories was their desire to use birth control and their partners' refusal to allow them to do this. Some women covertly acquired varying forms of birth control at community health posts. One woman reported secretly having an abortion to end an unwanted pregnancy.

During one of our conversations at the shelter, twenty-six-year-old Ana described her and her husband's views on having children. The difference in perspective between Ana and her husband became apparent early on and was mirrored in other women's narratives:

> CRISTINA: And when you began to live together, did he want to have children?
> ANA: Lots.
> CRISTINA: Oh, he wanted to have lots of children?
> ANA: He wanted children.
> CRISTINA: And you?
> ANA: I didn't because, well, I wanted to have only one. Well, ok, that's one, the little girl, right? But not to have more children. But he always forced me to have sex with him. He didn't want me to use any birth control.

CRISTINA: And did you want to use birth control?

ANA: Yes. I didn't want to have children. No, I didn't want to. What for? For example now, if I'm pregnant, what do I do with another child? I didn't want to at all. But he would say like, "What will they lack? They won't lack anything here. They have everything." But when he got upset he would beat me. He always beat me.

As in other women's narratives that touched on the subject of children, for Ana her desire to become a mother did not negate the use of birth control. For her husband, however, the desire for children negated the use of birth control. As mentioned in the Introduction, in workshops with men in rural areas of Peru, Movimiento Manuela Ramos found that men's greatest fear regarding their partners' behavior was infidelity, and that the suspicion of infidelity could be sufficient to trigger abuse (2003). The women I interviewed stated that their partners did not want them (the women) to use birth control because the men feared that birth control would encourage the women to have affairs. Based on her analysis of *autodiagnósticos* (self-diagnostic evaluations) by residents of Huancavelica in the late 1990s, Boesten similarly finds that "some husbands seemed to be concerned about losing control over their wives' sexuality, and associated modern contraceptives with infidelity" (2007:11). None of the women interviewed reported resorting to birth control to have affairs.

Like Ana, Inés wanted to limit the number of children she had, in spite of her husband's demand that she not use birth control. Inés had envisioned waiting three to four years after getting married before having children, yet her husband insisted that they begin to have children immediately. After giving birth to her third child, Inés began to take the pill secretly. Inés told me that her husband found her pills and became angry, accusing her of taking the pill to sleep with other men. Although he forbade her from taking the pill, when he became angry he would tell Inés that if she became pregnant, it was her problem, not his. Racquel, thirty-eight years old and the mother of five young children, found herself in a similar situation. She did not want to have more children and began to use birth control pills secretly. She too stated that her husband would become angry and violent toward her when he found her pills. He accused his wife of using birth control to have affairs. According to the women's narratives, men punished women through their violence both because the women sought to prevent pregnancy and because they became pregnant.

Of the different forms of available family planning that did not require the cooperation of a partner, pills were easier for men to discover than other forms of birth control. Because of this, some women relied on periodic birth control injections at community health posts. In addition to pills and injections, women resorted to sterilization as a way to resist men's efforts to control their bodies and reproduction and to ensure control over the number of children they had.[8]

*Sterilization as a Form of Resistance*

When Maria's husband asked her why she, a thirty-five-year-old woman who had given birth to eight children, had not gotten pregnant since the birth of their six-year-old daughter, Maria responded that it was probably because she was getting too old to have children. The real reason why Maria did not become pregnant was that she had undergone sterilization immediately after the birth of her youngest daughter. Because, in Maria's words, her husband thinks "only slutty women do that [sterilization], in order to sleep with other men," Maria keeps her sterilization a secret.[9]

In 1995, the Peruvian Congress passed a law that legalized sterilization for both men and women. Around the same time, sterilization in Peru gained a bad reputation due to reports of the forced sterilization of poor indigenous women through a state-sponsored family planning program (CLADEM 1998; Ewig 2006). Through the program, initiated in 1995 under Fujimori, sterilization was offered free of cost. However, the government had turned to state-subsidized maternity hospitals, gynecological clinics, and community campaigns in marginalized areas for the promotion of sterilization. Reports of discriminatory treatment, coercion, cruelty, and misinformation by government health workers arose soon after the program's inception (Alcalde 1999; Boesten 2007; CLADEM 1998; Ewig 2006).

As noted in Chapter 1, hundreds of women suffered through the state-sponsored program, but it is worth noting that even in this largely oppressive environment, women who were not coerced benefited because they had access to a free and efficient form of family planning. In this way, and following Foucault (1978), it is important to recognize that sites of oppression can also become spaces of resistance (Sawicki 1991:84). For the women who willingly underwent sterilization, the procedure became one path to empowerment within a generally constrictive environment. Through sterilization, the women were able to translate into reality their desire for a limited number of children and to silently but sternly reject men's demand for more children.

Among the women I interviewed, four underwent sterilization without their husbands' knowledge, and against their husbands' wishes, and at least four others either expressed a strong desire to undergo sterilization or had unsuccessfully attempted to have the operation. Economic and health concerns were among the most commonly cited reasons. Daniela was one of the women who wished to undergo sterilization because of financial and health concerns. She confronted several obstacles in her attempts to have access to the operation:

> DANIELA: No. He wouldn't let me [use birth control]. I even wanted to be operated on [be sterilized]. I had pains, the doctor said, "If you, *señor*, will allow your wife to undergo the operation" [to relieve the pain]. He became angry. He said, "What?! No. Things are not done that way" he said. "No, she will not undergo the operation."
>
> CRISTINA: What did he want?
>
> DANIELA: He wanted to fill me with children.
>
> CRISTINA: And how many children did you [plural] want to have? That is, how many children did he want and how many—?
>
> DANIELA: I wanted the two children I had. The pair. I already had a pair, apart from my oldest son [from a previous relationship]. I didn't want to have more. But he said no.

Daniela's experience exemplifies how institutional violence and intimate violence may work together to promote male control over women's bodies. In her case, these two forms of violence converged in the institutional requirement of the husband's consent for a procedure on a woman's body. Although Daniela's doctor suggested that she undergo sterilization in part to relieve pain, her husband's refusal to allow her to be sterilized forced Daniela to put aside her health concerns. Without her husband's consent, the doctor would not perform the operation. When Daniela attempted to undergo sterilization, she had three children—one son from a previous relationship and a daughter and son with her husband. When I met her in 2001, she had five children.

Unlike Daniela, four other women (Maria, Marina, Jacinta, and Carla), also in their thirties, successfully underwent sterilization. They did not tell their husbands about their plans before they underwent sterilization. Instead, they creatively found ways to get around the required husband's signature—one woman asked her son to forge his father's signature on the consent form. Had their husbands been asked if they would allow their wives to undergo sterilization, the women believed they would have reacted like Daniela's husband.

For Maria, health concerns were also one of the main factors influencing her decision to have the operation. After giving birth eight times and having one miscarriage, Maria felt certain she should not have more children. Before opting for sterilization, Maria tried different forms of birth control, always without her husband's knowledge.

Unlike Maria, who never revealed why she could not have more children, Carla told her husband about the operation after the fact:

> No, my husband didn't want [birth control]. With my last daughter, I tied my tubes. Because with my last one I had twins. The little boy died and I kept her. But I've always had high-risk pregnancies. My three pregnancies. My second daughter was born at seven months. And the last one, eight months. That's why I always said, three and no more. I don't want more children. And I tied my tubes. But I also suffered a lot because my husband, when I got sterilized, said, "You are probably running around with another man" since I went out, was out on the streets. And sometimes when I didn't want to be intimate with him, he would say, "Sure, you come home tired, you come relaxed." [*laughs*] He, always with a morbid mind. I just let him talk.

Like Daniela and Maria, Carla viewed sterilization as a way to protect her health by resisting her husband's control of her body. For her husband, sterilization was a dangerous reminder of the limits of his power and control over his wife's body and of her own power and control over her body.

Among the women I interviewed, a recurrent theme was that of the men's insistence on having more children than the women wanted. The women were suspicious of their husbands' statements that they (the women) should not worry about the risks of having more children because their husbands would support the family financially. The women knew all too well how little they had with which to cover existing expenses, how easy it is to become unemployed from one day to the next in Lima, and how some men stop contributing money to the household even when they are employed.

## Sex and Money

Even when the women could not prevent men from forcing them to have sex, they resented being forced to have sex. The violence the men used to force the women to submit to their demands worked to further alienate the women from those men, and sometimes women from their bodies. The growing frustration and resentment women felt because their husbands violently imposed their demands for sex on them is apparent in the following conversation with a group of women in the main room of a neighborhood *wawahuasi* (communal childcare facility) in a shantytown in northern Lima. The women, whom I had met with on a previous occasion, were eager to speak about their experiences, yet also concerned that our meeting not last too long. Each woman needed to continue her numerous daily chores, which for some included serving their families lunch just an hour and a half after our meeting began. After sending her six-year-old daughter, who had accompanied her to the *wawahuasi*, back home to make a light *refresco* (non-alcoholic beverage) for the group, Natalia began to speak about her husband's demands for sex:

NATALIA: They want to be with you by force.
ESPERANZA: If you don't want to be with the man, it's just that with all the violence with which he hits you—
LAURA: After all that, how can you be with a man like that.
CRISTINA: Sure, if they don't respect you—

NATALIA: You begin to feel anger.
LAURA: Resentment, right? And you don't feel anything. But how could you with so much violence?

In spite of the women's objections to and anger over men's demands for sex and use of violence to obtain sex, they reported that men continued to expect and demand sex from women who were clearly not interested in sex with those men.

Within the women's narratives of marriage and forced sex, a script of marital duties surrounding sex emerged. According to this script, men should be breadwinners and women caretakers. Wives obey their husbands and have sex with them as part of their marital duties even when the women do not want to have sex. In cases in which the pact is broken—for example, when men refuse to contribute to the household—women may question whether or not they should fulfill their part of the pact. Some women felt justified in refusing to have sex when their husbands did not live up to their end of the pact.

In most cases, the women stated that the men either did not contribute money to the household or, more often, their contributions were sporadic and the amount of money insufficient. Some women openly recognized their partner's difficulties and stress in finding reliable work in an environment in which men are also discriminated against by their employers and can be fired from one day to the next, but they did not consider these to be justifications for withholding money during times of employment.

The women also complained that sometimes men explicitly demanded unlimited access to women's bodies in return for their economic contributions. The connections between men's monetary contributions and access to women's bodies was made explicit by Virginia. In describing her demands to her *conviviente* that he provide money to purchase gas for the stove so she could cook, Virginia stated that her *conviviente* would respond by telling her that he would only give her money for gas if she had sex with him. According to Virginia, she responded, "So, I'm going to buy the gas with my body?" Because Virginia refused to have sex with him, her *conviviente* refused to buy gas for the stove.

Teresa, thirty-two years old and a mother of two, used the money her husband contributed to buy food to provide meals for her husband and children. She avoided having sex with her husband because she knew he was having an affair. Every night, she would go to sleep early with their young children in the children's bed. In Teresa's case, her refusal to have sex with her husband resulted in her being punished through forced sex on some occasions and through the withholding of money for household expenses on others. In both cases, Teresa's husband appeared to punish her for not fulfilling her obligation to have sex with him. For Teresa, sex was something she wished to avoid; yet, as she told me, she did not feel she was right in refusing her husband's demands (even though she did refuse them), even when they went against her will, during periods in which he contributed money to the household.[10]

## The Virgin and the Whore

The expectations placed on women's sexuality resulted in particularly negative treatment of women with children from previous unions. In these cases, the children marked the women's bodies as "used" and as dangerous reminders of the limits of men's control over their partners' sexuality. The children from previous unions became clear, public statements that the men with whom the women lived in the present had not always controlled their sexuality. Thus children from previous relationships may threaten what many Peruvian men have been taught to expect: control of and unlimited sexual access to the women with whom they live (Fuller 2003).

In women's narratives, having children from previous unions appears as a form of men's justification for heightened control and abuse of women. Daniela, thirty-eight years old and a mother of five, had dropped out of school as a teenager when she became pregnant with her first child. Years later, she met the man with whom she had four other children. Even before they met her, her second *conviviente*'s parents and siblings refused to consider Daniela as a suitable partner. According to Daniela, they referred to her as a sexually loose woman and even as a whore because she had a son from a previous relationship. Daniela explained that her *conviviente* tormented her by reminding her of his family's opinion of her and by bringing up her past sexual experience as justification for constraining her movement.

Daniela's *conviviente* forbade her from opening the door to any of his guy friends who stopped by the house when he was not home. She followed his instructions, yet he accused her of having let men in every time he found out a friend of his had knocked on the door while he was out. "When he came home, he would say, 'You probably let him in.' 'Open your legs!' he would say. And he wanted to check me!" In Daniela's account of events, because she had been with another man before meeting him, she could never be trusted to remain faithful to her current partner.

Kristina, forty-five years old and a mother of two, had a similar experience to that of Daniela. Because she already had one daughter when she met the father of her second daughter, her husband subjected her to extreme forms of surveillance and demands. Near the beginning of their relationship, and before exhibiting violent behavior, Kristina's husband demanded that her older daughter live with Kristina's parents once he and Kristina moved in together. Kristina had to give up her closest family— her daughter—in order to form a new family with her new partner. I interpret such requests as possible indicators of a man's desire for ownership over the new family. By asking a woman to separate from the children of previous unions, a man may be seeking to dissolve her pre-existing family ties and secure complete ownership over the new family.

### Self-Ownership and Setting Limits

In spite of the various forms of violence that directly affect how women experience and control their bodies, reproduction, and sexuality, my interviews with women underscore their desire, attempts, and successes in keeping men out of their bodies. Women attempt to regain control of their bodies, sexuality, and reproduction in the context of relationships in which their partners' demands for control greatly diminish their ability to decide on how many children to have, when to see their children, and how to protect their health. Women take substantial risks to regain control in oppressive and limiting home environments. They speak to their children and encourage them to behave more openly regarding sexuality, they refuse to have sex, and they secretly use birth control and undergo sterilization. In coping with men's sexual violence and the potential for pregnancies from this abuse, women secretly use birth control, since resisting their husbands' forceful demands for sex is not always a viable option because it could lead to an escalation of violence.

Men's violence, however, continues to negatively affect and limit how women experience their bodies. That women resist men's violence does not mean that they are able to stop it or keep men and men's demands out of their bodies permanently. In most cases, women's everyday resistance brings immediate, short-term relief. For example, while sterilization results in the permanent end of women's ability to reproduce, it does not permanently stop men's violence against women, men's use of force to obtain sex, or men's demands for more children, nor does it protect women from sexually transmitted diseases. The burden of thinking of and acquiring birth control in a violent environment continues to fall on women. The women I interviewed did not expect men to think of and use birth control, but they hoped that their husbands would not prevent them (the women) from using birth control. In that sense, the women's actions contain "elements of resistance" (López 1994) in that they contest the everyday workings of men's privilege but do not necessarily defy the social conditions that allow and reinforce men's privilege. To expect women to actively defy the vast social conditions that perpetuate men's privilege would be unrealistic, given the limited resources available to women in abusive relationships. What they do to survive, end violence, and transform the future for their children takes more courage and creativity than popularly imagined.

# PART II

# Leaving the Relationship

# CHAPTER 4 ﴾ Families, Children, and Mothering

﴾ THE MAJORITY OF THE WOMEN I interviewed turned to—or attempted to turn to—their families for help before seeking assistance from state and nonprofit agencies. Some families assisted the women in leaving while others pressured the women to stay with abusive partners. Although studies exist—and more are needed—on women's experiences in seeking assistance from women's organizations, nonprofit agencies, and state agencies in trying to leave abusive partners (for Peru, see Boesten 2006; Güezmes, Palomino, and Ramos 2002; Movimiento Manuela Ramos 2007. For elsewhere, see Hanmer and Itzin 2000; Hautzinger 2007; Santos 2005), research on the role of women's families of origin and by marriage in aiding and blocking women's efforts to cope with or leave an abusive relationship is still underdeveloped (but see Abraham 2000; Raj et al. 2000; Van Vleet 2008).[1] Additionally, in Peru, as in the United States, "the mother, not the father, is likely to be held responsible for child abuse or neglect either because of her presumed failure to protect her child or because of her silence" (Schneider 2000:148) in abusive home environments, yet our understanding of women's own views of mothering within a violent home environment is an area of research in need of further attention. In all of the cases with which I became familiar, the women referred to their roles and responsibilities as mothers in discussing their decisions to leave, stay with, or return to an abusive partner.

This chapter examines the realities of having—and not having—families and children for women attempting to survive within an abusive relationship or to leave it, and pays particular attention to how women understand their roles as mothers in these contexts.[2] It discusses the existence of various forms of helpful, not-so-helpful, indifferent, and hostile families, and how a woman's efforts to cope with or leave an abusive partner are supported or thwarted through interactions with her three families: her nuclear family, made up of the woman, her husband or *conviviente*, and their children; her family of origin, made up of her parents, siblings, and (sometimes) other relatives (such as grandparents, aunts and uncles, and godparents or co-godparents); and her family by marriage, made up of her parents-in-law and brothers- and sisters-in-law. Jimena's experiences, as narrated to me during her shelter residency and during phone conversations after she and her children returned home from the shelter, are the main vehicle in this chapter for the discussion and analysis of the role of families, mothering, and children in the lives of poor women in abusive relationships.

For Jimena, as for many other women in Peru, the nuclear family is the ideal family form. In practice, as in other parts of the world, only a minority of families in Peru conform to this ideal: 34 percent of Peruvian families are nuclear families (Ponce 2007:99).[3] Although it may be generally true that, as a popular introductory textbook on Latin America states, "for the poor, the [extended] family is not a mechanism to control resources, but an institution to turn to because of the scarcity of resources," and that "their kinship networks . . . provide help in times of hardship" (Cubitt 1995:107), this was not generally true for the women I spoke with in Lima. In the cases with which I became familiar, including Jimena's, it was more common for a woman's nuclear family, family of origin, and in-laws to be unavailable or to play an active role in preventing the woman from leaving an abusive partner.

## Meeting Jimena

As I opened the locked gate and then the front door to the shelter, a little boy I had not met before greeted me. After an excited "*Hola!*" and "You know what?" the skinny, bright-eyed boy began to describe how his father threw and broke things in his house when he became angry. A few seconds into the boy's narrative, a young woman rushed in. Jimena, the boy's mother, wanted to know whom her son was speaking with about these things. It was Valentine's Day 2001, and my day at the "Women's Harmony House" shelter had just begun.[4]

After a couple of informal conversations and lots of playtime with the children at the shelter over the next two days, Jimena and I sat on one of the benches in the back patio to talk. Her two children, six-year-old Carlos and three-year-old Maribel, played in an upstairs bedroom so that Jimena could speak freely. Jimena left the bedroom window slightly open to make sure we could hear the children as they played, and the children yelled down every few minutes and we answered them as part of an elaborate game they created. After about half an hour, the children became bored with their game and came down to convince us to stop talking so much and play with them. I had brought soft drinks and some snacks to the shelter to share with everyone that day, and, with Jimena's permission, I offered the children some of these snacks. Those snacks provided us with an extra ten minutes of uninterrupted interview time. After turning off the recorder, we joined the children as they drew, and then we played hide-and-seek with them. On the following days, we repeated this routine as Jimena little by little told me about her life and about the events that had led to her flight from Juan, her *conviviente*.

A week before Jimena's arrival at the shelter, her *conviviente*'s violence had escalated to an unbearable level emotionally and physically. As Jimena spoke of how Juan's violence had affected her everyday life, she narrated an episode that had happened that week:

> After [the beating], my head hurt. And I told my husband, "I'll be right back. I have a headache, I'm going to go walk [to buy medicine for a headache] nearby." And I went out to walk. And, I don't know, I must have walked like that for about four blocks or so, but [when I realized where I was] there was a road and everything. And I really don't remember. I don't remember what happened. My mind went blank. I ended up way down. There's a sports field near my house, but it's about eight blocks away. And to get there you have to go through a field where they would take girls to rape them. And I walked through there! But I don't know how I went through there. . . . It was about eight at night already [and dark]. And I wasn't feeling right. I don't know how I could have ended up there. There was a big house nearby where they had found the bodies of girls before. And I had gone out to walk to buy a pill because I had a headache. . . . And I got scared and started to cry. That was the first time that my body trembled all over from fear.

To treat the headache that had resulted from Juan's violence, Jimena tried to go to a pharmacy, but instead became disoriented on the way there and ended up in an area in which women and girls are targeted for violence. Juan's violence in the home is directly tied to her exposure to other forms of violence outside her home, thereby underscoring the interconnections between intimate and public violence in her life. Jimena's heightened vulnerability to violence at home and on the streets led Jimena to tremble all over from fear.

At age twenty-five, Jimena had spent almost half her life working. She was an organized and outspoken third grade teacher at a school in a large, established shantytown in northern Lima. As a teacher with three years' experience at the school, Jimena earned minimum wage (about US$117 a month). Before arriving at the shelter, she and her children had stayed first with a friend and then with her grandmother as she worked on a long-term plan for herself and her children. Having felt pressured to leave both her friend's and grandmother's houses, her stay at the shelter was filled with guilt about having her children in a place (the shelter) in which she did not feel able to satisfy her maternal obligations to feed and shelter them properly.

Jimena became especially concerned that she was failing in her role as their mother because of the shelter's limited resources. Whereas in their home the children had taken warm showers, the shelter only had cold water and the children cried because they were not used to taking cold showers. Similarly, the squeaky bunk beds, worn sheets, and bedroom door with a broken lock provided little that reminded her children of home or with which Jimena felt able to comfort them. Jimena told me she was "accustomed to better food for my children" and explained that her children had tasted but refused to eat the food provided by the shelter. Partly because they refused to eat, she felt increasingly worried that she had not made the right decision in coming to the shelter. When her daughter had a temper tantrum, Jimena told me she was surprised because her daughter did not normally do this, and she worried that this too was a sign that she had not made the right decision.

Jimena felt that by coming to the shelter, she had placed her children in a situation in which "I have made them feel hunger, cold" and she found it difficult to justify subjecting them to this. She also believed that the shelter staff was routinely absent and, when they were there, too busy to address her and her children's needs. In part, her experiences had to do with the fact that her stay coincided with a particularly busy time for the already understaffed shelter. Less than a week after her arrival at the shelter, she had made up her mind to return to her house within the next couple of days, if not sooner, in order to better provide for her children.

After she left the shelter, we spoke on the phone on two occasions. The second conversation took place three months after she left the shelter. She informed me that her situation had improved a little. Her *conviviente* had ceased all physical abuse, although he continued to abuse her verbally. She hoped that their relationship would improve. At the same time, she knew from past experience that Juan could become violent at any moment. Although Jimena knew of the shelter's existence, she felt certain she would not go there again because she did not think it provided sufficient resources for its residents. Jimena's brief stay at the shelter, her experiences prior to her arrival at the shelter, and her return to Juan are part of a larger story of the many problems women may face when attempting to leave abusive partners, and the role families play in women's decisions to stay, leave, or return home.

## Convivientes *and Forming a Family*

Jimena had lived with the father of her children for six years before going to the shelter. Although she was not legally married to Juan, she referred to him as her *esposo* (husband). Jimena and Juan were not alone in their status as *convivientes*. Among low-income couples, it is common to live together but not marry. Among the women I interviewed, the majority (71 percent) were *convivientes*. As Barrig (1982) noted, and it is still the case today, *convivientes* live together and form families and often refer to their partner as *esposo/a*. Women *convivientes* generally feel the same responsibilities as married women toward their partner and children. High costs connected to the marriage certificate and ceremony posed serious obstacles for many of the women I interviewed who had originally hoped to marry.[5] These costs make *convivencia* a common response among the poor to the wish to form a family.[6]

Peru's 1993 constitution legally recognizes *convivencias* that last for at least two continuous years. Peru's Family Violence Law similarly recognizes physical, psychological, and sexual violence in *convivencias* as well as in marriages. The law refers to violence between ex-spouses, ex-*convivientes,* and between men and women who have had children together, even if they never lived together.

To better understand *convivencias,* I asked a group of women to speak with me about their views on *convivencias.* The women were from a recently established shantytown in northern Lima and had agreed to discuss with me the obstacles they faced in attempting to lead violence-free lives. The following conversation during the group interview clarifies some of the reasons for becoming *convivientes.*

> CRISTINA: And why do you prefer to be *convivientes*? Why *convivientes* and not marriage?
>
> JACINTA: Being married is too difficult. [*everyone laughs*]
>
> NATALIA: Also because of the cost.
>
> JACINTA: But when you start, or when you first have a partner, you say, "Let's save," right? Because of the cost.
>
> NATALIA: Oh, yes.
>
> JACINTA: It ends up being expensive. That's why to get married you need lots [of money].
>
> NATALIA: You have to offer some sort of party, something—
>
> JACINTA: First and foremost is the economic situation.
>
> CRISTINA: And what about to be able to separate?
>
> JACINTA: No!!
>
> NATALIA: At that moment, you're in love, you have illusions.
>
> JACINTA: And, also, who wouldn't want to get married in white?
>
> NATALIA: *Convivencia* is forever, isn't it? But the years go by and that's not the way it turns out.
>
> JACINTA: Later, when you want to get married, the man doesn't want to marry you.
>
> ESPERANZA: That's what happened to me. I wanted to get married at first but later he didn't want to marry me.
>
> NATALIA: It's a very pretty dream, to be married in white, but—
>
> JACINTA: But after you live together for a while, you don't think of getting married in the future anymore. Or the years go by and there are more and more problems. You get to know each other

and then the problems come. "I didn't marry you and now I can just leave you" [says the man]. Because now to be married and to separate requires a lot of money. And if the man doesn't want to give you anything—

NATALIA: You save a lot [by being *convivientes*]. [*everyone laughs*]

As Natalia comments, *convivencia*, like marriage, is supposed to last forever. Although a woman may decide to *convivir* rather than marry, her decision may be largely based on economic rather than affective factors, given the costs that prevented her and her partner from initially getting married.

Although women expect their *convivientes* to use their income to maintain the household, most of the women I interviewed reported that their partners refused to give them money directly or to allow them to manage the household budget. Among the women whose partners covered household expenses on a regular basis, some reported that their partners did all the shopping for the house in order to avoid giving them money. The women also complained that their partners spent the money they earned mostly on themselves, that they ignored the children's needs, and often—particularly when the women worked (secretly or with the man's knowledge)—that they took away the women's money.

When Jimena met her *conviviente* through mutual friends, she was eighteen and he was nineteen. Jimena believed she had found a mature, gentle, intelligent partner. According to Jimena, Juan stood out because he seemed smarter than the rest of their friends, and because he offered to help her with school assignments. Within a few months of almost daily conversations, she had fallen in love with him. She introduced him to her parents and two sisters, and they too liked him. Juan and Jimena decided to become *convivientes* and moved into a room in her parents' house a few months after they began to date. After living with Jimena's parents for about half a year and Juan's parents for the rest of the year, the couple moved into their own apartment. Financial difficulties forced the couple to move back to her parents' house within a year, but this time they built a room adjacent to the house with money they had saved. However, finding a suitable place to live was not the couple's biggest problem.

After they started to live together, "little by little, I began to discover his ignorance, uhm, that he was *machista*, that he believed that machismo still exists, you know?" It didn't take long for Jimena to see in Juan the opposite of the man she had dated. What Jimena experienced—the change from the calm, loving, and attentive man she had dated to the abusive and controlling man with whom she lived—is something many other women experience cross-culturally (Mooney 2000). By the time Jimena realized Juan was abusive and controlling, she was pregnant.

### Becoming a Mother and Empowered Mothering

According to Adrienne Rich, we must differentiate "between two meanings of motherhood, one superimposed on the other: the *potential* relationship of any woman to her powers of reproduction—and to children; and the *institution*—which aims at ensuring that the potential—and all women—shall remain under male control" (Rich 1986:13, cited in O'Reilly 2006:11; emphasis in original). While the patriarchal institution of motherhood may be oppressive, the practice of mothering has the potential to be empowering for both mother and child (Rich 1986; O'Reilly 2006).[7] According to O'Reilly, "empowered mothering" means that "the mother lives her life and practices mothering from a position of agency, authority, authenticity, and autonomy," thus transforming motherhood into "a political site wherein the mother can effect social change" through the ways in which she rears her children and through her own autonomous acts of social justice (2004:12).

For Jimena and other women, the institution of motherhood within an abusive home and a broader social environment characterized by racism and poverty constituted an oppressive space that allowed women little room for effecting social change. At the same time, women found ways to exert agency through their mothering practices in order to protect children even within this constrictive space. For those women who permanently left abusive partners, the sort of empowered mothering O'Reilly describes was not without challenges, because racism, poverty, and additional forms of violence continued to impact the lives of the women and their children even after they left abusive relationships. Many women, including Jimena, ultimately rejected mothering outside of the institution of the two-parent family because they did not consider it to be in the best interests of the children.

Significantly, in North America, research on "mothering as a site of empowerment and social change" has been rare (O'Reilly 2004:3), whereas in Latin America, mothering has been studied and publicly performed as a site for resistance and social change for several decades. In Argentina, the Mothers of the Plaza de Mayo have since the late 1970s constituted an internationally known group that has challenged the State's use of violence against its citizens—particularly the disappearances of its citizens—through its members' public self-presentation as mothers concerned with the well-being (and therefore whereabouts) of their children. Women have underscored their role as mothers to create similar groups and engage in protest against violence throughout Latin America (for El Salvador, see Stephen 1997; for Mexico, see Bejarano 2002).

As has been the case with state violence, the experiences of the women I interviewed point to their role as mothers as significant to their decisions of if, when, and how to resist domestic violence. Yet their actions cannot be reduced entirely to this role. Women's multidimensional identities include but are not limited to a single role. Thus, to understand women's resistance in connection with abusive relationships, we must recognize motherhood as one among the many roles practiced by the women I interviewed.

### Children

As mothers, the women believed it was inevitable to make sacrifices. However, they strongly protested against sacrifices their partners imposed on their children. As Jimena explained in relation to Juan's failure to give her money for the children each time they temporarily separated, "I told him: 'I'm not waiting for you to support me. I have always looked for a job and I can spend two, three days without food, and that's fine. But I can't make my children go through that.'" The theme of women as self-sacrificing mothers came up repeatedly in interviews and conversations. For example, during a group interview with women who worked at a communal daycare center in a northern shantytown, one of the women, Esperanza, emphasized the extent to which a woman will sacrifice her well-being in order to uphold the unity of the family for the sake of the children. When I asked why she thought women stay with abusive partners, she replied, "It's better to respect the children and wait [to separate] until they are grown up, until they have formed their own homes." According to Esperanza, even when the husband demonstrates that he no longer loves his wife, the woman should stay with him for the sake of the children because children should grow up in a two-parent nuclear family. Other women agreed that being a mother involves pain but that when a partner demanded that children also experience pain because of his violence it was time for the woman to exert her position of agency as a mother by standing up to that man.

The women who left their partners cited their children's well-being as the main reason for leaving. In their cases, the ideas of motherhood as restricted to the nuclear family had initially pressured them to stay, but the difficulty of mothering in a violent environment ultimately motivated them to leave. Children, especially very young children who did not understand the violence toward their mothers as a threat to their own well-being, were strongly attached to their fathers and resented their mothers' attempts to separate them from their fathers. Mooney describes one case in London in which "a woman went to a woman's refuge, but her little boy, aged five years, missed his father so much that he became ill" (2000:175). The women in Lima faced similar dilemmas in separating children from the fathers. One woman at the "Women's Harmony House" reported that her son became ill while at the shelter, but the doctor could find nothing wrong with him. It was only when she and her son returned home to her husband that her son was well again. Another woman described how thinking of her children made her feel guilty about filing charges against their father. She worried about "what my children will say now, because my son, the second one, he asked, 'Is my father going to jail?' And he cried.'" As in Jimena's case, these women stayed with or returned to their partners because they believed it was in the best interest of the children and because they believed that as mothers they should be willing to sacrifice their own well-being for that of their children.

In the cases in which women returned to or never left their

partners, it was common for the women to protest if and when men abused their children. The women occasionally used physical punishment ranging from a slap on the hand to a slap in the face to discipline their children. They contrasted this to their partners' use of hands as well as belts and household objects to discipline children all over their bodies on a regular basis. Jimena and Juan had different views on disciplining children. According to Jimena,

> What I do is slap them [on the hand]. I believe there are ways of speaking. I have always started with that [speaking to them]. And if they misbehave I tell them, "You know what? Don't talk to me, don't say anything to me, I am very upset at you." Or sometimes I'll tell them, "I'm going to hit you" [if the child continues to misbehave] and I go over and *pum*, a slap in the hand. But it's enough for them to see me coming toward them for them to stop. Because I don't talk to them [when they misbehave], I pretend I'm upset at them so that they understand. But more than that, no. Yet he would [go beyond a slap in the hand].

While at the shelter, Jimena reported that Juan had beaten the children all over their bodies. Three months after she returned home, Juan had yet to beat the children again, but Jimena felt that a resurgence of violence toward the children would again force her to leave with them. Studies in the 1970s and early 1980s point to an emphasis on blind obedience and discipline of children within poor, working families in Lima (Scott 1994:93). However, the women I interviewed shared Jimena's concern for their children's safety at the hands of their children's fathers and openly disagreed with their partner's disciplining tactics when they believed these tactics endangered their children.[8]

Among the women I interviewed, only one woman reported regularly beating her children. She explained that she used to beat her children as a way to vent her frustration and anger at her husband, who beat her. After attending workshops on domestic violence offered by local feminist organizations, and after her husband stopped abusing her physically (but continued to abuse her verbally), she began to communicate more with her children and this led her to stop beating them. By the time we met, she spoke of her violence toward her children as a problem in her past she felt proud to have overcome.

Maria, thirty-five years old and the mother of eight children, stated that she repeatedly confronted her partner about his use of violence against their children. She summed up what she viewed as the problem with how her husband treated their children by stating, "I told him, 'You are not going to hit my children with your anger. You have to speak to them and gain their trust. Your children don't respect you, they fear you, and that's ugly.' I told him, 'Your children should have respect for you, not fear you.' Since then he doesn't beat them. He didn't use to beat them too much, but still." I asked Maria what advice she would offer women, like Jimena, in abusive relationships and with young children. She responded that it was important for women to stand up to their partners, stating that if a woman allowed her husband to beat her or her children once, he would do it again and again. This, she explained, was a lesson women needed to learn.

When women decided to leave permanently, it was often because they had reached a point at which they felt unable to protect their children. Jimena had not reached that point in 2001. Another woman I met at the same shelter, Amada, had reached that point. One of the ways in which Amada's partner had abused her was by demanding that she show him her hands and remain still as he made small cuts on her hands using a kitchen knife. When he began to do the same thing to their three children, Amada felt certain it was time to leave. She reported her husband's abuse of their children to the police, and they referred her and her children to the "Women's Harmony House" shelter.

Two other women spoke of how their teenage daughters from previous marriages convinced them to leave. In both cases, the daughters did not live with their mothers but had observed and complained about the abuse they witnessed in their mothers' homes each time they visited. As she analyzes the contradictions of patriarchal law in her book on the life of a Mexican peddler, Behar highlights how "the 'master of the house,' it turns out, is not much of a master anywhere else. When children witness the disjuncture between social and domestic power, they gain critical tools for taking apart the very terms of gender hierarchies that are inextricably embedded in class hierarchies" (1993:280). Behar's observation helps explain the disjuncture the daughters witnessed between, on the one hand, the little power and control their mothers' partners exerted outside the home due to their low class status and, on the other hand, the power the men claimed and the violence they used to enforce this power inside the home. In this sense, the daughters understood that rather than being "the experience of power," masculinity for these men became "the experience of entitlement to power" (Kimmel 2000:241). These two teenage daughters offered their mothers a different, less tolerant, view of men's violence. Slowly, they convinced their mothers to leave secretly with the other children.

Mothers, both in cases in which they left and in cases in which they stayed, also encouraged daughters to be less tolerant of men's violence in their lives. Although the women's priority for all of their children was for them to go to school in order to facilitate the children's upward mobility as adults, the women were especially concerned about their daughters' futures. They urged their daughters to stay in school and be independent because they did not want their daughters to depend on men in the same way they had. As Maria explained,

> I talk to my daughters and tell them to study. That they never become like me because I did not study. I tell them, "Take advantage of this time, study early in life. When you have finished your studies, then you can work." So that they learn to support themselves. "You are not going to depend on anyone, you are going to have a job, my daughter." I always tell them, "You have to go to school, graduate, then you go to a university or institute, and then you can have a boyfriend. Not now. Men deceive women. They take advantage of you." . . . I send them to school with the money that I've earned.

For many women, the accomplishments they are most proud of are keeping their children safe, sending them to school, and seeing them graduate. It is in these ways that women exert the agency, authority, and autonomy inherent in empowered mothering and thereby effect social change through their daughters' education. Women are particularly proud of children, especially daughters, who plan to pursue careers, because careers can allow those children to become self-sufficient and upwardly mobile. As is exemplified by Maria's advice to her daughters, mothers want their daughters to be safe and advise their daughters about the dangers of depending on men. At the same time, mothers may reinforce the image of men as necessarily violent, and thereby ignore the diverse forms of practicing masculinity in the Peruvian context, by teaching their daughters that "[all] men deceive women."

*Resistance and Balancing Roles as Wife, Mother, and Teacher*

The role of mother was not the only role women practiced in their everyday lives. In Jimena's case, she balanced roles as wife, mother, daughter, and teacher. As time passed, Jimena became increasingly concerned about the dangerous situation she and her children lived. During our second interview at the shelter, she explained that when Juan went out with his friends to drink, he often came home drunk and revealed episodes from his childhood that he had kept secret while they dated, describing abuse he had experienced as a child. Juan also became progressively more verbally and physically abusive and insisted on having the children witness his attacks on Jimena when he drank. Jimena regretted not having known more about Juan's past and family before they moved in together.

I asked Jimena about the most recent violent episode she had experienced. She responded, "I was supposed to be the servant and he was the master of the house. So then he started breaking things, throwing things, throwing the electrical appliances, throwing me out, hitting me, insulting me, humiliating me. *So then I stayed quiet.* But what made me most indignant was that my son, who is at the peak of his development, that he witness all this." Jimena discussed what Juan expected of her in her role as his wife, and contrasted it to what she expected of herself in her role as a mother. On many occasions, these two roles conflicted with one another. Juan's expectations of how a wife should behave were not shared by Jimena. According to Jimena, he wanted someone to serve him and she wanted someone with whom to communicate and share responsibilities. As a mother, she wanted to protect her children from Juan's violence and felt increasingly frustrated because he forced them to witness his violence.

Rather than interpreting Jimena's silence as an expression of passivity, resignation, or subordination to Juan, I see Jimena's purposeful silence as strategic resistance to what she perceived as unjust—her husband's violence and her son's witnessing that violence. As Stanko reminds us, "silence is a *declaration*. Factors such as concern for others . . . encourage silence" (1985:19; emphasis in original). Jimena's resistance took the form of rational, conscious strategies that replaced more overt and potentially deadly forms of resistance—in her case, talking back or getting up and walking away. Her silence served to end the immediate danger of further, possibly lethal, violence against her. It also served to protect her children, because she curbed her husband's power to force them to witness his violence by stopping—or at least cutting short—the violent episode through her silence.

Jimena was not alone in using silence to resist and curb her husband's escalating violence. Her silence was successful in that it was a declaration of her power to stop her husband from abusing her in front of her son in this episode, but it will do little to challenge the subservience Juan expects of her and may actually reinforce his power over time. Rather than showing him she has power, her silence may persuade him that he is in control and that she obeys him (even if only as a way to stop his violence).

More broadly, women's silence during episodes of violence similar to the one Jimena described reminds us that accommodation may include resistance (Olmedo 2003:376). Women's silence can be interpreted as a form of accommodation to mainstream values of feminine passivity in that women's gendered reliance on silence is embedded in the submissive, subordinate behavior abusive men expect of women. It is, after all, through gender socialization that women learn to use silence as outward displays of respect to their supposed "superiors"; in the case of the women I interviewed, these were often their husbands and the middle-class, white(r) employers in whose homes they worked. Women's silence can also be interpreted as a form of resistance. In Jimena's case, her silence challenged the partner's power by producing the desired effect in his behavior: the cessation of violence, and therefore an increase in her power and ability to protect her children from witnessing violence.

As in Jimena's case, many of the women I met stated that being a wife or *conviviente* meant very different things for them compared to the men with whom they lived. Focusing on attitudes regarding gender and sexuality among adolescents in Lima, Yon examines the different attributes women and men value in women in intimate relationships.[9] For women adolescents, she finds that the most important characteristics of the ideal woman are honesty and faithfulness, sympathy, affection, intelligence, and the desire to get ahead in life. For men adolescents, the most important attributes of the ideal woman are "a good body" and beauty (1998:32). Whereas the women's responses reveal a range of characteristics that are equally important for the ideal woman to possess, the men's responses focus on two related, superficial, and objectifying characteristics as more important than all others. The findings from this adolescent study and my interviews with women underscore that within an intimate relationship, the categories "man" and "woman" rarely refer to two different but equal types of partners. These categories mark gendered beings typically reared to have unequal positions within society and within intimate relationships. Many of the attributes the women adolescents described in Yon's study are irrelevant for the type of woman the men in her study envisioned as an ideal partner.

It is not unusual for men and women's expectations of each other to conflict within intimate relationships. Like Jimena, Inés worked as a teacher. Inés is an independent, forty-six-year-old mother of three teenagers who separated from her husband in the mid-1990s. In discussing the beginning of the years of violence, she described how she had danced with a male cousin at her wedding party. Although she saw nothing wrong with this, and did not think her husband would expect her to refuse her cousin a dance, her husband became visibly upset, and then dragged her into their room by her hair and beat her on their wedding night. Inés recalls that he called her a whore and demanded to know why she had danced with another man after becoming his wife. Surprised and overwhelmed by her husband's behavior, Inés tried to convince herself that maybe that was what marriage was supposed to be like, but hoped it would not happen again. Like Jimena and Inés, other women felt surprised by violent episodes early in their relationships, and they slowly began to develop ways to cope with violence in their daily lives. When forms of everyday accommodation and resistance no longer worked to keep the violence to a tolerable level, women who were able to do so left. After leaving her husband, Inés stopped feeling like a prisoner in her home.

Jimena and other women who married young had not been given any advice by their parents or anyone else as to what to expect or do in an intimate relationship. When violence erupted, many women, hoping to be good wives and mothers, worked harder to fulfill their husbands' expectations. They tried to focus on the feminine qualities their husbands commonly demanded of them—to be gentle, maternal, and obedient—to keep their husbands happy and as a way to stop the violence. Forty-seven-year-old Ester remembered some of the things she did and accepted in the hopes of making her marriage work and keep her family together:

> ESTER: Unfortunately my husband is very *machista*. He is a man who at home gives orders, destroys things, and no one else in the house has a voice or a vote. No one could give an opinion, no one could answer back. And like I was telling you before, I sort of also blame myself for letting it happen.
> CRISTINA: But, how old were you when you got married? You were very young—
> ESTER: I was eighteen. And what happened? That I said yes to everything he ordered me to do. I would say yes and remain quiet. Yes, yes, yes. Until one day [recently] he told me: "You are the one to blame. You said yes to everything. You should have reacted." But I would tell myself, it's to get along, for the sake of harmony.

Ester followed the script she had been taught at home, at school, and through the media: good wives obey their husbands. However, as in other cases, the attention and care she wanted to give her children in her role as their mother was often inhibited by her husband's demands that she serve him first. In other cases, as in Jimena and Juan's, men insisted that the children witness men's violence or directly abused the children. These sorts of behaviors reinforced the power of the men while at the same time undermining the women's roles as mothers by making the women's protection of their children during these episodes difficult.[10]

The women had a tough time balancing their competing roles as wives and mothers. The men insisted that the women play their primary role as wives while at the same time prohibiting them from using birth control and expecting them to have children. It was almost impossible for the women to find time and energy to fulfill their husbands' expectations of them as wives and also their own expectations of themselves as mothers. Twenty-six-year-old Ana worked at a juice shop near her home when she met her *conviviente*. Early in their relationship, she began to experience conflicting expectations in her roles as mother and *conviviente*. After stating that her partner pressured her to become pregnant, Ana told the following story:

> He started being jealous when I became pregnant. Why? Because that man [a customer at the juice shop] would also come drink juice and then later when we moved in together that man would walk by, talk with me, look at me. And everything changed since then. When I became pregnant he [the *conviviente*] said it wasn't his child, that it was the child of that man. And that man was black! And my baby. [*She looks at her baby, whose skin is not dark, and lifts her baby's arm.*] So that's when it started. He would make me sleep on the floor, "No, I don't want you on the bed." That's when everything changed, until now. He says, "He doesn't come by now, your husband [the juice shop customer] doesn't come by anymore, does he?" And I say to him, "But, love, why do you speak that way? The fact that he had juice while I was there does not mean that he was something of mine." But he always says the same thing. . . . Two days after coming home from the hospital [from giving birth], he threw me out of the house [because he said the baby was not his].

According to this narrative, Ana's *conviviente* wanted Ana to be a good wife. He wanted her to be under his control and become the mother of his children. Her interactions in public spaces with other men appear to have threatened his sense of ownership of Ana. Ana underscores his jealousy by stating, "The fact that [the customer] had juice while I was there does not mean that he was something of mine." Although Ana found her *conviviente*'s attitude extreme, there was little she could do to convince him that she was not being unfaithful.

After quitting her job at the juice shop and moving in with her *conviviente*, Ana was constantly under his watchful eye, working with him in his welding shop daily and being locked in the house when he left. On the one hand, motherhood was necessary for Ana to fulfill her role as a good wife. On the other hand, Ana's potential motherhood—her ability to become pregnant (through her *conviviente* or any other man)— was out of his direct control and threatened to challenge his view of her as his. Their daughter could be viewed as a symbol of his control over her, yet she could also symbolize Ana's independence from—and possible betrayal of—her *conviviente*. Ana's potential for motherhood served as a reminder of the limits of his power.

Although the women's roles and hopes as wives were difficult to give up, some of the women found that leaving their partners was one way to claim a space in which they could exert more agency by autonomously working on defining and practicing what it meant to be a mother. Although the women highly valued their roles as mothers, and motherhood provided an important source of fulfillment for them, most of the women I interviewed had not been given any sort of advice by their mothers regarding what to expect in an intimate relationship or as mothers. The primary de facto message the women had received from parents, teachers, neighbors, and even strangers was that they were destined to be mothers and should strive to be good mothers.

Looking back at the periods of cohabitation and violence, several women who had separated from their partners commented on the tension they had experienced between being wives and mothers. Some women stated that they felt they had behaved as "more woman than mother" while in abusive relationships, unable to protect their children because they had dedicated so much time and energy to satisfying their partners' demands. As has also been noted by other researchers (see Itzin 2000:363), the women reported that men forced them to choose between their roles as wives and mothers by demanding that children from previous unions be kept with the women's parents. The men's justification was that it was for the good of the family (i.e., the new family the man wanted to form with the woman), yet their demands in reality broke a family apart (i.e., the family the woman had before living with the man).

*Being a Teacher (and a Wife and Mother)*

Balancing the roles of wife and mother at home proved to be a difficult task. When women worked outside the home, they faced even more challenges and dangers to practicing and satisfying the different roles in their lives. Some men did not want their wives to work, so the women either did not work or worked in secret. When women secretly worked, they commonly used their earnings to supplement the money men contributed to the household to meet household expenses and saved any remaining money for emergencies. In some cases, as in Juan and Jimena's, the men expected their wives to work and cover all household expenses so that they would not be asked to contribute their income to the household and could instead spend it on themselves or their families of origin.

Both in the cases in which women secretly worked and those in which men pressured women to work, the men's violence threatened the women's ability to work and provide for their families. Juan's abuse made it very difficult for Jimena to work as a teacher because she had to conceal the abuse to keep the job she depended on to cover her children's expenses. Her triple role as wife, mother, and teacher proved increasingly difficult to maintain. In part, her belief that what takes place inside one's home is private and should not be disclosed to outsiders made balancing her roles as mother, wife, and teacher more challenging because it prevented her from initially seeking assistance to cope with the violence. Jimena's view that what goes on within the home is private is common among women in Peru as well as among women elsewhere. Writing on domestic violence in the United States, Merry notes that "the idea of the private domain of the family, insulated from state supervision by the patriarchal authority of the husband (although constituted by the state in its capacity to marry and divorce) exists at the level of the taken-for-granted world" (2006:187). In Peru, the privacy of the family is similarly part of the taken-for-granted world. This privacy has been historically maintained through laws concerned primarily with men's public behavior that considered what men did to women within marriage and in the "privacy" of their home outside of the state's purview.[11] In contemporary Lima, the majority of women believe family issues should only be discussed within the privacy of the home and with family (Güezmes, Palomino, and Ramos 2002:79).

The people closest to Jimena—her family of origin, in-laws, and co-workers—reinforced her feeling that her *conviviente*'s violence against her was a private matter and facilitated her self-blame through their indifference. The ideal family life Jimena was expected to have stood in stark contrast to the reality of the everyday life she felt unable to discuss with others. As she described, "For a job, and more so as an educator, you aren't supposed to have any problems, right? Because they say that if you have problems, you are not going to pay attention to your work. . . . I always tried to appear as if I were fine. My house was my house and in my house I had to leave all my problems and my place of work was my place of work, right?" Jimena was aware that many families had problems and that the image she was supposed to project was unrealistic, yet she could not find a way to balance all her roles and admit the violence she experienced at home without risking losing her job as a teacher.

Inés also worked as a teacher and faced difficulties in attempting to conceal the abuse from her boss and co-workers: "Because my face was swollen, I was embarrassed to leave the house and I practically didn't even go to work because of my face. And I had problems at work because I missed work too much and I arrived late . . . and that forced me to quit my job because I couldn't continue to work under those conditions." Like Jimena, Inés initially believed that her husband's violence was a private matter even when it affected her life outside the home. In the end, Inés lost her job because her husband's "private" violence left her with physical marks she had to conceal from her co-workers by missing work or arriving late. The violence also caused chronic headaches. Even after separating from her husband, the consequences of years of abuse continue to impact her life. She continues to have migraines and feels unable to concentrate, which makes working as a full-time math teacher very difficult.

*Family of Origin*

Jimena grew up in a violence-free home. She considers her family to be close and to value communication highly. When she began to experience violence in her relationship with Juan, however, she decided to keep it a secret because she felt ashamed that she was in a relationship so different from that of her parents. For years, Jimena kept up the appearance of normalcy to keep her job and to spare her family of origin shame and trouble.

Because Jimena and Juan lived in a room adjacent to her parents' house, she worked hard to conceal the abuse from her parents. Her living situation also led her to worry about who would keep the room they had built if she and Juan separated and how this would affect her parents. Dobash and Dobash (1992) have noted that it is common for persistently violent men to use physical threats and intimidation. According to Jimena, Juan threatened her by telling her that the only way he would leave their home was by destroying the room and taking everything with him. Juan's threats prevented Jimena from kicking him out because she did not want him to damage her parents' property or hurt her parents.[12]

Jimena and Juan separated for a few days on three occasions during the four years before she went to the shelter. Each time they separated, he promised he would change and she gave him another chance for the sake of keeping the family together. During these temporary separations, Jimena was able to convince Juan that he should leave the house so that she and her children could stay in their home and not disturb the children's routines. Juan would leave but, as described by Jimena,

> He would always take everything with him. I mean, he would take all my things. I mean, to me he was being materialistic, right? No, it didn't seem to me, I was certain that he was materialistic. Because anyone, the first thing that I would do is grab and take my children with me instead of the things, right? It was supposed to be that the father, if you can call him a father, has to, the first thing he should take care of are his children, right? But not him. He would take everything and would leave me like that with the bed and some pillows for my children. And he wouldn't send me any money [for the children].

Jimena's salary was barely enough to buy food for her family and cover the costs of the children's uniforms and school supplies. She had no money to use if the children got sick or needed something extra. Juan knew this, and Jimena interpreted his taking all their things and refusing to give Jimena money for the children as a sign that he was not willing to fulfill his role as a father.

Jimena did not request assistance from her parents when she decided to leave Juan in 2001 because she wanted to spare them any trouble, and because she blamed herself for her situation and wanted to solve it independently of her parents. She decided to go to her grandmother's house for refuge. The advice she received from her grandmother and her grandmother's inability, or unwillingness, to understand the gravity of Jimena's problem reinforced Jimena's belief that she needed to solve her problem on her own. The following description of her grandmother's reaction to Jimena's decision to leave Juan exemplifies the little assistance a woman may receive from a family that is in other ways close and helpful:

> I said to her, "Mama—because I call my grandmother 'Mama'—I want to separate from Juan." "My little daughter, is your problem that serious? Don't forget that you don't know what it is to raise children on your own. Try to talk it over with him. Tell him to come and I will talk to him."

The grandmother's response to Jimena represents a common view on the importance of keeping a family together even in situations of abuse.

After Jimena again explained to her grandmother that she did not want to reconcile with Juan because the situation was very difficult, her grandmother agreed to let her stay at her house for a few days. However, her grandmother provided very little support, claiming her religious beliefs prevented her from lying if Juan asked her about Jimena's whereabouts, even if it was to protect Jimena. As Jimena described, "I would tell her, 'Mama, but it's as if you were doing a good deed. You are not lying, take it as a joke." 'No, I can never lie.' 'Mama, look at it as helping your neighbor.' And afterwards I left on Tuesday [the following day]." Although Jimena's grandmother may be unusual in her strict interpretation of the religious teaching to not lie, she is not unusual in suggesting that Jimena talk things over with her husband in spite of the severe abuse she had experienced and her desire to leave, and in prioritizing family unity over individual women and children's well-being. In her work on domestic violence in the Peruvian Andes, Estremadoyro (2001) similarly finds that women's families and community leaders encourage and play an active role in promoting reconciliation with the husband. Other women I interviewed similarly reported that they had been advised by their pastors to talk things over with their husbands and to uphold the unity of the family.

Two weeks after Jimena left Juan, he went to Jimena's family to ask for forgiveness for having used violence against Jimena, to find out where she was hiding, and to ask for help in convincing her to return home: "This morning I spoke with my mother and she said that on Sunday he spoke with my father and she says he got on his knees in front of my father and my mother and asked them to please help him. That he could not take another day without sleep and thinking that I am on the streets with my children. That's what she told me. So he asked my mother, my father for help in finding me." In Jimena's description of events, Juan manipulated Jimena's family by presenting himself as a concerned father and good husband and Jimena as the "bad mother" who had taken the children away from their home. Jimena's parents and sisters promised Juan to assist him in his efforts to reunite his nuclear family. Although Jimena had separated from Juan before and knew that in the past he had promised to change but never had, because he asked her parents for forgiveness Jimena wondered if this time he would change.

Faced with pressure from her family to reconcile with Juan, Jimena decided to tell her mother about the full extent of Juan's physical and psychological abuse against her and the children. Her mother listened but ultimately responded that she believed Juan was being genuine in asking for forgiveness and wanting to change. Jimena's mother then asked Jimena to return home to Juan with the children. Like many women, Jimena felt embarrassed and blamed herself for "allowing" herself to be abused. Pressure from her family to return home further fueled her self-blame. After a brief stay at the shelter, Jimena and the children went back to Juan.

Although one of the main reasons women reported for not telling their parents and siblings about their partner's violence was shame and self-blame, another important reason was the fear that siblings or parents would retaliate against their partner by using violence. Amada, thirty-six years old and the mother of three, had the opposite problem. She told her brothers about her husband's abuse, expecting that they would offer to protect her by physically threatening her husband. Amada stated that her brothers reacted instead by asking her to please not seek refuge in their houses if she ever left him because they did not want her husband to follow her and hurt them or their property.

She then went to her *comadre* (the godmother to one of her children) to ask if she and her children could stay there if she left her husband, but her *comadre* gave her a bag of food and sent her on her way.

For other women, turning to their family of origin in Lima was not an option. Many of the women were migrants and did not have close relatives in Lima. This was the case for Daisy, whose experiences are discussed in detail in Chapter 6. She had sent her sons to live with her stepsister in Cuzco while she got back on her feet in Lima after her abusive partner abandoned them. A short time later, she found out that the sister (the only family she had) had stolen the monthly money Daisy had sent for her boys, depriving them of clothing and education while in Cuzco.

Other women had more positive interactions with—and were offered support by—their families of origin. Some women's sisters, when they lived close by, were particularly helpful and intervened in situations that were or had the potential to become violent. Some women had family near them, but their families could offer only limited support. Lucia, a forty-two-year-old woman with two young children, worked as a secretary until her husband made going to work impossible due to constant beatings (as in Inés's case). When she decided to separate from her husband, her mother stood behind her and provided emotional and limited financial support. Lucia's mother visited Lucia at the shelter every day and brought her and her grandchildren food and gifts. She also helped her look for a job and a place to live. However, her mother could not offer Lucia and her grandchildren a place to stay because Lucia's mother worked as a live-in domestic worker and had no home of her own. Although she had worked for the same family for over thirty years and Lucia had grown up in that family's home, the nature of the employer-employee relationship with the family prevented Lucia's mother from asking the family to let her daughter and grandchildren stay with them.

## The In-Laws

Women reported telling their husbands' families about the abuse almost as frequently as they reported telling their families of origin. One explanation for this is that couples could not afford their own homes and so lived with the man's family almost as often as with the woman's family, making privacy and secrecy difficult in both cases. Far from playing a homogenous role, women's in-laws, like families of origin, played varying roles in women's efforts to survive within or leave violent relationships. As compared to a woman's family of origin, however, a woman's family by marriage appeared to be more hesitant to intervene and tended to side with the woman's partner. As women described to me the years of abuse they endured, they regretted not having met their husbands' families before they started to live with their husbands. Many women claimed that if they had known more about their future in-laws, they would never have moved in with their partners (Vega-Centeno 2000; Movimiento Manuela Ramos 1998; Warwick 1997). The majority of the men had been abused as children, and the women believed that these earlier experiences of abuse greatly influenced their partners' violence against them.[13]

When I asked Jimena if her parents-in-law had intervened when she and Juan lived with them and Juan became violent, Jimena responded that although her parents-in-law had had good intentions and intervened the first couple of times, they later opted to protect themselves from Juan's violence by not intervening. Ironically, Jimena's father-in-law, a man who had also been violent toward his wife for years, was the one who intervened when Juan and Jimena first moved in.

Jimena did not receive assistance or advice from her mother-in-law. Sisterhood, based on "the idea that women as a group share certain similar life experiences and social roles" (Olson and Shopes 1991:189), did not typically define the mother-in-law/daughter-in-law relationship among the women I interviewed. In her work in the Bolivian Andes, Van Vleet (2008) identifies the mother-in-law and daughter-in-law relationship as a major site of conflict. Similarly, according to the accounts of the women I interviewed, mothers-in-law more often reacted in their role as mothers—protective of their violent sons—than as women and potential "sisters" who were sympathetic to and protective of their daughters-in-law. In analyzing the dynamics between mothers-in-laws and daughters-in-law, it is important to understand women's actions in the context of the power that comes with each position. Although both refer to women, "mother-in-law" and "daughter-in-law" signify different social positions that include distinct privileges and obligations within the family. These different positions within the family may facilitate competition and hostility between women.

In her discussion of women in abusive relationships in Brazil, Hautzinger describes a case in which the mother-in-law takes on the role of "token torturer" of her daughter-in-law:

> Typically an older woman, frequently a mother-in-law, a token torturer reproduces oppression and abuse, reinforcing the same patriarchal values used to subjugate her in her youth (Campbell 1999). She is a "token" in that she advances, by age and often widowhood, to be able to stand in for the same forces that socialized her into feminine constraint, thus serving as the ultimate hegemonic agent for patriarchy and working against a social category of people—women—to which she belongs. (2007:60)

Women work hard to achieve their status as both mothers and older women, and may not want to lose their position in the family power structure. If they protected their daughters-in-law and thereby turned against their sons, they could jeopardize their status as mothers to their sons (because of the risk that their sons could break off the mother-son relationship) and possibly encourage a relationship of equality between themselves and their daughters-in-law. The women I interviewed described experiences in which their mothers-in-law played active roles in encouraging their sons to beat their wives to assert their authority over them as men. The bond between mother and abusive son made life for many daughters-in-law very difficult.

Otilia, a forty-eight-year-old woman and the mother of four, was in an abusive relationship for twenty-two years. She, her husband, and their children had lived with his parents for several years. When I met Otilia, she had been separated for six years. She was trying to convince her daughter, who was in an abusive relationship, to stay with her at her house rather than move in with her in-laws. Although Otilia felt she had not been able to successfully resist her husband's violence as a wife earlier in her life, she was determined to protect her daughter from her son-in-law's violence. Otilia describes her mother-in-law's response to Otilia's experiences of abuse: "I knew that if I told her [about the abuse], I am certain that she as a mother would have stood behind her son. And, really, my mother-in-law sometimes said to me, 'Fuck you, it's your fault, why did you come to this house?'" Otilia's mother-in-law blamed Otilia for the violence, telling her she was not good enough for her son. In encouraging her daughter to stay with her rather than move in with her in-laws, Otilia sought to protect her daughter from the sort of potentially abusive living arrangement she had experienced as a young wife and daughter-in-law.

The relationships between mothers and sons and the actions of mothers-in-law affected daughters-in-law in varied ways. One man reminded his wife, who complained of his abuse and that he gave his mother all his money, that if there was ever a choice that had to be made, he would always choose his mother and his mother would always choose him over her. Another woman reported that although she and her mother-in-law had gotten along very well for over twenty years, her mother-in-law refused to speak with her after she placed a domestic violence complaint against her husband. Her mother-in-law told her that the only reason she had liked her was because she had taken good care of her son. Now that she was causing trouble for the son, her mother-in-law saw no reason to continue a relationship with her.

Although mothers usually sided with their sons, the sons did not always support their mothers' expressions of power over their daughters-in-law. Maria, thirty-five years old, described how her mother-in-law tried to slap her in the face. Maria's husband stopped his mother from hitting her, pointing out, "She is not your daughter, you can't hit her." Although mothers-in-law encouraged—or did little to discourage—their sons' violence, they themselves did not usually beat their daughters-in-law because, as Maria's husband pointed out, they were not related to them by blood. Like their partners, the women believed that the only people who could legitimately use violence against them were their parents. It was not uncommon for women to resist men's violence by declaring that "you are not my father or mother" or "if my father never hit me, you won't either."

Of all the women I interviewed, only one woman said her mother-in-law had made a significant effort to help her. Carla, a thirty-three-year-old mother of three, described how soon after she moved in with her partner, her mother-in-law had advised her that if her son ever hit her, she should hit him back. According to Carla's mother-in-law, if a woman allowed a man to hit her once, he would then go on to do whatever he pleased with her. Following her mother-in-law's advice, Carla fought back by hitting her husband the day he hit her for the first time. Carla reports that her husband did not try to abuse her after that day. Although hitting back proved to be an effective form of resistance to physical abuse, Carla continued to have problems because of his verbal abuse and refusal to allow her to work.

## Women and Their Families

The women who turned to their families for help or who received unsolicited advice from their families faced an upward struggle. Although some families supported women's decisions to leave, other families encouraged women to uphold the unity of the nuclear family regardless of the personal cost and long-term negative effects of violence on the women and children. Women were wary of telling their families about the violence due to concerns for their families' safety and the real possibility of additional violence toward the women or others who became involved. Guilt about breaking off children's attachment to their fathers also prevented women from leaving permanently. The women who had moved in with men or married them had had dreams of forming families and growing old together, but the realities of the men's expectations and violent behavior had shattered those dreams and made mothering very difficult.

In addition to the strategies discussed in previous chapters, the women's resistance strategies examined in this chapter include preventing children from witnessing their fathers' violence through the strategic use of silence, temporarily leaving, empowering daughters to finish school and have careers to avoid depending on men who could potentially be abusive toward them, and mothering outside of the nuclear family. Yet, even as many of these strategies result in immediate and even short-term relief from abuse, they do not erase the widespread belief—among women and their families—that the best place for a child is within the intact nuclear family, even when the father is abusive. In an environment in which women receive little support from families, workplaces, or the police, the belief that the best place for children is within a nuclear family plays a significant role in women's experiences of violence. And, for those women who left abusive partners and thereby exerted more power over how to mother their children, racism, poverty, and additional forms of violence have continued to impact their lives and those of their children.

CHAPTER 5 ◼ Resources (Un)Available:
Institutional Aid and
Institutional Violence

◼ IT IS NOT UNCOMMON FOR WOMEN who are unsuccessful in their attempts to cope with and stop their husbands' violence on their own or with the help of relatives to seek assistance from resources outside their families as their situations worsen. The previous chapter discussed how women's families and family roles help shape their experiences of abuse and ability to leave. This chapter shifts the focus to institutions outside the family and to service providers within these institutions who act as gatekeepers. It explores how these institutions assist or injure women during their attempts to access needed services to cope with or leave abusive partners. It illustrates that in many cases during the process of seeking assistance from their families and from external resources, "women developed a double consciousness of injury, both as people whose relatives failed to treat them properly and as people whose rights had been violated" (Merry 2006:183) by institutions charged with helping them.

Just prior to her latest separation, after repeated attempts to stop her husband's violence on her own and by seeking assistance from friends and relatives, Jimena sought assistance from state agencies. She found it impossible to receive assistance from these agencies because of office hours that were incompatible with her work schedule and because of the indifference and violence she and her children encountered within these institutions. One afternoon, after the end of her shift as an elementary school teacher, Jimena traveled an hour downtown to visit the Ministry of Women's Advancement and Human Development, also known as PROMUDEH (Promoción de la Mujer y Desarrollo Humano).

The PROMUDEH was created in 1996. Its vision is "to achieve a great cultural change in which women and men share the same opportunities and are in charge of their own destinies, in an environment of peace, democracy and solidarity" (PROMUDEH 2000). In 1999, the PROMUDEH created Women's Emergency Centers, where women could speak with police, lawyers, medical examiners, prosecutors, and social workers under one roof. The main headquarters for the Women's Emergency Centers is in the PROMUDEH headquarters downtown, where Jimena went.[1] On other occasions when her husband beat her, she had called the police. Jimena stated that she did not receive assistance either from the PROMUDEH or the police. As she explained,

> I didn't find anything [at the PROMUDEH], I mean, it was closed, they told me to come back later. So, I said to myself, "This is supposed to be an institution to help women, and they can't impose schedules during which the man can and can't beat his wife, that the man can only beat his wife from 8 to 4. No." [Women can't be told] to wait until the next day because the next day he might have already killed us, right? I would even call the police station when I had problems. [The police would ask me,] "*Señora*, are you hurt? Can you walk? Then come and place a complaint [in person]." But how could I leave if my husband was there? He wouldn't let me leave. But the police said it was a private matter.

Both the PROMUDEH and the police are "institutions to help" that women pass through for protection and to begin legal processes against their abusive partners.[2] Jimena was familiar with domestic violence laws but could do little to gain the legal protection she needed from either of these institutions. She could not go to the PROMUDEH because of her work schedule; going to the PROMUDEH during its hours of operation would require that she miss work and therefore risk losing her job. Her calls to the police were met by officers' indifference and lack of understanding of the dangers women in abusive relationships may face in attempting to leave.

Following her failed attempts to receive assistance at the PROMUDEH and at the police station, Jimena decided to go to the INABIF (El Programa Integral Nacional para el Bienestar Familiar) with her children to request assistance for the sake of her children. The INABIF is a state agency whose main responsibility is to improve the quality of life of at-risk children.[3] As she and her children waited to speak with one of the social workers there, her children became impatient and tired and complained that they were bored. It had been a long trip to the INABIF, and waiting was not what her six- and three-year-old children had in mind. After waiting for approximately thirty minutes, Jimena was approached by a young man and invited into his office. As they entered his office and she began to explain that she wanted to leave her abusive husband, the social worker stopped her to tell her she should first go to the police station to place a complaint if hers was a domestic violence case. Jimena became increasingly frustrated as she replied that she had been there and no one had helped her. After she and the social worker discussed where she should go next, the social worker referred Jimena to his supervisor.

As Jimena spoke with the supervisor, her children, who had followed her into the supervisor's office, finally found something with which to entertain themselves: a pile of sticky white labels. Jimena did not notice her children were playing with these and what happened next both surprised Jimena and her children and further alienated Jimena from state agencies. According to Jimena,

> And while I was talking my children had taken some labels, something like that, that they had put out there for inventory. My children saw them and put them all over their arms. And [when he saw them doing that] the man hit the table with his fist, got up, bitter, and I didn't know what to think. I really wanted to cry, I was feeling bad. And he grabbed my children by the neck and spoke to them with bad words, "*Carajo* [fuck]! Who do these children belong to?" and he threw them out of his office. I didn't say anything because if I had I would have broken something, I would have thrown his computer. He was supposed to help me and he had no business yelling and humiliating my children.

Jimena felt the supervisor had overstepped his boundaries by yelling and physically grabbing her children. According to Jimena, it was she in her role as mother, not the supervisor in his role as a staff member in an institution to help children, who was responsible for disciplining her children. Because he had the power to help her, she felt both threatened and further silenced by his actions. Her experiences at the PROMUDEH, with the police, and at the INABIF underscore that inadequate working hours, service providers' indifference, and even violence within institutions charged with assisting women and at-risk children constitute serious obstacles to the implementation of domestic violence laws and to women's access to needed resources.

Police stations (particularly specialized women's police stations), conciliation procedures (made mandatory between 1997 and 2001 and promoted until the present), shelters, and nongovernmental women's organizations are among the main resources women use as they cope with and attempt to escape from abusive partners. As when they turn to their families, when women turn to agencies charged with preventing and punishing violence against women, they may encounter the indifference, negative attitudes, and even violence that Jimena and her children experienced. An analysis of women's experiences within these commonly used institutions makes visible the ways in which some institutions support, alienate, or revictimize women.

## Legal Frameworks and Processes

In 1993, Peru became one of the first Latin American countries to pass a family violence law. As a result of modifications in 1997, 1998, 2000, and 2003, the Family Violence Law includes physical, psychological, and sexual violence as forms of domestic violence, regardless of an individual's class, race, or gender. The law applies to violence between spouses, *convivientes,* ex-spouses, ex-*convivientes,* and between those who have had children together, even if the man and woman never lived together. The police is the state entity responsible for receiving domestic violence complaints, carrying out the preliminary investigation, and notifying the parties involved. Women can file complaints in the family violence sections of regular police stations, specialized women's police stations, Women's Emergency Centers, and at the public prosecutor's office.

Beginning in the 1990s, under President Fujimori, the Peruvian government took several steps to condemn gender violence and discrimination publicly and to affirm its intent to prevent and punish violence against women. At the international level, Peru ratified the Convention on the Elimination of All Forms of Discrimination against Women (CEDAW) in 1982 and the

Convention of Belém do Pará in 1996, thereby formally recognizing violence against women as a form of discrimination and as a human rights violation. At the national level, Fujimori proclaimed 2000 as the Year of the Fight against Family Violence. By 2001, the PROMUDEH had created the National Program Against Family and Sexual Violence to carry out preventative actions and policies and to support victims of domestic violence. As these initiatives were enacted, the number of women

"Family Violence," a pamphlet explaining resources available in cases of domestic violence. The pamphlet was funded by UNIFEM (the United Nations Development Fund for Women), Centro de la Mujer Peruana Flora Tristán, and the National Police of Peru. The sign on the cover reads, "No more family violence."

reporting abuse by their partners increased. In 1996, police in Lima received 6,181 domestic violence complaints; in 2001, the number jumped to 32,821 (Fernández and Webb 2002:260). In 2006, there were 85,747 complaints filed nationally (Movimiento Manuela Ramos 2007:7).

In Peru, the police can legally detain an abusive partner for a maximum of twenty-four hours after the initial report of abuse. A woman's need for protection for herself and her children, however, exceeds a single day. Some women may have friends, acquaintances, or family on whom they can count on for sup-

"The Law Protects You," a pamphlet summarizing the main points of the Family Violence Law. The pamphlet was funded by the Women's Commission of the Peruvian Congress with the support of UNIFEM. The slogans on the signs on the cover include: "No more tears! I want to smile always," "I love you more because you no longer beat me," "If he hits you, report him," "A loved woman is a respected and valued woman," and "Don't allow them to abuse you. The law protects you." Courtesy of Lili Blas and Gina Yañez at Movimiento Manuela Ramos.

port and a place to stay. Other women, including women whose families live outside of Lima, have nowhere to go after placing a domestic violence complaint. Particularly in the cases of women who do not have relatives in Lima, being admitted to a shelter is essential for immediate and temporary protection from an abusive partner. In all cases, after a woman files the claim at the police station, she must decide whether she will return home, go to a shelter (if she is told of its existence, and if there is space for her and her children), or stay with family or friends. In the context of poverty and of few people willing or able to offer a place to stay, it is not uncommon for a woman to return home after filing a claim, and to face further violence as she waits for the legal process to begin.

In the United States, leaving a violent man is the most dangerous time for a woman because of escalating—and sometimes the onset of lethal—violence (DeKeseredy and Joseph 2006). According to the accounts of the women I interviewed, this is also the case for women in Lima: they said that their partners had become more violent after discovering that the women had reported them to the police. This appears to reinforce Merry's point that women's consciousness as individuals with rights may be interpreted by some men as a challenge to their power and identity as men (2006:185). When women seek resources that have the potential to provide them with power and protection, they are contesting men's use of force to control them, and therefore men's control of them. Alternatively, when men discovered that their wives had been turned away and that police officers did not pay attention to them, those men's power over the women they abused was reinforced.

When a woman places a claim, the police notify the man accused of beating her that a claim has been filed against him and that he must go to the police station to provide a statement. The police also refer the woman to a forensic doctor for an evaluation of her injuries. The doctor's report is often the most important piece of evidence against the man accused of perpetrating the violence. However, not all women are given appointments for medical examinations for the same day or even week of the domestic violence complaint. Delays between the date of the complaint and the date of the medical examination are particularly significant because they may negatively affect the woman's case: the more time that passes between a violent incident and a doctor's examination, the higher the likelihood that the injuries that must be documented will have healed or disappeared.[4] The claim will then go to the family prosecutor, who evaluates the claim and has the authority to issue orders for petitioned protective measures.

Between 1997 and 2001, prosecutors then set up mandatory conciliation hearings. As will be discussed later in this chapter, conciliation has continued to be promoted by police officers, prosecutors, and judges even after it ceased to be mandatory. If the woman and man did not reach an agreement during the conciliation, the prosecutor sent the claim to the family judge, and to the criminal prosecutor in cases of felony. In domestic violence cases, felonies are defined as injuries that medically require more than ten days of rest. If and when the judge hears the case, a sentence may be handed down. In cases in which documented injuries required between ten and thirty days of rest, the sentence is a maximum of two years. If the woman dies from injuries that required between ten and thirty days of rest, the sentence is between three and six years. Most of the women I interviewed did not know what happens after they filed a complaint at the police station and had few options for where to go between the date they placed the complaint and the date of the conciliation hearing. In the 1990s, a judicial process initiated through a domestic violence complaint took on average between twelve and eighteen months to be initially resolved (Movimiento Manuela Ramos 1998). In 2005, a study in Lima revealed that after ten months, the majority of domestic violence cases had not yet been resolved (Movimiento Manuela Ramos 2007:48).

Shortly after deciding to leave and filing claims against their partners, many women feel disillusioned by the difficulties they encounter in attempting to reach satisfactory arrangements that ensure their safety in both the short and long term. If they did not already know it, they soon learn of the prejudices against— and lack of funds to help—women and their children, and that the process of filing a claim is a long one replete with bureaucratic hurdles. In Mexico, many women prefer not to report their partner's violence against them because of the legal problems and extended bureaucratic requirements they would face when trying to file a claim (Hijar 1992). In Peru, women may face a similar situation.

Women learn early on in the process of leaving that the men who abuse them will rarely be punished for their violence. As Racquel and I sat on one of the bunk beds in her room at the shelter discussing what her next steps would be, she expressed her frustration at the difficult road that had led to her arrival at the shelter and on which she would continue on even after leaving it. As she stated, "They [the government and the police] should not allow that [violence against women and children]. The government should hand out sentences to all those men. There should be a sentence, a punishment for those men."

Racquel knows domestic violence laws exist, but her experiences—as well as those of other women she knows—tell her that men who beat their partners are rarely punished. Racquel feels certain that her husband will not receive a sentence and that she and her children, not her husband, will be the ones forced to start over without a home, money, or support.

*An Introduction to Police Stations (and Long Bureaucratic Procedures)*

Having heard from women, particularly the poorest women I interviewed, about the indifference and hostility they faced at police stations while trying to file domestic violence complaints, I was curious to see and speak with personnel from the main women's police station. A month after I arrived in Lima, I boarded a crowded *micro* for the bumpy ride downtown to visit the station. As I got on and handed the *cobrador* (fare collector) the *sol* (approximately 30 U.S. cents) fare, I quickly noticed that all the seats were taken, a common occurrence on this popular route. I stood and held on to the bar above me and tried to take up less and less space as the vehicle—originally intended for up to eight passengers—filled with ten, twelve, and eventually fifteen passengers during the thirty-minute trip, which felt more like a race. This form of transportation is the cheapest, if not quickest, in Lima. It is also the most popular, as *micros* can be found speeding up and down all the major streets as well as many minor ones. Without set stops, *micros* can be flagged down anywhere on a street with a nod or the lift of a hand. With each sudden stop to pick up a passenger or quick start to beat another *micro*, my body swayed, and it became impossible not to push or fall against other passengers.

After jumping off the *micro*, I only had a few blocks to walk to the main women's police station. As I attempted to open the door to enter the station, a uniformed guard stopped me. Although I did not know this at the time, it is the guard outside the station whom visitors first speak to and who directs those allowed to enter to the appropriate area inside the station. After briefly explaining my interest in meeting and speaking to officers responsible for handling domestic violence cases, he allowed me to go inside and told me to go to the counter, where every person who came in seemed to be directed.[5] As I entered the lobby, the first thing I noticed was a long, tall counter at the other end of the room. Behind the counter, three officers responded to women's queries. The office of the *mayor* (the head of the station), a man, was on one side of the lobby. A small room with a table and two chairs was on the opposite side. Further down the lobby was a doorway and stairs leading up to the second floor, where the offices of lawyers and social workers are located. After I briefly explained my research and requested to speak with an officer in charge of domestic violence issues, I sat in one of the chairs in the lobby and waited. Waiting is most of what I did during the month and a half during which I attempted to get permission to interview staff from the station.

The police station has a specific hierarchy that can be difficult to decipher but which must be respected and followed to gain access to those within the station. As I sat waiting to hear if I would be allowed to speak to and explain my research interests to the officer in charge of handling domestic violence complaints, the doors that led to the stairs opened and a neatly groomed and uniformed officer in her mid-thirties approached me. Officer Ramirez led me to the small room on the right side of the lobby, where I explained why I was in Lima and asked for permission to interview her about the women's police station at a later date. Having heard from the women I interviewed that officers from the women's police station gave educational talks on domestic violence to shantytown organizations, groups at beauty salons, schools, and community kitchens, I also requested to be informed of and permitted to attend these talks.

Following a question about where in the United States I had lived, Officer Ramirez explained that she had just gotten her visa to visit family in the United States and proceeded to ask me a series of questions about English and life in the United States. We spoke about life in the United States for several minutes and, then, with a smile, she said she would be happy to be interviewed and have me accompany her to the talks she gave, but she also warned me that she could not be interviewed or allow me to accompany her to the talks until her supervisor, the *mayor,* gave his permission. Without her supervisor's permission, Officer Ramirez explained, she could only answer a limited number of general questions. To receive the *mayor*'s permission to interview Officer Ramirez, or anyone else who worked for the women's police station, and to be informed of and attend the talks, I needed official clearance from the main police headquarters, located several blocks away.

Officer Ramirez then lowered her voice to tell me that it would be very difficult to receive permission because of what had happened a few months earlier. According to Ramirez, two people, who, like me, had claimed to be students working on a project on domestic violence, had received permission to interview her from her supervisor. They had brought recorders (similar to mine) and taped everything she said and even photographed her in front of the station. The next morning, her picture and a story about the police station appeared in the widely read newspaper *Liberación.*[6] According to Ramirez, the "students" had been reporters and printed a story critical of how the police station functioned. Her supervisor was not likely to allow her to be interviewed again, even with all my official documentation as a student and researcher and her willingness to be interviewed.

After spending many hours over the next few weeks traveling to and from and waiting at the police headquarters, where I had submitted paperwork requesting permission to interview staff at the main women's police station, I became convinced that I would never receive clearance to interview Ramirez or any other officers.[7] Officer Ramirez's experience with the two "students" appeared to have made the supervisor acutely aware of how vulnerable the police could be to criticism and suspicious of outsiders. Because of this, most of my information about women's experiences in police stations comes from interviews with women

who visited these stations rather than from my direct observations at police stations. In this way, this chapter privileges
women's perspectives on seeking access to state agencies.

## Women's Police Stations

Women's police stations were specifically created to respond
to women's complaints of violence against them. The first and
main women's police station opened in downtown Lima in 1988,
largely as a result of the efforts of local women's organizations
to push for more and better resources for women trapped in
violent relationships. The opening of the first women's police
station in Peru came only three years after the creation of the
first women's police station in Latin America in São Paulo, Brazil. By 2002, six women's police stations had opened in Lima
and seven more in other parts of the country. Each of these stations is designed to include a lawyer, a psychologist, and a social worker. However, insufficient funds prevent some stations
from including one or more of these professionals. Most regular
police stations also have a small, specialized family violence
section in which women can file domestic violence complaints.
Within stations, officers work long hours and receive very low
salaries. To help the police station's personnel cope with the
personal fatigue and stress resulting from working with violence on a daily basis, staff members are invited to attend mutual help sessions twice a week as well as occasional workshops
facilitated by women's nonprofit organizations.[8]

In 2000, the Peruvian Congress approved a modification to
the legal definition of domestic violence to include sexual violence as a form of domestic violence. According to my conversations with officers at the main women's police station, however,
and as noted in Chapter 3, a woman could only file a claim for
physical or psychological violence. If the woman referred to incidents of sexual violence, her claim was filed under psychological
violence. The reasoning behind this practice, according to the
officers with whom I spoke, was that the personnel at the police
station did not see themselves as specializing in sexual violence
and that sexual violence involved humiliation, which could also
be considered to be a form of psychological violence.[9] A recent
study of women in Lima further points to women's own feelings

of shame and belief that their partners have a right to demand sex as additional reasons for the low levels of sexual violence reports (Movimiento Manuela Ramos 2007:50).

## Women's Experiences in Police Stations

Among the women I interviewed who spoke of interactions with police officers, fifteen women described their negative experiences at police stations or had heard of other women's negative experiences, and as a result were less likely to seek help from the police; five women mentioned placing complaints at police stations but offered few or no details of these experiences; and two women reported that they were treated well at police stations and received the assistance they needed. Of these two women, one woman's brother was a police officer and had played an active role in assisting his sister to place a complaint.

The discussion of women's experiences at women's police stations is especially relevant in a book that underscores the multidimensionality of identities and how gender is one among several identity markers that inform women's experiences of violence. It underscores that having a police station staffed by women has its merits but cannot guarantee women the right to be heard or protected from their partners' violence (Nelson 1996; Hautzinger 2007). In Lima, as in other settings, individual police officers may interpret existing laws through the filter of personal biases on race, class, language, and sexuality when interacting with individuals of the same, or different, gender. Not all women share the same opportunities or ideas, and gender solidarity cannot be assumed once we take into consideration issues of class, race, education, and economic standing (Mohanty 1991).

In focusing on women's interactions in police stations in this section, I do not intend to suggest that the police as an institution is solely to blame for the violence women suffer, or that all police officers treat women in ways that prevent women from finding alternatives to living with violent partners. In addition to the intimate violence experienced at home, the women I interviewed faced structural violence in the form of racism, sexism, and class prejudices outside of police stations. All of these forms of violence permeate women's lives and also constitute obstacles to women's ability to protect themselves and their children in their attempts to cope with or leave an abusive relationship. For some of the women I interviewed, however, police stations played a significant role in prolonging the amount of time they remained in abusive relationships.

An examination of the experiences of Ester, Inés, Jimena, and Ana helps shift the focus from gender to the intersecting identities that informed their experiences at police stations. I begin with a discussion of Ester's experiences. Ester had asked me to meet her at her apartment at two in the afternoon. It was not until 2:30 PM, as I was writing her a note explaining I had been waiting for thirty minutes and had to leave, that Ester opened the gate so I could walk up the stairs to her apartment on the third floor. Although I had rung the doorbell four times, she had not heard it because she did not have electricity. As Ester explained during our interview, her apartment had not had electricity for the past year because her job working in the kitchen of a friend's small neighborhood restaurant did not provide her with enough income to cover the apartment's monthly maintenance bills.

As I walked into the apartment, I could see other signs that the apartment had not been maintained due to a lack of money: the cabinets and tiles on the floor were cracked and missing pieces, the paint on the wall was peeling off, and the legs on the small round kitchen table—the only piece of furniture I could see in the two bedroom apartment—were wobbly and cracked. Ester explained that her husband had recently taken and sold all their furniture, even her bed, without her consent. The only pieces of furniture her husband had left in the apartment were the kitchen table and their teenage son's bed, which she and her son now shared. Ester then explained that her husband wanted her to leave the apartment but she refused to do so because it was the only property they owned, and she and their son had nowhere else to go. Ester also explained that over the last few months her husband had been coming and going from the apartment whenever he pleased, verbally abusing her each time. She could not afford to change the locks on the doors to prevent him from entering.

Ester's living situation was precisely the reason why she felt she needed to separate from her husband permanently and legally. However, she did not want to leave because she feared he would keep the apartment if she did and she and her son would have nothing left. Toward the end of our meeting, she asked if I knew anyone at the main women's police station who could help her with mandatory paperwork she feared was not being processed. She had been to the police station several times since filing the domestic violence claim, but was told to come back later each time. The longer she waited, the more desperate her living situation became. I had just spent several days speaking with Officer Ramirez at the station, and I suggested to Ester that she ask for Officer Ramirez next time. A few weeks later, Ester informed me that although at first the officers would not help her, once she asked for Officer Ramirez and told her I had sent her, things changed. Officer Ramirez told the other officers to help her because she was "a relative," and from that point on Ester was treated very well.

Although Ester ultimately received the assistance she needed to begin the lengthy judicial process against her husband, her experience illustrates the indifference women may face at police stations if and when they do not have personal contacts (which most women do not have). Several of the women I interviewed believed they had been treated with disrespect and turned away because they were poor and did not know anyone inside the station. Ester also believed this. How police treated the women had real, negative effects on the women's ability to protect themselves and their children. In Ester's case, the longer the domestic violence complaint took to be processed, the longer the judicial process would take, and the longer she had to tolerate her husband's abuse in the empty apartment. The women agreed that they confronted more indifference and discrimination at regular police stations than at women's police stations and that women's police stations were "the best option." Yet, as Ester's case illustrates, treatment at the main women's police station also negatively affected some women's efforts to cope with abusive partners. In her case, being a woman did not guarantee her fair treatment by women officers. It was the claim that she was an officer's relative that allowed her access to needed resources.

Inés's experiences at the police station also bring attention to factors beyond gender that affect women's treatment at wom-

en's police stations. It took several years for her to decide to
go to the police station to report her husband's physical, psychological, and sexual abuse. In part, she had been waiting for
her children to grow up so that she would not deprive them of
a father figure during what she considered to be their forma-
tive years. She had also been hesitant to go to the police station
because she had heard from acquaintances that "when people
went there they treated them badly and so many of them did not
want to return out of shame. The police will say, 'Why do you
let yourself be hit?' or maybe use vulgar language. So then, that
was my fear." In the mid-1990s, Inés decided to report the abuse
in order to leave her husband and have access to her belongings
legally, regardless of how the police treated her. At the police
station, the psychologist she spoke with blamed Inés for the violence by suggesting that Inés enjoyed being hit. Feeling angry
and disillusioned, Inés left the station. She knew her rights and
she resented being revictimized by the state institution responsible for protecting these rights. She told me that the experience
made her so angry that she felt even more determined to leave
her husband afterwards. As was the case for other women in
Lima, Inés felt injured both by the man closest to her and the
state entity responsible for protecting her rights. Inés's experiences suggest that the myths of the acceptance of violence as a
form of affection as expressed in *"más me pegas, más te quiero"*
and of the masochistic woman who seeks out violent men persist in the minds of some professionals responsible for helping
women in abusive relationships.

Unlike Ester and Inés, Jimena, Ana, and Amada initially requested assistance at regular police stations that were close to
their homes instead of making the long and more logistically
complicated trip downtown to the main women's police station.
Jimena's experiences took place in the family violence section of
a regular police station. They illustrate the sexism some women
may experience at the hands of officers whose personal views
shape how they treat women in a professional setting. Like Inés's
experiences, they point to the need for better training and sensi-
tization among service providers who interact with individuals
in situations of domestic violence. Jimena wanted to place a
complaint for physical and psychological violence against her
*conviviente*. When the officer asked her if she lived with her *con-*

*viviente*, Jimena replied that she had left her home with her two young children a few days earlier and was staying *"en la casa de un amigo"* (at a male friend's house) because her *conviviente*'s violence had recently become extreme. According to Jimena, the officer then disapprovingly exclaimed, "But, *señora*, why is the first thing you do to go live with another man?!" Jimena explained to the officer that her friend had a wife and children and that she and her children were staying with the entire family, but she felt the officer did not believe her. Jimena successfully placed the domestic violence complaint, but the personal scrutiny the officer subjected her to indicates that officers' personal views—in this case on women's sexuality—may influence how women are (mis)treated.

Ana's case illustrates both her wish to escape her husband's violence and the effects of the police's emphasis on family unity at the expense of individual women's well-being. Ana described her experience at a police station:

> ANA: I always reconciled [with my husband] at the police station. They would make me see, *"Señora*, what are you doing separating?"
> CRISTINA: Before you placed the claim?
> ANA: Yes. Before filing the claim they would speak with me, "What are you doing?" they would say. "Look at those babies. Think, you alone can't provide for them." That. They always put my daughters in the middle of it. "What are you doing?" they would say. "Because of you, because of you your daughters are going to suffer."

When I asked Ana what she would have liked the police to have done when she asked for assistance, she replied that she wanted officers "to support me" instead of telling her to return to her husband. Even after Ana had explained to the police that she was an orphan and had no family to turn to, the police had failed to mention the existence of shelters. Her experiences exemplify how officers prioritized their personal investment in family unity over the application of laws designed to protect victims of violence and the women's individual well-being. The patronizing manner in which the police officers treated Ana directly affected Ana's chances of leaving her partner by denying her state protection and reinforcing her submissive and self-sacrificing role as wife and mother within a violent home.

Ester, Inés, Jimena, and Ana were not the only women who

reported negative experiences at police stations. During a group interview, Mariana, a *dirigente* in a northern shantytown, echoed and elaborated on women's complaints regarding police stations: "Sometimes we take them [women from the shantytown] to the police station or to the DEMUNA [Defensoría Municipal del Niño y el Adolescente] and they [the service providers] make fun of them or they make them wait too long and don't help them.[10] So then people really become tired. Because it's a problem that they're living and they get tired of not being paid attention. So they return, stay with their partner, and so that problem that was small becomes bigger." Mariana felt frustrated because the police ignored and turned away women she and other *dirigentes* had convinced to file claims. Like Ester and other women I interviewed, Mariana believed the women were ignored because they were poor and therefore seen as unimportant. As she listened to Mariana's comments, Esperanza, also in the group of women who had agreed to speak with me that day, explained that when she went to the police station with her children, a policewoman advised Esperanza to return to her house quickly with her children so that her husband would not become more upset and beat her for reporting him.

In some cases, after facing police indifference, the women took additional steps to challenge police behavior. This was the case for Amada, who went to demand that the police arrest her husband because he was in violation of a protective order. He had beaten her, and the fresh bruises on her face constituted the evidence. Amada described how the police chief initially ignored her request:

> AMADA: He said, "No, there's no law for that," he said. "Just go home. And don't yell at him, don't say anything to him, just go back."
> CRISTINA: He said for you to not yell at your husband?
> AMADA: Uh-huh. So, for me to not complain about anything to him, to not say anything. That I should be very calm and that I shouldn't look to fight with him. To not do anything because it would just make it worse. So I said, "How is it that some women, because they have friends here or because they have boyfriends or I don't know what, acquaintances, as soon as they come in, as soon as they speak, all they have to do is open their mouths and a police car is there. And I, because I am a poor woman, or because I am not dressed up, or because the policemen haven't fallen in

love with me, you don't pay any attention to me." I said that to a
woman [officer].

Amada began by describing her interaction with the chief and
concluded by eloquently identifying the flaws in the treatment
she had received and detailing her response to a woman officer with whom she had spoken. She succinctly identified the
myths, injustice, and misinformation to which women may be
subjected at police stations. Amada demonstrated her knowledge of her rights and the extent to which these rights are denied by the institution responsible for protecting those rights. In
Amada's account, both the man and woman officers she spoke
with blamed her for the violence, misinformed her about laws,
dismissed her requests, and told her that the best thing was for
her to be calm to avoid exacerbating her husband's violence.
Fully aware of the importance the police placed on hierarchies
within the organization and of her low status as a poor woman,
Amada nonetheless answered back. Her response to the police
echoes other women's identification of police indifference toward poor women ("because I am poor") and toward women
without family or romantic connections to officers ("because
the policemen haven't fallen in love with me") as key problems
in police treatment of women.

Among the women I interviewed, Amada's behavior is unique
because after leaving the station, she went to the office of a
small newspaper to denounce the police. She told a reporter
there about her case and described how she had been mistreated.
The reporter took pictures of her bruised and swollen face and
promised to publish the story and the photograph the next day.
Amada thus achieved her goal of doing what she could to shame
the police publicly. Nonetheless, after denouncing the police's
indifference, she had no other option but to return home.

As women's experiences at police stations illustrate, there
is a great difference between the rights women should have as
citizens and the way police have treated them as poor women,
wives, and mothers. Other women I spoke with reported that
the police would not pay attention to them unless they had severe and visible injuries and bruises and that they asked them
for money for office supplies and snacks to process or speed up
their claims.

My findings that some police officers are biased and negatively affect women's options for protecting themselves from abuse reinforce similar findings for both urban and rural parts of Peru (Boesten 2006; Movimiento Manuela Ramos 2003, 2007) and cross-culturally (for Brazil, see Nelson 1996; Santos 2005; for China, see Tam and Tang 2005; for Mexico, see Hijar 1992; for the United States, see Abraham 2000; Anderson et al. 2003; Wolf et al. 2003).[11] In light of cross-cultural findings of inadequate police responses, in exploring why women stay with or return to abusive partners, we should remember that for some women, "in the absence of real protection, it is rational to want to put more faith in the promises and apologies of their batterers" (Anderson et al. 2003), as in Jimena's case. For other women, as in Amada's case, even in the absence of promises and apologies, there are few or no other options but to stay with or return to an abusive partner.

*Asymmetrical Conciliation Procedures*

After placing a domestic violence claim at a police station, one of the most common next steps is a conciliation hearing. Peruvian feminist organizations have consistently rejected conciliation as a solution in domestic violence cases in part by arguing that conciliation presumes two equal partners whereas situations of domestic violence are characterized by unequal power relations between partners (Boesten 2006:363). The mandatory nature of conciliation hearings between 1997 and 2001 and continued promotion of the procedure even after it was no longer mandatory in cases of domestic violence communicate the false message that domestic violence that has gone on for months or years can realistically be expected to end suddenly after one short hearing mediated by a family prosecutor. Forcing women to undergo a conciliation session in which they face the men accused of beating them in an unprotected setting at a time when they feel especially vulnerable does little to help them and may instead increase their feelings of powerlessness, guilt, and fear. Conciliation procedures may also delay the prosecution of abusive men and prolong women's and children's homelessness.

According to a study in Lima in 2005, four years after conciliation stopped being mandatory, family prosecutors continued to consider their greatest successes those cases in which an agreement was reached through conciliation (Movimiento Manuela Ramos 2007:42). Family prosecutors stated that they believed conciliation was successful in solving domestic violence cases because they observed "aggressors accept the blame and sign agreements to continue life as a couple without violence" during the conciliation and were convinced that couples who had been through conciliation rarely returned to court (Movimiento Manuela Ramos 2007:42). In contrast, the women I interviewed and women interviewed by the feminist organization Movimiento Manuela Ramos in 2005 insisted that conciliation agreements do not work because the men they lived with continued to be violent. The women further stated that they filed additional domestic violence complaints against their partners after the initial conciliation. However, because the time between the initial conciliation and the time the man and woman reappear before a family prosecutor is typically one to three years, magistrates may not realize they are dealing with the same couple (Movimiento Manuela Ramos 2007:42).

Agreements reached during conciliation have the same legality as those passed by a judge during judicial hearings, yet they are rarely enforced. In conciliation, it is not necessary, or usual, to be represented by a lawyer. In cases of domestic violence in which the woman is in the process of separating from her partner, the conciliation session may be the first time the woman sees her partner after leaving him. Each woman I interviewed spoke of her anxiety during the days leading up to the conciliation hearing. She worried about arranging childcare in order to attend the hearing and about how to control her emotions and fear upon seeing the man she had recently left. She was concerned about what the man might say or do before the conciliation started and about the possibility that he would attempt to harm or follow her after it ended. On many occasions, women went to the conciliation hearing only to find that the men accused of the violence had not shown up. When the man did not show up, another notification, with a new date and time, was sent to that man. Meanwhile, more time passed, and for women in a shelter or other form of temporary housing, the time they were allowed to stay drew closer to an end.

When both parties showed up for the conciliation procedure, the proceedings frequently reflected the family prosecutor's personal beliefs and prejudices and reinforced the asymmetry of power between the woman and her partner. Ester, forty-seven years old and the mother of three, had participated in three conciliation hearings and was about to participate in a fourth one when I first met her. When I spoke with her a day after she attended the fourth conciliation hearing, Ester told me she had not been able to stop crying during the night. During the conciliation, the prosecutor persisted in pressuring her to sign the agreement he proposed. Ester refused to sign anything, telling the prosecutor, "I do not trust that man [her husband] at all" because he had ignored the previous conciliation agreements. During the latest conciliation, the prosecutor suggested to her husband that he buy Ester flowers and that in return she should forgive him. Upset and outraged by the suggestion, Ester replied that she would not go back with him "even if he brought me a whole garden, because I do not trust him." In spite of Ester's efforts to demonstrate to the prosecutor that she wanted to prosecute, not reach an extrajudicial agreement, the prosecutor ignored and then simplified Ester's statements and situation, thereby prioritizing family unity over her well-being and rights.

Ester's experiences during the conciliation session are not unique. Many of the other women I interviewed, and other women whose files were reviewed by women's rights organizations, reported similar experiences. Women reported being blamed for the violence, asked to agree to fulfill their role as wives to avoid further violence, and pressured to accept blame for the violence and to uphold the family for the good of the children in conciliation agreements (Movimiento Manuela Ramos 1998).

### Shelters

Following the filing of a domestic violence claim and during her wait for a conciliation hearing, Kristina and her two daughters stayed at a shelter. When I asked Kristina how she would describe a shelter to women who had never been to one, after she and her daughters had been staying at a shelter for one month, she replied, "It's like a home, like your home. They will welcome you, they will help you, they will give you advice, you will have moments during which to speak with the psychologist. They will give you some peace of mind, right? At least a shelter, now that I am living it, it's like a, like hope. Look, something that like tells you that you are going to be something in the future, right? It helps you to reflect."

Kristina and her daughters had a generally positive experience at the shelter. Not all women shared Kristina's view of shelters. For example, Jimena, whose experiences were discussed in Chapter 4, described her and her children's stay at the shelter as a difficult time that did not provide any of the comforts of home and during which shelter workers had little time to listen to residents. Overall, however, the women I interviewed described shelter personnel as supportive and viewed their shelter residence as an empowering period during the process of leaving an abusive partner.

The police did not initially inform several of the women I interviewed who placed complaints at police stations of the existence of shelters. When police officers referred women to shelters, it was often not until after several visits to the station. Racquel found out about the existence of shelters only after several attempts to file claims against her husband. According to Racquel, during her visits to the police station, officers advised her to return to her husband because that was her duty as a wife. During the fifteen years she lived with her husband, Racquel experienced severe beatings and briefly contemplated suicide as her only escape. At the shelter, she and her children felt safe and were given the opportunity to speak to a psychologist about their experiences.

Shelters play an important role in women's ability to leave abusive partners and feel safe. This section examines the shelter system available to women, the views and experiences of shelter workers, and the obstacles workers face in attempting to meet the needs of residents. During my fieldwork, I regularly volunteered at one shelter and visited two others several times.[12] To protect the identity of each shelter, and to discuss more freely the obstacles each faces, in this section whenever possible I refer to them as Shelter 1, Shelter 2, and Shelter 3. In practice, shelters have names such as "Women for Survival" or "Shelter of the Association of Women for Justice."

In 2001, there were seven shelters in Lima and three more in other parts of the country.[13] Shelters have space for anywhere from five to twenty women and children. However, lack of resources, particularly food, can force shelters to limit drastically the number of women admitted during any given period. In Lima, each shelter is in a different district. In a city of almost ten million people, shelters can be very far from one another. For example, from the shelter at which I volunteered to another shelter I regularly visited, if there was only light traffic the trip took approximately one and a half hours by *micro*. Shelters in Lima have typically been founded by women community leaders who opened their homes, or who secured funds to build a shelter from private agencies and city administrators. It is not uncommon for individuals who run shelters to experience poverty on a personal level. Because of the precarious resources on which they rely for their operation, shelters cannot regularly provide women with needed medicines, money for transportation costs, or other necessities. To be admitted to a shelter, a woman must first file a claim, or she may be admitted on the condition that she will file a claim. At Shelter 2, personnel routinely offered to accompany residents to the police station and offered support during the process of filing a claim.

Shelters are not state-run and since 1997 have sought to organize themselves through RECARE (Red Nacional de Casas de Refugio para Mujeres y Niñez Victimas de Violencia Familiar y Sexual) to work together on issues dealing with domestic violence, improve their services, secure grants and other forms of funding, and meet at an annual national meeting of member shelters.[14] RECARE was founded and is led by Rosa Dueñas, a native Quechua speaker from Ancash and respected leader on women's and human rights issues. In 1982, Dueñas founded the first shelter in Peru by opening the house in Lima she had inherited from her mother to women and children seeking to leave violent homes.

Coming together through RECARE has also allowed shelters to create common rules and regulations for member shelters. Today, regulations for member shelters state that residents can stay for a maximum of fifteen days. In practice, however, the length of a woman's stay is often decided on a case-by-case basis. Shelter workers often go to great lengths to extend residencies and to help the women find other forms of temporary housing after they leave. Shelters recognize that fifteen days is not enough time to complete the complicated and long bureaucratic processes women must undertake in attempting to leave abusive partners. At the same time, they insist on keeping the fifteen-day rule in their written regulations in case they need to enforce the rule due to the lack of resources to support all residents for longer periods of time.

During one of my visits to the shelter founded by Dueñas, she and I spoke about the fifteen-day rule and she offered several examples of how she and her staff worked with women to make sure residents received the attention and assistance needed during that time, as well as beyond the fifteen days. Before speaking about the shelter's rules, however, we spoke about politics, which had become usual for us. As mentioned in Chapter 1, the year 2001 was an election year and politics was a common topic of conversation. For Dueñas, this election was particularly important because it was the first time a self-identified indigenous Peruvian, Alejandro Toledo, had run for president, and because Toledo came from her hometown, Ancash.

Dueñas believed that with Toledo, it was the *pueblo* (the common people) who supported him rather than the upper and middle classes as had been the case for most incoming presidents in Peru's history. According to Dueñas, both Toledo and his wife, Eliane Karp, a Belgian Jewish anthropologist and economist, appeared to be more committed to helping the largely poor indigenous majority than maintaining the status quo. The content of speeches and interviews given by Toledo and Karp appealed to Dueñas, whose own political grassroots work had focused on marginalized indigenous peoples and women over the past three decades.[15] Although she did not allow any sort of political propaganda inside the shelter, in her work outside of the shelter she decided to support Perú Posible, Toledo's political party—a position common among several shelter workers with whom I spoke. Dueñas was also hopeful that a Toledo presidency would be more open to hearing about the needs of shelters and to providing more state assistance to shelters and other institutions working on issues of domestic violence.

Seamlessly turning from her political views outside the shelter to her grassroots work within and on behalf of shelters, Dueñas began to speak of the fifteen-day maximum stay at shelters:

> They stay here for fifteen days, those are the rules. So, if they stay a few more days, even a month sometimes, it's more because they need to get better. Or sometimes they don't want to leave because they've found their niche here. They don't want to leave. Plus there's a whole schedule. Here no one has special privileges. Here, yes, they don't cook the first day. We don't make them do anything [the first day]. Almost always they want to sleep. Because almost always a woman who comes from being tortured wants to sleep all day. *Uy*, my God, that woman doesn't even feel like eating. They lie down and sleep. Maybe the next day [they get up]. Until they themselves ask to do something. They take turns, the one who came in on Monday, the one who came in on Tuesday, to do the cleaning. There's always someone from the staff here to be with them at all times, one in the morning and one at night. No one can be alone in the shelter. They can't be alone. They are terrified of being left alone. They are afraid, they think that at any moment their batterer might come and kill them, right? So then, one has to offer them trust. Once they begin to trust us, they too begin to want to do something for themselves, to earn money, or they teach us what they have lived.

As Dueñas states, shelters have regulations but they also practice flexibility to satisfy women's needs. In practice, being at a shelter is a deeply personal journey for both staff and residents. Shelter workers provide assistance to as well as learn from residents, and ideally residents find the space and resources to begin to cope with their fear and plan a new stage in their lives.

The day starts early at shelters. Residents take turns preparing meals and cleaning common areas. For breakfast, residents prepare and serve food between 6:30 and 7:30 AM. At Shelter 1, breakfast typically includes bread, butter, and watery oatmeal poured into plastic cups. During the winter months, which are characterized by high humidity in Lima, it is especially difficult to get the children up, bathed, and dressed so early in the morning because shelters cannot afford to pay to heat water and, occasionally, when a shelter does not have enough money to pay the water bill, the water is shut off for one or more days. In spite of the Peruvian custom of having lunch around 2 or 3 PM, in shelters lunch is served at 12:30 PM so that children who do not start school until 1 PM can eat before leaving the shelter. At Shelter 1, lunch typically consists of rice and beans or lentils and cold tea. Dinner, served at 6 PM, consists of leftovers. Condiments are sparse because all food supplies, including salt and oil, must be rationed to last through the month. Fruits and vegetables only accompany a meal when there is money for them. Every day, before each meal begins, a different person is responsible for saying a prayer. After dinner, the children at Shelter 1 go into the meeting room, where there is a small television perched high on the wall, and watch a show before going to bed.

Shelters typically include two to three staff members. At Shelter 1, the staff positions include those of coordinator, assistant coordinator, and nocturnal assistant. Both the coordinator and assistant coordinator are psychologists and counsel residents as well as perform administrative duties. The nocturnal assistant arrives just before dinner and leaves just after breakfast each day. Her main responsibility is to keep company with the residents at night in case of emergencies.[16] Work shifts for staff at the shelter rarely overlapped. On any given day, just as the coordinator arrived, the assistant coordinator left, and, just as the assistant coordinator left, the nocturnal assistant arrived. In the morning, the cycle started again as the coordinator arrived just after breakfast as the nocturnal assistant prepared to leave. Each staff member wrote down the events that took place during her shift and any important issues to be addressed by the staff member during the next shift in a shelter log kept at the coordinator's desk, and each staff member read this log as soon as she walked in and before entering the common areas to greet residents.

Because of the scarcity of funds at shelters, salaries are notably low. In 2001, the nocturnal assistant at Shelter 1 earned approximately three-fourths the minimum monthly salary set by the Peruvian government, while at Shelter 2 one of the two workers (apart from the director) earned one-third the minimum monthly salary. In spite of the low salaries and workers' personal economic hardships, during my fieldwork I never heard a shelter worker complain that what she was paid was too low. They all knew what they earned was very low, but they also knew that funding was limited. For the two workers who reported how much they earned during their interviews with me, part of the appeal of working at these shelters was that they were provided with food and, for the nocturnal assistant, a place to sleep, thereby lowering personal expenses. Additionally, both women received financial assistance from family members and depended on *comedores populares* to help offset their families' food costs. Both also felt personally committed to helping women in situations of domestic violence even as they struggled with significant economic hardships in their lives as a result of their work at the shelters (and grim employment opportunities citywide).

Each shelter typically receives small amounts of aid from the State in the form of monthly installments of food (usually sacks of beans and rice) and/or assistance in paying for some bills (such as telephone, water, or electricity), yet these contributions cover only a small portion of its residents' expenses and needs. Donations from local and international organizations as well as the residents' own initiatives help generate additional money for basic expenses such as transportation costs to and from police stations or hospitals and medicines. At each of the shelters, it is common for residents to collaborate to purchase ingredients to bake cakes or other sweets and then to sell these baked goods in the neighborhood and divide the earnings among those who participate.

Shelters 2 and 3, together with three other shelters in Lima, further emphasize economic activities through a series of talks and economic initiatives that help women acquire job skills and earn money during and after their shelter residency. In Shelter 2, women crochet shoes, purses, vests and belts. Once women learn how to crochet from more experienced participants, the shelter provides them with enough raw materials (plastic soles, thread, and accessories) to make shoes for their children and themselves. A woman may take anywhere from one day to one month to make a pair of shoes, depending on her skill, the amount of time available to dedicate to the project, and how quickly she will be paid after she turns in the finished product. The shelter offers women a fixed amount for each article. The difference between the fixed amount and the selling price for each item helps defray shelter expenses. The women take pride in their newly developed skills and their ability to earn money, and they sell their handicrafts at fairs, in the neighborhood, and

to friends. Participation in the program is not mandatory, but the majority of women decide to participate in it and to continue their participation after leaving the shelter.

Once it is time for a woman to leave a shelter, because she has exceeded the maximum stay or because she has found a place to go, she must leave the room in which she and her children stayed in the condition in which she found it. The rooms, which at Shelter 1 and 3 each included two to four bunk beds, must be swept and cleaned. At Shelter 1, women must also wash all the used bed sheets and covers. There is no washer; the women use cold water and a patio sink. When there is little or no water, the women ask neighbors for water in buckets. I once saw a woman take two hours to wash her and her children's bed sheets because she had to stop washing to go next door and ask the neighbors for buckets of water every half an hour.

The majority of women in Lima shelters come from Lima, are poor, and have children. Because of the lack of follow-up programs, it is unclear how many women in shelters leave the shelter to return to their abusive partners and how many permanently leave their partners. Women are most often referred to shelters by police, the PROMUDEH, or DEMUNAs. Through information campaigns in recent years, more and more women have become aware of the existence of shelters through the media. For example, Kristina first heard of shelters on a daytime television talk show and "kept that [shelter] phone number for three years" hidden behind a picture frame until she felt prepared to leave her husband.

When I asked the assistant coordinator, Yesenia, and coordinator, Elena, at Shelter 1 on separate occasions what they believed to be the most challenging aspect of working in a shelter, they each responded that the most difficult part was not having sufficient funds to meet the shelter's and residents' needs. Yesenia also mentioned that sometimes she felt frustrated because "each woman has a different schedule so organizing a workshop that would be useful to them, or a support group, is almost impossible. Women don't show up." Over the course of a year, Yesenia had organized workshops and support groups at the shelter. She had prepared for these events by dedicating many hours of her time off from work to learn more about topics she had identified as relevant to women staying at the shelter. While she understood that the women had to go to doctors' appointments and to speak with police officers, social workers, and lawyers, she also felt disappointed because each time she organized these events, either no one showed up, or only one woman showed up. The women expressed interest in the workshops and groups, but the long list of things the women needed to accomplish during their short shelter stays made it very difficult for them to attend these events.

Yesenia came from a mestiza working-class background and began working at the shelter in her mid-twenties, soon after graduating from college. She had worked at the shelter for a little over a year when I met her. In discussing why she decided to work at the shelter, Yesenia explained that she had been interested in "women's issues, equality, discrimination against women" as far back as she could remember because "my father is *machista*" and she had grown up feeling it was unfair that she and her sisters had to clean, stay home, and cook while her brother went out partying. Her college classes had further opened her eyes to gender inequality, but it was not until she began to work at the shelter that she "saw the full extent of what machismo and gender discrimination can do to women." At the shelter, her biggest sense of fulfillment came from working with children on issues that she and Elena identified as obstacles to the children's development. For Elena, a psychologist in her mid-thirties whose family background is also working-class and mestiza, her goal as coordinator was to provide women with "a peaceful environment so that women can visualize and internalize a new type of life, a totally different one from the one they are living which is filled with violence." Because of this, for Elena the most fulfilling part of her job was "the process, to see the evolution, the change in women and children during their stay at the shelter" from a state of fear to a more peaceful, tranquil state of mind in which they could define specific goals for a new stage of their lives. Elena and Yesenia, like Rosa Dueñas, were committed to assisting women begin a new stage without intimate violence in their lives, yet they were acutely aware that women with children who are poor, unemployed, and lack housing also face other forms of violence and discrimination in Lima.

*Women's Organizations*

As part of my fieldwork, I contacted and visited several feminist and women's organizations to find out more about their work and the services they provided to women facing domestic as well as other forms of violence. Over the last four decades, feminist and women's organizations in Peru have played a pivotal role in bringing violence in the home to the public eye, researching and treating violence, and getting legislation passed. These organizations have also tackled issues related to health, political participation and political violence, employment, and rural development.

Among the principal organizations that have pushed the Peruvian government to address violence in the home, the Centro de la Mujer Peruana Flora Tristán, Movimiento Manuela Ramos, the Women's International League for Peace and Freedom (WILPF), CLADEM, and Estudio para la Defensa de los Derechos de la Mujer (DEMUS) have held prominent roles.[17] At the main women's police station, lawyers from Flora Tristán, Manuela Ramos, and DEMUS take turns counseling women in domestic violence situations. Flora Tristán began to offer legal assistance at the main women's police station just a year after the station opened. In addition to staffing the main women's police station with lawyers, these organizations offer free legal counsel at their main offices and work on multiple projects related to women's rights. For example, Manuela Ramos has offered free legal counsel since the mid-1980s and counseled over 15,000 women between the mid-1980s and 2001 at their main office. In the late 1990s and early 2000s, the number of women seeking legal counsel from Manuela Ramos increased as a result of media campaigns on women's rights and domestic violence.[18] The women I interviewed offered positive assessments of their experiences asking for information and receiving assistance from feminist and women's organizations.[19]

During my fieldwork, my contact with Flora Tristán and WILPF was more extensive than with the other organizations. I contacted these organizations during pre-fieldwork trips to Lima and they generously agreed to allow me to become affiliated with them to apply for the fellowship I ultimately received to conduct research in Lima. During the first three months of my fieldwork, Flora Tristán put me in contact with a small community reproductive health clinic sponsored by the organization. The clinic is a small, old two-story house in the middle of a dirt road near a very busy main avenue in northern Lima. At one end of the room sits the main desk, with a very full file cabinet. On top of the file cabinet, there is a small, plastic white bucket with holy water. At the other end of the room, the walls are lined with educational posters offering information on family planning. The small waiting area is equipped with a sofa, two chairs, a coffee table, and a television set and VCR. Nine middle-aged women from the surrounding community staff the clinic. The women, who were originally trained by personnel from Flora Tristán, started volunteering at the clinic when the clinic opened in the early 1990s. Together with one paid doctor, they keep the clinic running. The clinic charges minimal fees for services, and women who cannot afford to pay are treated for free. Women call or visit the clinic for a variety of reasons that range from vaginal infections (the most common reason) to information on emergency contraception. Men occasionally visit the clinic, usually for condoms or to accompany a partner.

The women I interviewed at the clinic, as well as other women I interviewed through personal contacts, are usually invisible in domestic violence research. They are invisible because many have not visited police stations and shelters, and they have not filed domestic violence claims. Because of this, no published record of their experiences and of how they deal with everyday violence exists. Although the clinic is not specifically for women in abusive relationships, it is a space where women who suffer violence can go, be heard, and receive information on available resources. It is also a space in which women can learn about their bodies and reproductive rights. The clinic coordinator is Carmen, a married fifty-eight-year-old woman with six children. As she explained to me, the volunteers at the clinic work there "so that women learn that they too have rights. Not only to not be beaten but that they also have sexual rights, reproductive rights. That they are the only ones who can say, 'I don't want to, I don't feel like it,' right? And that they also have the right to say, 'Today I do [feel like it],' right?" The experience of volunteers at the clinic strongly suggests that economic hardship and lack of access to educational opportunities prevent many poor women

from adequately caring for their health and bodies and asserting their rights. Women's organizations and small clinics such
as this one work to change that.

*Multiple Institutions, Multiple Barriers*

In Lima, inadequate funds and discriminatory practices within
institutions responsible for helping women in domestic violence situations are among the reasons why women who want
to leave and attempt it end up staying with their partners. In
addition, there is little networking and sharing of information
among the various agencies and institutions charged with helping women in abusive relationships. At a roundtable organized
by Shelter 1 in 2001, representatives from various state and
nonprofit entities in the shelter's district came together. One of
the representatives was the chief at the nearby police station.
He had only found out about the shelter's existence through the
invitation to the roundtable two weeks earlier. The shelter had
been in his district for several years.

Women who want to leave their abusive partners face many
obstacles. They may lack family and community support as well
as money and personal identification documents. They may have
no way to leave the house, or nowhere to go. They may feel dis-
couraged from pursuing legal redress by stories they have heard
from other women who went to police stations to attempt to file
claims. Women who are not legally married may also fear that
they may be blamed for the violence due to the nature of their
relationship or that they may be considered unworthy of protection or help (García Ríos and Tamayo 1990:247). This chapter
has explored women's experiences in institutions women commonly use, the ways the institutions function, and the effects
of the attitudes and actions women encounter in these institutional settings on the women's ability to protect themselves and
their children from violent partners. It has approached wom-
en's struggles to access external resources as overt forms of
resistance to men's violence. In the next chapter, the discussion
moves on to women's attempts to rebuild their lives in Lima
after leaving abusive partners.

# PART III
# Rebuilding Lives

CHAPTER 6 ◊ The Everyday
Experiences and Dangers
of Starting Over

◊ BY 2008, IT HAD BEEN SEVEN YEARS since Daisy and her sons left her abusive *conviviente* and the shelter at which we met. Daisy had been employed in the same household for five years and supplemented her main source of income as a domestic worker in that household with occasional work in other homes as well as with small entrepreneurial ventures with her sons. Her eldest son, Yonatan, had graduated from high school and begun to train to become a mechanic. Her three younger sons were enrolled in school and were all doing well in their studies. Daisy felt proud of her sons, and of herself, for overcoming so much adversity in their lives as they continued to struggle to *superarse*. Although her sons' successes bring Daisy joy, the family's poverty and the boys' continued education result in additional obstacles to overcome. To ensure that her children can concentrate on schoolwork, Daisy forbids her sons from working during the school year. This means that during the academic year, all school supplies and professional training fees come only from Daisy's work cleaning homes, and that in the summer, the whole family works long hours to purchase supplies to begin the academic year.

Like other women I interviewed, Daisy is courageous, strong, and creative. Yet, as the previous chapters suggest, it would be naïve to present an unequivocally optimistic portrait of the path taken and obstacles encountered in the process of starting over by very poor women who have little or no family or institutional support. Daisy escaped two abusive relationships successfully, yet her and her sons' lives continued to be informed by other forms of violence long after these abusive relationships ended. While women are capable of solving many problems on their own, escaping an abusive relationship and starting over is a complicated process that often necessitates assistance from outside resources. Once a woman leaves her home, a shelter, or other form of transitional housing, she faces an upward struggle with no definite end. She must find and maintain a home and job and protect her children from other forms of violence in the midst of poverty, discrimination, racism, and few job opportunities.[1] In this chapter, I focus primarily on Daisy's experiences to provide a dynamic picture of the process of starting over and the multiple ways in which intimate, institutional, and structural violence intersect with women's lives long after they leave abusive relationships. I incorporate data from a 2005 interview with Yonatan, Daisy's then fifteen-year-old son, to provide a unique young man's perspective that complements Daisy's rendition of events, places, and moments that have affected the family's livelihood.

### Daisy, and Our (Unequal) Relationship

In 2001, twenty-nine-year-old Daisy lived with her four sons: twelve-year-old Yonatan, ten-year-old Alfredo, five-year-old Jesús, and three-year-old Richar. As described in the first part of the Introduction, she and I met at a shelter at which she and her children were residents and I was a volunteer and researcher. It was early February 2001 and I had just begun my fieldwork. I had spent a significant amount of Daisy's shelter residency searching for a job for another shelter resident, Ana, and had not had any significant interactions with Daisy. It was not until after Ana left the shelter that the relationship between Daisy and me began to develop.

Daisy's exit from the shelter was facilitated by her part-time cleaning job, daily work selling candy on the streets, and some additional money and supplies contributed by an agency and by various acquaintances and relatives of mine who became familiar with Daisy's situation. Daisy bought—and built a house on—a piece of land in a *pueblo joven* far from the shelter and from her former home. Over the course of the following year, in the midst of rebuilding her and her sons' lives after leaving her second abusive relationship, Daisy narrated her life story during at least ten interview sessions. We have continued to communicate with each other and engaged in follow-up interviews and numerous conversations during the past eight years via telephone and in person during my annual visits to Lima.

Daisy now regularly works in my relatives' homes. I receive news of her and her children through my relatives and through Daisy, and she receives news of me and my family through my parents and other relatives, as well as directly through me. Our relationship has moved well beyond a research relationship, but although we care about each other, our relationship is not one of horizontal friendship. The relationship between Daisy and me is an inherently unequal relationship in which mutual care intersects with class, educational, and cultural differences.

In discussing relationships she developed during her field-work with poor people in Honduras, Pine comments that her position as a privileged North American researcher "made it difficult for me to have the kind of friendships with them that I am used to enjoying in the United States, in which power dif-ferentials are subtly negotiated so as to appear trivial or non-existent" (2008:7).[2] Similarly, both Daisy and I are aware that "inequality is a core principle structuring domestic servant/ employer relationships" (Sagaria 2000:101). Although I have never been Daisy's employer, by assisting her in finding employ-ment and ultimately facilitating her employment as an *empleada* (domestic worker) within my relatives' households, I have con-tributed to the solidification of an unequal relationship that is partly maintained through her work in settings that emphasize power differentials and in which I am directly connected to the individuals with power over Daisy.

Two years after I finished my fieldwork, Daisy began to work regularly as an *empleada* at my parents' house in Lima. A year after that, she also occasionally worked at my grandmother's and uncle's houses. When Daisy became unemployed after she left the shelter, my parents had agreed to ask her to work at their house part-time until she found something else to help her make ends meet. Months later, Daisy had not found any other employment. Although my parents had initially agreed to hire Daisy as a favor to me, they had come to count on the ser-vices she provided, they trusted her, and they were concerned about her and her family's well-being. I initially felt uncomfort-able when I heard from my parents that Daisy needed such-and-such amount of money for her sons' schools or medicines and that they had given her that amount (in addition to her salary), because I felt I was transferring a responsibility I had developed with Daisy on to them. However, after several months, I realized that my parents and Daisy had developed their own relationship that, although it became possible because of my relationship with Daisy, was now separate from me, my responsibilities, and my research. And, as a result of Daisy's employment with my parents, my relationship with Daisy has developed in some unforeseen ways.

Behar has noted that traditionally "we [researchers] ask for revelations from others, but we reveal little or nothing of ourselves; we make others more vulnerable, but we ourselves remain invulnerable" (1993:273). Through Daisy's work relationship with my parents, I became "vulnerable" in a sense to revelations about my personal and professional life two years after our initial meeting. During summer visits to my parents' house, my interactions with Daisy included early morning conversations (while I was still in my pajamas) that did not deal directly with her situation or experiences of violence and midafternoon lunches together. She observed my interactions with my parents, husband, and son in ways not previously available to her. In short, Daisy became familiar with many details of my life and the lives and gossip of my family members as a result of her work in my parents' home.[3] In this way, my "private" life became part of Daisy's public life as an *empleada*. Earlier, it had only been her "private" life that had been part of my public life as a researcher.

Significantly, my becoming more vulnerable to Daisy's observations and knowledge of my "private" life does not erase inherent differences in power in our positions in Lima and in our relationship. While part of me remains uncomfortable with the knowledge that the unequal relationship of *empleada*/employer now indirectly informs our relationship, I am cognizant that our relationship before that was also unequal and that ignoring inherent power differences does not erase or make one less accountable for these differences, nor does it provide employment. The experiences I discuss in the following pages are those that Daisy recounted to me primarily in 2001 but also during the following years, during breaks and days off from and after work days at my parents' and other relatives' homes.

*Early Experiences of Violence*

When Daisy was three, her father passed away, and her mother took her and her two older brothers to Cuzco from their small rural community in the neighboring department of Apurimac. Her mother remarried in Cuzco, and Daisy and her brothers suffered repeated violence at the hands of their stepfather and mother. She remembers watching her mother and stepfather get drunk together while she and her brothers worked in the fields. She does not remember her mother ever providing affection or advice. At age seven, Daisy began to work as a domestic worker near Cuzco. When she was in third grade, she dropped out of school to work full-time. There is little of her childhood that she wants to or can hold on to. Even the small plot of land her family had owned in Apurimac—on which she lived during the first few years of her life, and to which she might have returned to escape her first or second abusive partner—was taken from her family in the conflict between the State and Sendero Luminoso in the 1980s.

When Daisy was thirteen, she met a twenty-three-year-old man who expressed an interest in dating her. She paid little attention to him, but he kept his eye on her as she matured. When she turned seventeen, he forced her to have sex and she became pregnant with their first son.[4] Because she had no one to turn to for information and support, she began to live with this man and continued to do so even after he began to beat her regularly. Although Daisy wanted to space apart her pregnancies, her *conviviente* did not allow her to use any form of birth control. According to Daisy, he was convinced that she would cheat on him if she used birth control. As time went by, Daisy began to go to the community health center secretly for birth control injections to space out her pregnancies since she could not control his demands for sex.

*Daisy in Lima*

In 1997, when Daisy was twenty-five, she, her *conviviente*, and their three sons moved to Lima. "He brought me to Lima from the highlands through deceit," she explained. He had promised her land, a job, and a good education for their children. Instead, a month after they moved to Lima, he abandoned her and their sons. She did not know anyone in Lima, did not have a job, and, as she would later find out, the piece of land on which she had built a new home was on government property and she would soon be evicted. Daisy struggled to learn her way around Lima and worked at different jobs to make ends meet. She had been a domestic worker in the past, but her position as a migrant woman and newcomer to Lima with three young children made finding such work especially challenging.

While it is common for women migrants to come to Lima to work in full-time domestic service or commerce, for many of the women I interviewed, neither of these avenues of work was a viable option. First, to work as independent vendors or engage in most types of commerce, women need economic capital. None of the women I interviewed had money to invest. Second, to be full-time domestic workers, especially live-in domestic workers, women must be away from their children for five to six days at a time. Without family support networks in Lima, it was impossible for Daisy to be away from her sons for that long.

For Daisy, her difficulties in earning enough money to feed and clothe her children in Lima led her to send them to Cuzco to live with her stepsister.[5] In this decision, Daisy followed a pattern practiced and recognized by many Peruvians of sending children to live with relatives who are better off to improve the children's options in the future (Leinaweaver 2008a, 2008b).

Without children to care for from day to day, Daisy had a better chance of finding a full-time job. She planned to work and save money to move to Cuzco eventually, where she would start a business and live with her children. To achieve this, she spent as little as she could on her own food and transportation, both to save money and to send money to Cuzco for her children's food and education every month. After a year-long separation from his mother, Daisy's eldest son, Yonatan, complained during a phone conversation that he and his brothers did not have shoes and that their aunt did not allow them to attend school. Feeling betrayed by her stepsister because she had neglected Daisy's sons in spite of the money Daisy had regularly sent her, Daisy used some of her savings to travel to her stepsister's home and bring her sons back to Lima. In Lima, she used the rest of her savings to buy a piece of land, on which she and her sons built a small straw-matting shack.

By mid-1998, Daisy had found work as a cleaning lady at a library. While she had been fortunate to find a job, the amount she received and the pay schedule did not allow her to meet her daily expenses. Like many paid jobs, the library job paid her only after a month's work. For a middle-class person with savings, or even for a poor person with support networks through which to acquire a temporary loan, waiting a month to receive payment for services rendered in advance may not pose significant problems. As a migrant single mother, Daisy had no one to turn to for a loan, yet she had children to feed and her own transportation costs to and from her job to cover on a daily basis.

In 2000, the legal minimum salary in Peru was US$117 a month, the poverty line was set at approximately US$45 per person per month, and it was common for women's incomes to fall below the poverty line. In Lima, as in other urban centers, women earned on average about 54 percent of men's incomes (Canadian International Development Agency 2002). Most of the women I met during my fieldwork did not come close to earning the minimum wage in any given month, and few earned more than US$45 per month on a regular basis. At the end of each month, Daisy earned about two-thirds the minimum wage at the library.

As the days passed, Daisy found it increasingly difficult to provide food for her sons, and the family's situation became progressively worse. To get to and from work without paying bus fare, Daisy sold candy on the bus routes to her job. To avoid paying fares, she only stayed on each bus long enough to sell a few pieces of candy. Because of this, Daisy often arrived at work late. One evening, she offered bus passengers pieces of candy and asked for donations. With tears rolling down her face, she began to tell the people on the bus about her situation:

> And people, when they saw me, in a single bus I earned almost twenty *soles*. And that brought me so much happiness, because God is generous, isn't he? So then I got off the bus and jumped up and down from happiness. I said, "Now I have money." And I went to take them [my sons the money]. At that time I had no stove, nothing. I collected branches, little sticks [to make a fire with which to cook]. I went to the shack where we lived. And

I cooked, and in the afternoon I didn't go back to work [at the library]. I didn't go there anymore, I went to the streets to sell candy. And my children ate every day. But then people stopped believing me and I didn't earn money.

Daisy's relief at finding a way to support her family was short-lived. Today it is common to encounter several individuals, including very young children, selling candy on a single bus, and adults may have a difficult time competing with young children for passengers' attention and money. In this setting, this sort of work cannot support a family.

A year after Daisy signed the papers for the piece of land on which she and her sons were living, the government evicted her; whoever had sold her the land had done so illegally.[6] She and her children had nowhere to go and no one to turn to for help. At around the time that she was evicted, Daisy met the man who would become the father of her fourth son. Referring to this man, she tells me that during this difficult period, "I believed I would form a new home with him. But it didn't go well for me." According to Daisy, like her previous partner, he did not want her to use any form of birth control. Soon after she became pregnant with her youngest son, she discovered that her *conviviente* used drugs regularly.[7] At her insistence, he entered a drug rehabilitation program. After only two months in the program, he abandoned the program. He began to abuse her soon after he dropped out of the program. He beat her for the first time when she tried to defend her sons from him. Daisy recounted that "he wanted to beat my sons. He says that a father needs to beat or use a belt to discipline children. Like a father. But I didn't like that." Daisy explained that she also disciplined her sons physically, but that she slapped them on the hand or occasionally hit them. She viewed his use of a belt and his emphasis on physical punishment as excessive and harmful to her children.

They moved into a room in his father's house, and, according to Daisy, within a few months of the move, he stopped working but continued to demand that she work and provide food for him. She worked during the day selling candy on buses and came home to cook for her sons and *conviviente* in the evenings. Daisy tells me that although she hid her money, her *conviviente* always found it. Daisy suspected that her *conviviente* spent the money on drugs; sometimes she came home to discover that he had sold their belongings, including the boys' clothes, yet he had no money. What most disturbed Daisy, as she recounted her *conviviente's* behavior, was that while she worked, he would beat and threaten her sons, telling them that he was going to throw them out of the house but not before he killed one of them. According to her sons, when the boys responded that they would tell their mother that he was beating them, he threatened to kill them all if they told Daisy about the abuse.

When Daisy's sons told her about the abuse anyway, she decided to leave with her children. She and the father of her youngest son had been together for one and a half years. Daisy explained that when she told him of her decision, he taunted her, reminding her that she had no place to go. She said she would leave anyway and that she would take her children, including their son. Her partner became very angry and grabbed a kitchen knife and tried to kill her oldest son, Yonatan. According to Daisy, it was only because her partner's sister came in and managed to take the knife away from him that Yonatan is still alive today.

For Yonatan, this episode changed his view of his life. In 2005, as he and I sat together at a small café having lunch, I did not bring up the knife episode Daisy had discussed with me years earlier, yet Yonatan brought it up within seconds of my asking about what he thought of his family's experiences up to that point. Putting his ham and cheese sandwich down on the plate, but still looking down at the plate, Yonatan explained that his stepfather had "almost killed me with a knife" and asked if his mom had ever told me about the incident, to which I replied that she had but that I would like to hear his thoughts on what happened if he wanted to talk about it. Yonatan stated that the actions by this man, whom Yonatan had trusted, "changed my life." Yonatan believes he survived because God has something better in store for him. Soon after the knife incident, Yonatan decided he wanted to begin to go to church (something his mother and brothers did not do). By our lunch meeting in 2005, Yonatan had become a devout Christian whose main activities outside his home revolved around the evangelical church in his neighborhood.

Having taken the knife from Daisy's partner, the sister called the police. By the time the police arrived, Daisy's partner had gotten hold of the knife once again and had thrown the knife at Daisy, barely missing her back and her youngest son, whom she carried strapped to her back. The police detained Daisy's partner for twenty-four hours. During those twenty-four hours, Daisy had to leave the house and find a new place for her and her four sons. After she placed a domestic violence claim at the station, the police referred Daisy to the shelter at which we met.

Looking back at their time at the shelter and comparing it to the months that followed, Daisy described the shelter residency as "a holiday." Yonatan remembered the shelter differently. When I asked him what he thought of his stay at the shelter, he responded that "the woman there [the nocturnal assistant] yelled too much. She discriminated against my mother. She would take all the good food and would only give us the leftovers." Daisy also remembered unpleasant aspects of the shelter, but her overall view is that the shelter provided her and her sons with a safe place to stay when they most needed it. For her son, however, the shelter stay was a poignant reminder of how people outside of his home also mistreat his mother. When, toward the end of our lunch, I asked him what he would like to do when he is older, he responded with certainty that he wants to become a lawyer "to defend people who suffer a lot of injustices." Yonatan's directly experiencing and witnessing multiple forms of violence have clearly influenced his goals in life.

At the shelter, because there was no child care and women could not leave their children there unsupervised, Daisy had to find a place to leave her sons while she sold candy during the day. She left her three older boys at a nearby park in the afternoons so that she and her youngest son, strapped to her back, could go to the police station to check on the progress of her domestic violence claim when necessary and sell candy on buses and on the street. It was a matter of days until one of her sons spotted Daisy's ex-*conviviente* near the park where they spent hours each day. When her sons told her they had seen their stepfather near the park, Daisy befriended a security guard at a nearby large department store. The guard allowed the boys to stay in the television section of the store very quietly for a few hours each day while Daisy worked.

While at the shelter, Daisy had gotten up very early, gone out to sell candy, and gone to bed late, yet made little progress in finding a more reliable job and a home. Reluctantly, she decided to place her three eldest boys in state care so that she could find a job as a domestic worker—or any other job—and save money with only her youngest son in tow. [8] Once she was back on her feet, she would reunite with her sons. However, the state home in which she had hoped to place her children refused to take her sons. The home required original birth certificates, which Daisy did not have and could not acquire because her three oldest children had been born outside of Lima. It also required her to supply clothes and shoes for each son, and she could provide neither these nor the required immunizations.

Recognizing that Daisy and her sons had nowhere to go, the shelter allowed them to stay beyond the customary fifteen days. After two months at the shelter, Daisy told me she felt pressured to leave by some of the staff but still had nowhere to go. Through acquaintances and family contacts, I was able to assist Daisy in finding and buying a piece of land in a far away *pueblo joven*. Daisy and her boys moved in and built a house with the help of neighbors.

At this point, Daisy's life, in broad strokes, is a success story: a woman who left her partner, rallied others to help her, found a place to live, and is now "safely" away from her abusive partner. But as discussed earlier, especially in Chapter 1, Lima is not always a hospitable place, and starting over with four boys in an empty house in an unfamiliar neighborhood and selling candy on buses cannot guarantee the end of violence or poverty. Successful, in this context, does not mean living without significant obstacles.

*Starting Over*

I visited Daisy's new home in a relatively new *pueblo joven* that had secured water and electricity for its residents shortly after she moved in. Barking dogs were territorial about the steep, arid hill that leads to Daisy's home. As we walked up the hill, I could see homes in various stages of completion and of varying materials: wood, straw, metal, and bricks. Daisy's new home was almost at the top of the hill, and by halfway up I was already feeling out of breath. Daisy could have made it up the hill in half the time had it not been for my slow pace.

In Daisy's house, a large blue piece of plastic sat on top of the straw and wooden walls to protect the inside from wind and rain. One of the walls could be lifted to function as a door. The house was divided into two areas. The kitchen/storage area was largely empty except for a small, portable kerosene double burner for cooking and a rectangular table with the boys' schoolwork piled on top, and various wooden boxes for storage on either side of the table. The second area was the bedroom. There was a light bulb hanging from the ceiling in one corner, and a small rectangular mirror and comb in another corner of the room. The two older boys used the mirror to comb their hair carefully before school. In the middle of the room, taking up most of the space, were two twin beds, set up tightly one against the other, surrounded by four metal chairs. The family slept on those two beds. A poster of the movie *Kill Bill* was taped to the wooden plank wall.

*View from Daisy's house. Photograph by the author.*

Just a little further up past Daisy's new home was the communal "bathroom"—a piece of undeveloped land. The dirt was littered with human excrement and toilet paper. Daisy told her children not to play up on the hill because it was dirty, and because at night men congregated there to use drugs. She also cautioned them about not leaving the house unattended. Sometimes that meant that one of the boys had to miss school, but because their home had already been burglarized, keeping it guarded at all times was important. So the boys went to school on most days, tried to stay away from the top of the hill at night, and regularly guarded their home. They no longer experienced their stepfather's beatings, but other forms of violence continued to affect their everyday lives.

When Daisy moved to this community, only ten families lived there. Four months later, at least ten additional families had moved in. Some of her neighbors, she told me, were single mothers fleeing abusive husbands. Sometimes the women came from outside of Lima, and they were now the poorest of the poor in the capital. She did not know all her neighbors, and she felt suspicious and fearful of some of them.[9] She also felt sympathetic toward other neighbors. She told me about one of her neighbors, a single mother with two toddlers who lived just a few feet away from them and whose small, straw matting shack provided little protection from the wind and cold. Whenever Daisy received clothing from acquaintances that was too small for her children, she passed it on to this neighbor.

Like other shantytown communities, Daisy's community had a board of directors. The board decided who could and could not live there and what the residents had to do to maintain their community. Every Sunday there was a mandatory community meeting at which issues such as acquiring sewage service, dividing the community into lots, and obtaining legal property titles were discussed. Failure to attend the weekly meeting resulted in a fine. For Daisy, the fine was the equivalent of a whole day's earnings. After the meeting, residents worked together to clean the community. Participation in community work was also mandatory, and failure to participate resulted in a separate fine.

Community meetings, work, and solidarity are important to keep an emerging community organized and safe. Carla, a thirty-five-year-old mother of three who lives in a more established shantytown at the other edge of the city, identified unemployment and gang violence as the two biggest problems in her community. The children, Carla explained to me, "have so many illusions when they finish school, and they have nothing" when they start looking for jobs and therefore sometimes join gangs. Other women echoed Carla's concerns. A group of women from her community described to me how they had seen their neighbors' children, now in gangs, break into the communal kitchen and steal their stove and pots. Other problems shantytown dwellers face include land disputes with neighboring communities and lack of childcare centers (especially in newer settlements).

For many women, living on a hill can also mean lack of state protection from violence. Homes near the top of hills are not often accessible by car, and this can facilitate the isolation of women and children in those homes and the continuation of violence against them. As García Ríos and Tamayo (1990) observe in their study of domestic violence in a poor district of Lima, interviews with police revealed not only that some police considered the home as the most violent place, but that they viewed the shantytowns in "the hills" as especially dangerous and violent. Group interviews with women from two shantytowns made clear to me the uselessness of calling the police for intervention in domestic violence disputes or incidents of gang violence when the event took place on "the hill." The women who live in those areas most often do not have the money for bus fare to and from a police station and the police refuse to go to their homes. These women thus experience violence at home in addition to structural violence through lack of access to state protection, and this further marginalizes them.

Daisy believes she cannot count on the police, family, or neighbors to help her or her children. She worries that her children depend on her so much. One incident in particular has made her especially anxious about her ability to support and protect her children. As she first described it, she, with her baby on her back, had fallen out of a moving *micro* to which she was trying to get on to sell candy. What had actually happened, she later revealed, was that the *cobrador* pushed her out as she was trying to climb on. She fell, and her ankle and foot were swollen for over a week, making working that week particularly challenging and painful. This experience made her wonder what would happen if something happened to her: how would her children survive? Selling candy was not very profitable and it could be dangerous, yet it was one of the only jobs Daisy could find to make money during her first year after leaving the shelter. Daisy tried working in various homes cleaning and cooking, but all these jobs were part-time and short-term. On one occasion, she was offered a higher-paying job on Sundays. She had to turn it down because of the mandatory meetings she had to attend in her community. She would have had to use her entire day's earnings just to pay for transportation to and from the work place and the fines for not participating in the meeting and communal work.

## Strategizing and the Essentialized Battered Woman

Even before facing the obstacles previously discussed, there had been many obstacles to overcome when Daisy and her sons prepared to leave the shelter. Daisy searched far and wide for ways of acquiring basic materials and resources for her new home and for her sons. She spent one day walking around downtown Lima looking for state and nonprofit agencies from which to request assistance. The social worker in one agency offered Daisy several cases of powdered milk for her sons. To receive the milk, Daisy needed to write a signed statement to document her situation. Daisy used the money she had with her to buy a white piece of paper from a nearby bookstore and spent the next two hours carefully handwriting the following letter:

> I Daisy Mamani López with national identification number xxxx with residence in xxxx come before you with the proper respect to present myself and say the following that because my *conviviente* is a drug addict he beat my sons and when I defended them he beat me too. The 3rd of February he attempted to kill my son who is 12 years old and my son who is one year old with a kitchen knife the police detained him for 24 hours and sent me to the xxxx shelter it's a shelter for 15 days it is located in xxxx in this shelter I have been for 2 months and they have already told me that I have to leave the shelter. I acquired a piece of land in xxxx but don't have money to buy construction materials I don't have a bed or bed sheets or clothes for my sons I practically have nothing. The father of my son sold all my belongings. I went with the police to the house where I used to live and I didn't find anything.

And also I would not want my sons to miss school. I found space for them in the XXXX school but what they ask from me is to provide the uniforms supplies and I don't have money to buy them. I am working selling candy so that my sons can survive I have 4 children who are 12-10-5-1 year old.

Please I ask with all my heart help me for my sons
Daisy Mamani López [translation by author]

To receive assistance she could not secure from her family or acquaintances, Daisy had to perform gender (Butler 1990), and, more specifically, gender as popularly believed to be performed by poor mothers in abusive relationships. The stereotype of a poor battered woman is that of an uneducated, needy, dependent, dirty, physically bruised woman with many children. The stereotype of the poor battered woman worthy of being helped has certain added elements. She should be courteous, subservient, respectful, humble, and a good mother. Daisy had to adapt to the stereotype of a poor indigenous woman while also showing how she was different from it and therefore worthy of being helped. This is not an easy task. In reality, she was very needy, yet had she explained that she had already received assistance from individuals, she might not have received help from the agency.

As in the United States, mothers in Peru are expected to be able to protect their children from all sorts of harm, even when the mothers are also being victimized. These expectations lead to the blaming of women in abusive relationships for their children's experiences of violence and to negative assumptions about these women's ability to mother (Schneider 2000). Thus, on the one hand, Daisy had to show she had several children to support, and thus had "irresponsibly" not planned the number of children to adapt to the popularized image attributed to poor indigenous women. On the other hand, she had to make clear that she loved her children and was concerned about their welfare and education to show she was a good mother worthy of public sympathy and assistance.

Writing on indigenous women beggars and their children in Quito, Ecuador, Swanson (2007) points out that rather than acknowledge the oppressive socioeconomic conditions that force indigenous women into begging, in the national imagination "indigenous women and children are regularly described in terms of child exploitation/child delinquency, false manipulation of public sympathies, ignorance, laziness, and filth. They are further described as being 'out of place' in urban areas" (705). Indigenous women beggars are expected to respect the racialized class hierarchy through subservience and docility in urban areas (710–11). Similarly, Daisy had to show the agency that she was asking for aid "with the proper respect." When she sold candy on the streets, she had to show she was a "good" indigenous woman through her subservience. At the time she wrote the letter, she had received two twin beds, bed sheets, some money for construction materials, and miscellaneous kitchen utensils and pots from acquaintances. Given the scarcity of resources with which many agencies must function, a poor woman who has received this sort of aid would not typically be given additional assistance.

Like Daisy, other women I interviewed described how performing the role of the essentialized battered woman can serve as a strategy to bring attention to their situation and receive assistance. During a conversation with women in a northern shantytown, Carla described how "one of my friends, her husband beat her so much but the police didn't pay any attention to her. Would you believe that she hit herself one time?! She disfigured her face [with a hammer]. 'Now they'll pay attention to me,' my friend said. And she went [to the police station] and they really did pay attention to her. And she had to beat herself!" Carla's friend believed that evidence of physical violence through fresh bruises would facilitate her access to the police to file a domestic violence complaint. By filing a complaint, Carla's friend could bring attention to a situation that included physical violence as well as less visible forms of sexual and psychological violence.

Performing, and accommodating to, roles expected by institutions from which they sought aid helped Daisy and Carla's friend achieve their immediate goals. Once women acquire the resources they request, they are in a better position to move on with, begin, or continue the process of rebuilding their lives. Thus, as also discussed in the Introduction, in Chapter 2 in the case of Virginia, and in Chapter 4 in the case of Jimena, accommodating to a stereotype founded on dominant values can be liberating when used as a strategy to resist or escape the reality imposed on those individual women. Daisy presented herself as a poor woman devoid of any sort of help, and this action

had the liberating effect of allowing her to acquire needed resources to facilitate her transition to a new stage in her life. In
the case of Carla's friend, adapting to the police's expectation
that women in violent relationships show fresh physical bruises
had the liberating effect of at least temporarily separating her
partner from her.

At the same time, the women's performances were not without personal costs and consequences. In accommodating to stereotypes, women's behaviors may also unwittingly contribute
to the reproduction of ideas and behaviors that keep women
vulnerable to violence. More specifically, in performing expected
behaviors, the actions of Daisy and of Carla's friend's reinforced
the stereotype of poor women in abusive relationships as subservient, docile, and physically bruised.

Adapting to stereotypes is often required of minority individuals who seek access to institutional resources. In the case of
Colombia, for example, Jackson (1995) examines how Tukanoan
Indians reconstructed their past by going through a process of
"becoming [stereotypically] Indian," to satisfy the requirements
of NGOs and state agencies for aid to indigenous communities.
To do this, Tukanoans recreated and essentialized themselves
and the prehispanic past to present it in a way that could be
easily understood by NGOs. In Ecuador, Crain (1996) suggests
that Quimseña women take part in the "sale of self" by conform-
ing to and projecting the image of "Indian authenticity" the upper classes and foreign tourists expect in order to gain economic
and symbolic capital through their work in hotels in Quito.

In Lima, women's strategizing through accommodation to
essentialized images may allow them to receive needed aid, yet
it does not offer long-term relief from many of the obstacles and
dangers they face after they acquire needed resources to begin
to rebuild their lives. In the weeks after she left the shelter, Daisy
worried about running into or being tracked down by her former
partner. Kristina, a forty-five-year-old woman with two teenage
daughters, panics every time she sees a yellow cab because her
partner used to drive a yellow cab. Every time she left the shelter
and every time she leaves her new home, she fears she will run
into her ex-conviviente. Other women have similar fears. Still
others attempt to start over for months and never find a place
to live, and must return to their partners.

Amada, a thirty-six-year-old mother of three, could not find a place to live after she and her children left the shelter. Every time she found a room she could afford, the rent went up after she mentioned she had three children. Eventually she worked out a plan with her husband under which she and their children stayed in the house and he went to live with his sister. The arrangement did not last long, however, because her husband eventually decided he no longer wanted to live with his sister and returned to live with Amada and the children. Amada had little choice in deciding whether or not her husband could move back in; she had nowhere to go. The last time I heard from Amada, she had returned to the shelter.

*Persistent Obstacles, Daily Struggles*

Following up on women's lives since 2001, it has become clear that for those women who begin to rebuild their lives, the obstacles they face change rather than diminish over time.[10] As was the case for other women, for Daisy being a single parent has involved balancing increasingly difficult tasks. Three months after moving into her new home, a typical day for Daisy began at four in the morning. Until she saved enough money to buy a portable kerosene stove, she made preparations for each day by walking from neighbor to neighbor asking if she could borrow a portable stove. Once she found a neighbor willing to lend her a stove, she waited for that person to finish cooking for the day on it. On most days, she did not have access to a stove until ten in the morning. If she made money the day before, she bought oatmeal for her children and prepared it on the stove. She also prepared lunch, which generally consisted of some sort of beans or soup. At night, the boys usually had a piece of bread. Sometimes none of Daisy's neighbors would lend her a stove, or she had nothing to cook because she had no money, and she and her sons ate very little or not at all. Even when her sons ate, Daisy ate very little. After she finished cooking, Daisy went out to sell candy with her youngest son. Her three other sons stayed home and got ready for school, which did not begin until one in the afternoon for the two oldest boys. Six months after her move, Daisy appeared to have lost a significant amount of weight.

Recounting a typical day for him in 2005, Yonatan explained that he woke up at six in the morning, washed dishes and helped his mother cook for the day, and then he and his second-oldest brother prepared breakfast for their two youngest brothers as their mother prepared to leave to go work. After helping his two youngest brothers get ready, Yonatan walked them to school. It took approximately twenty minutes from their house to the school, and they could not afford to ride a *micro*. He then walked back to his house, did work around the house, and walked another forty minutes to and from his own school. In the evenings, after getting home from school, the family ate, he did his homework, and if there was time, he attended church events.

### Creating a Safe Environment for the Children

Similarly to other women I interviewed, seeing how domestic violence affected her sons led Daisy to her decision to leave her *conviviente* permanently. Cross-culturally, other researchers have also noted that children are frequently a woman's primary reason for leaving an abusive relationship and rebuilding her life (see Hoff 1990). After leaving her *conviviente*, Daisy did what she could to rear her sons in a safe environment and encourage their continued education. Although her sons did not attend school while at the shelter, once they moved into their new home one of the first things Daisy did was to secure spaces for them at a nearby school. The public school was free, but it did not provide the state mandated uniforms, books, notebooks, or other school supplies. Daisy purchased these items little by little, often receiving late notices from the school. At night, after she came home from selling candy, she helped her sons with homework. On several occasions Daisy confided in me that as her sons got older, she found it increasingly challenging to help them with their schoolwork because of the degree of difficulty of their assignments.

Soon after they left the shelter and moved into their new home, a gang member approached Daisy's oldest son to ask him his name and where he lived. When Yonatan told his mother what had happened, Daisy decided to go speak to the gang. Daisy spoke to the gang about her situation as a single mother who had just left an abusive man. She explained that her sons had experienced a lot of violence and that she did not want them to be involved in any other form of violence. Whatever her exact words were, they made a lasting impression on the gang members. Daisy's boys were never bothered by the gang. The drug users that gathered a little further up from their house did, however, approach and assault her sons. On one occasion, one man pushed and hit one of Daisy's sons, breaking the boy's wrist.

Daisy's efforts to keep her sons out of gangs and in school are concrete ways in which she protects her children from violence outside their home after having made certain domestic violence no longer affects them by leaving her *conviviente*. Yet there are other ways in which violence permeates her sons' lives and she has little power to protect them from these other forms of violence. When her children are sick, Daisy is not always able to take them to a doctor. She tells me that even when she takes them to the community health post, the care they receive is inadequate or the problem they have is left undiagnosed. In 2005, when I asked Yonatan if there was anything that especially worried him, he looked down and lowered his voice as he responded that he was scared of dying young. Yonatan felt certain that he will die young because "in my neighborhood, many die young from illnesses." The poor access to medical resources Daisy, her sons, and others in her neighborhood have is an example of structural violence. As discussed in the Introduction, structural violence is indirect violence embedded in unjust societal structures that are hegemonic and taken for granted by those in power, even as they negatively affect those in marginalized spaces (Farmer 2004), through, in this case, lack of access to adequate health care.

Having experienced domestic abuse, knowing his mother is discriminated on the streets and in institutions—including shelters—because she is undervalued as a poor, indigenous woman in Lima, and feeling especially vulnerable to diseases because of his family's lack of access to adequate health care, at age fifteen Yonatan was well aware of the practical consequences of intimate, institutional, and structural violence on his life and on the lives of those around him. After telling me that he was afraid of dying young, he went on to say that another fear he lived with was one which "I have felt since I was a little boy, the fear that goes from the tip of my toes to the top of my head." With an especially somber expression on his face, Yonatan told me that "every time my mom leaves [to work selling candy on the streets] my heart aches because I think something is going to happen to her." Daisy leaves home "very early, and I spend hardly any time with my mom," explained Yonatan. He felt powerless to end the multiple forms of violence that have shaped his life as far back as he remembers, and his sense of fear was heightened by his knowledge that his mother is also exposed to the same potentially lethal forms of violence.

Awareness that violence and poverty limit their ability to *superarse* and protect themselves, however, does not mean that Daisy and her sons do not struggle to *superarse* and challenge different forms of violence and discrimination. In their new home, Daisy and her children would sometimes talk and laugh about an event that took place at the shelter. One of the workers, with whom almost all of the residents had trouble and who was an anomaly in an environment of generally helpful and caring staff, expected Daisy not only to clean up after herself and her sons but also to clean this shelter worker's dishes and room. The shelter worker, a nocturnal assistant, attempted to impose an artificial hierarchy between the shelter workers and residents and in doing so intimidated several residents. As recounted by several residents, at meal time the shelter worker would insist that the children eat everything on their plates, even when the food had fallen on the table or floor, and would not allow the children's mothers to intervene.[11] One afternoon, Daisy stood up to the worker by telling her that she was not her *empleada* and would not clean the shelter worker's dishes and room. She did this in front of her children, signaling to them that this treatment was unacceptable. Daisy continues to teach her sons that just as they must respect others, other people should respect them.

Daisy's emphasis on mutual respect was something Yonatan found continuously challenged at school. Although he was doing well in all his classes, Yonatan dreaded going to school because there was a group of students that bullied and harassed him by telling him that he won't ever amount to anything in life because he's a *cholo*, a *serrano*, and his mother is a *caramelera* (candy seller). I asked him why he thought those boys insulted him, and he responded that it was "because they are ignorant. And they pretend they're rich." Although all the students at his school came from nearby neighborhoods, all in newer shantytowns characterized by extensive poverty and recent migration from indigenous parts of the country, the students differentiated between various levels of wealth and whiteness among themselves. This discrimination of the poor against the poorer was an everyday reality for Yonatan, who recounted how, just the week prior to our meeting, a boy in his class had teased him by showing him his new pair of tennis shoes and stating, "Look at these! Your mother will never be able to buy you anything like this."

Recently, as Daisy and I sat in my parents' house talking about what had happened since the last time we had seen each other, Daisy began to tell me about one of the times someone had insulted her on the street as she sold candy, calling her *india* and yelling at her to go back to where she came from (i.e., leave the city). Daisy turned to me, clearly perturbed by the person's insult, and said, "I don't know who he thought he was, here we are all *cholos*!" This is a lesson Daisy teaches her sons: All Peruvians are of mixed heritage and no one has the right to treat another Peruvian as inferior. When Yonatan told his mother about being bullied at school, she told him to be patient and ignore them. Yonatan's religious beliefs and association with an evangelical church in his neighborhood also influenced his reactions to how others treat him. He believes that as a Christian he cannot react with violence, yet regrets that because he did not stand up for himself by using violence, he was "left without friends at school." Although, according to Yonatan, "Among men, we are always looking to see who is the strongest and whoever seems to be the weakest, he gets picked on, they do whatever they want to him, they disrespect him," he rejected violent forms of masculinity because of what his mother and church had taught him and because of the support for nonviolent forms of confrontation he received from his church friends.

Research on men who are abusive toward women suggests that violence is transmitted intergenerationally, so that boys who witness or experience violence as children are more likely to be abusive toward women as adults (Buvinic, Morrison, and Shifter 1999:10; Finkelhor, Hotaling, and Yllö 1988; Graham-Bermann and Levendosky 1998; Murrell, Christoff, and Henning 2007). More specifically, some studies suggest that boys who are abused feel powerless and stigmatized and have difficulty trusting others, and because of this, are more likely to develop violent coping mechanisms in intimate relationships (Finkelhor, Hotaling, and Yllö 1988). Like the women whose lives I discuss in this book, however, Yonatan's life is multidimensional and, although he experienced and witnessed violence as a child and sometimes feels powerless and stigmatized, his experience of childhood abuse does not necessarily mean he will develop violent coping mechanisms. In contrast to Virginia's sons (and as discussed in Chapter 2) who are encouraged to use violence to defend themselves and their mother by their mother, Yonatan has learned to follow a nonviolent path in dealing with others' abuse both through his mother and through his church. Thus, although childhood experiences of violence clearly impact boys' lives, parental coping mechanisms, resources outside the home, and individual beliefs also influence boys' relationship to violence.

### Different Paths, Continuing Struggles

In July 2001, a proud Daisy informed me that her sons had passed their end-of-year exams. Given that they had missed school during their shelter residency and because of subsequent moves from one neighborhood to another, their success in school was a significant accomplishment. By November of the same year, Daisy was less enthusiastic. Christmas was approaching and her sons were wondering if and how they would celebrate Christmas, and if this new stage in their lives meant they would receive gifts this year. The family was becoming more and more settled in their new home, but they were very poor and could not afford a special Christmas meal or gifts.

Yonatan, who had just turned twelve, continuously complained to his mother that he was tired of being so poor. He told her he wanted to quit school and begin working. Although at that point his goal was to study to become an electrician, he was considering work as a cook's assistant in a restaurant to earn money and have guaranteed meals on the days on which he worked. Daisy talked with him and convinced him to wait a little longer to get further ahead in school. She offered to begin a small business venture with him, one in which he could play a central role after school and on weekends. With his help, she bought bananas wholesale and sold them on the street. It was a more logistically complicated business than selling candy, but less risky and more profitable, and one in which her son felt he had a clear role.

Selling bananas proved to be a profitable yet short-lived endeavor. By November 2002, Daisy and her sons were back in a shelter. Unable to guard her children and home twenty-four hours a day, Daisy and her family suffered two major blows. First, an adult neighbor threatened and severely assaulted one of her younger sons. Second, many of the family's belongings were stolen from the shack (presumably by gang members). After reporting her son's assault to the police, Daisy faced increasing pressure from the assailant to leave the neighborhood. Unable to otherwise guarantee her and her children's safety, Daisy left her home. Through Daisy's resourcefulness and courage and the aid of wealthier acquaintances, Daisy began to build yet another home, in another part of town.

Other women also continued to struggle long after beginning the process of rebuilding their lives. For Kristina, 2003 proved to be a very difficult year. Kristina's husband kidnapped their youngest daughter, taking her outside of Lima. After months of inquiry and distress, Kristina located her daughter through her husband's relatives. Reunited with her daughter, Kristina decided to help other women begin the process of rebuilding their lives. Although Kristina makes very little money at her part-time job at a photocopying business, she has found the time and energy to volunteer at an Emergency Center for Women in her district where women can file domestic violence complaints. Her volunteer work results in additional transportation expenses to and from the center and in accompanying women to police stations and court, yet Kristina feels intense satisfaction through her volunteer work and hopes to be able to continue it. With one daughter on her way to becoming a nurse and another soon to graduate from high school, Kristina's efforts to rebuild her and her daughters' lives have resulted in significant accomplishments in spite of the many obstacles they encountered.

## Complicated Successes

In spite of the various obstacles Daisy and other women face, women and their children are able to and do leave abusive relationships and rebuild their lives. It is not an easy task, and not all women who are ready and want to leave a violent relationship are able to do so. Many women have nowhere to go, lack money and a job, and have no one to help them. For the women who are able to leave and begin to rebuild their lives, the road ahead is difficult.

Of the thirty-eight life stories I collected during my time in Lima, Daisy and her family's is one of the few about which I have detailed accounts over a relatively long period of time. Although the experiences of Daisy and her sons may be unusual in some ways, their struggles are common to many women and children attempting to survive and leave abusive relationships. It is extremely difficult to start over while trying to avoid an ex-partner and to provide food and shelter for oneself and several others. It is even more difficult if the woman is poor and has no social support in Lima, as is the case for migrant women who cut ties with potentially supportive individuals also connected to their partners. For Daisy, as for many other women, neighborhoods can be dangerous and violent, new jobs through which to improve socioeconomic status difficult to acquire and maintain, and oppressive structures ever-present.

Daisy's life story illustrates that although leaving an abusive relationship is in itself challenging and dangerous, starting over also includes difficulties. After she left the shelter, Daisy faced many problems and obstacles: how to feed and clothe her children; how to get the materials necessary to build a house; how to furnish the house with basic items; what to do so her partner would not find her and follow through with his threat to kill her children; how to protect her sons from involvement in gangs and the family's few belongings from theft; where to work and what to do with the boys while she worked; and how to save enough money for notebooks, uniforms, and other necessary school supplies.

Like other women, while at the shelter Daisy needed to find a job to support her children and rebuild their lives, yet she had nowhere safe to leave her children while she looked for a job and worked—a situation illustrated by her attempts to leave the children first in a park and later inside a department store while searching for jobs. Because of her appearance (she is very poor, indigenous, and had limited access to water for baths, or to new or clean clothes), potential employers were hesitant to hire her as she searched for jobs during and immediately following her shelter residency. Yet she could not alter her appearance unless she found a job to finance, among other things, new clothes to wear at her job. Daisy and other women are often unable to escape this vicious cycle because of the overabundance of prejudice and discrimination against—and absence of aid for—poor women. Once women find a job and place to live, however, as in Daisy's case, the precarious conditions under which they rebuild their lives can change for the worse from one moment to the next. The effects of poverty on women's lives and the continued stereotypes and discrimination against nonwhite poor women make Daisy's story an individual success because of the obstacles she overcame. However, the obstacles she and her sons continue to face qualify this story as a complicated success that is better understood through attention to how forms of interpersonal, institutional, and structural violence inform the family's experiences even after permanently leaving an abusive partner.

# Conclusions

## Representing the Woman in the Violence and Approaching Violence in Women's Lives

**⋈ DURING ONE OF MY VISITS TO HER SHELTER**, Rosa Dueñas spoke with me about her views on academics' approaches to domestic violence: "While they [women academics], the majority of them, speak several languages and etcetera etcetera, they have more power to lobby [for their own projects rather than projects to benefit shelters directly] . . . we [activists] participate in everyday life. . . . It is a world which I believe those on top [academics] do not yet see." According to Dueñas, academics who focus on domestic violence tend to retreat to the world of academia and lose sight of the lived world of women at the conclusion of the research period. Although the academics' research deals directly with women's lived reality, the published pieces tend to stop short of addressing the complicated realities of women's experiences and needs.

Throughout this book, I examine how within a context informed by poverty, discrimination, and intersecting forms of violence, women struggle with and negotiate different identities and roles before, during, and after leaving abusive relationships. In making visible structures of racism, sexism, poverty, and class bias that influence women's experiences, I emphasize that even within constrained circumstances, women create spaces in which to exert agency. Yet, in order to caution against the "exaggeration of personal agency" (Farmer et al. 1996:28) and the romanticization of the options available to women I interviewed, I discuss both the persistence and limits of women's everyday forms of resistance.

I have attempted to make visible and to analyze the complicated everyday realities of women whose experiences of intimate violence intersect with institutional and structural violence. I believe I have seen—and I hope to have presented readers with— a view of the world "those on top do not yet see" by examining these experiences. Yet, as I sit on my sofa in the United States, looking over my notes and interviews with women and re-reading comments and suggestions I have received from academics on how to approach women's experiences in this book on women's lives in Lima—a book whose publication is necessary for and marks a milestone in my academic career—Dueñas's words continue to ring in my ears. Dueñas's words remind me, and hopefully readers, that even as we near the end of this book, many of the women in Lima, and many others, continue to experience violence and struggle to survive and resist intersecting forms of violence. And it is Rosa Dueñas and the staff at shelters, police stations, Women's Emergency Centers, and other institutions who will continue to participate in women's everyday realities after this book ends and we move on to the next book, the next class, or the next project.

## Representing Women's Lives

As with other scholars whose work has focused on domestic violence among marginalized peoples, one of my concerns has been that in my writing, representations of women's experiences "do not negatively affect marginalized battered women . . . or reinforce negative stereotypes about them" (Sokoloff and Dupont 2005:47). As stated in the Introduction, one of my goals has been to challenge stereotypes of poor women in abusive relationships. The women's narratives underscore that oppression does not signify the absence of agency, and that agency may result in actions that both contest and reinforce women's oppression. The women's strategies of survival and subversion range from not cooking to secretly using birth control to temporarily leaving. On the one hand, women employ these strategies to challenge their partner's violence. On the other hand, if we examine the beliefs that inform women's forms of resistance, it becomes clear that in some cases, women's actions and attitudes may also reify patriarchal, classist, and racist structures that facilitate violence against women. This book aims to represent women's experiences in a realistic manner so that these experiences are recognizable to Rosa Dueñas and other activists, and understandable to academics as well as to readers unfamiliar with the on-the-ground world of poverty in which some women in abusive relationships live in Lima.

I had originally met Racquel at a shelter in 2001. During a follow-up research trip to Lima in 2008, I met her for coffee. Just as we were getting ready to leave the restaurant, after spending almost two hours catching up on each other's lives, she looked at me and whispered that there was something she had wanted to tell me for a long time but had been embarrassed to bring up. She then asked me to promise not to think badly of her for what she was about to tell me. After several assurances that I would not think badly of her, whatever it was she was about to share with me, Racquel revealed that she had been involved in a secret sexual relationship with her neighbor for the last two years. It was secret because, as Racquel explained, although he was widowed and therefore "available," she was embarrassed to be seen with him in public. Noticing the confused expression on my face, Racquel nervously laughed as she stated, "Es feo! Y viejo, viejo! Me da nauseas cuando estoy con él" (He's ugly! And old, old! I feel nauseous when I'm with him). Nervously laughing in reaction to my failed attempts to conceal my puzzlement, Racquel blurted out, "He helps me out with money! He bought me a television!"

Unable to earn enough to provide fully for her family and meet her children's requests for a television, Racquel accepted her neighbor's request to be with him. In return, he promised to provide Racquel and her family with gifts. However, after two years of secret meetings, Racquel was beginning to seriously consider ending the relationship. On the one hand, she felt guilty about being in a sexual relationship with someone whom she did not want to be associated with publicly. On the other hand, her business (selling candy, cigarettes, and soft drinks on the streets and cleaning homes whenever she was offered the opportunity) had been particularly slow in recent months and she had come to depend on her lover's financial contributions to pay her family's bills.

As I listened to Racquel describe her situation, I wondered

how else she could make the money she needed to make ends meet and maybe even purchase some "extras" from time to time, but I could not think of any viable options. Thinking back to Racquel's "secret," I am reminded of Behar's admonition to avoid judging Esperanza, a Mexican peddler, on the basis that Esperanza—whose husband had beaten her earlier in her life—employed violence against other women. Behar asks, "From whose perspective, whose absolute scale of feminist perfection, are her attitudes and actions being judged?" (1993:296). Behar's question ultimately suggests that it is important to understand Esperanza's actions within their context, by considering the tools available to her, rather than from the context of feminist actions elsewhere and by others in substantially different situations. After all, in Esperanza's actions we not only see the oppression of other women by Esperanza but Esperanza's transgression of oppressive societal norms—in this case, the restriction of the use of physical force to men—and through this transgression an increase in power and control over her life. Similarly, it is important to understand Racquel's actions within their context. Racquel worked very hard, for long hours, and had been working most of her life. She had attempted to improve her economic situation through various business ventures throughout the years.

Racquel is unique among the women I interviewed in pursuing a secret sexual relationship in large part to guarantee economic support for her family, yet she is not alone in emphasizing the exchange of sex for material benefits. As discussed in Chapter 3, some women felt justified in refusing to have sex when their partner failed to contribute money to the household. In her work in a shantytown in Rio de Janeiro, Brazil, Goldstein (2003) similarly refers to one woman's "well-developed pragmatics of exchange" to describe how the woman would occasionally refuse to have sex with her lover if he did not assist her in providing for her family (237–38), thus transforming the lover from a "consumer of her body" to a provider for her family (240). Racquel's description of her relationship with her neighbor suggests that these situations are complicated and may include personal feelings of guilt, yet they are one way women may strategize to survive and get ahead in difficult situations.

Racquel's news underscores that in representing individuals

through our writing, it is useful to let go of false beliefs that the anthropologist or any other researcher can get to know one society, one city, or one person fully in order to begin to depict truthfully the dynamic, multilayered experiences in the societies, cities, and individual lives to which we are fortunate to be given access. These experiences may include views and behaviors that seem familiar or acceptable to others as well as those which seem unfamiliar, confusing, or unacceptable. While I cannot pretend to represent fully women's multidimensional identities, in this book I provide contextualized and theorized analyses of parts of the women's identities to which I had access.[1]

### Contributing Factors to Women's Experiences of Violence

As discussed in the Introduction, my approach to understanding women's experiences of domestic violence and the contexts in which these take place consists largely of examining women's accounts of these experiences and contributing factors, as proposed by feminist ecological approaches to domestic violence. Rather than focus on pinpointing specific causes, I suggest that a more productive approach is to analyze contributing factors to women's experiences of violence in specific settings, noting how in Lima women's lives are informed by the intersection of multiple systems of oppression and power.

I concur with others who have found that "there is no single factor that can adequately account for the high levels of violence in Latin America" (Buvinic, Morrison, and Shifter 1999:10) either inside or outside of the home. Among other factors, sexism, racism, and poverty inform women's experiences of structural, institutional, and intimate violence. In the lives of women in Lima, gender inequality—long privileged in feminist explanations of domestic violence—intersects with race and class as systems of oppression to produce situations in which women may be especially vulnerable to violence. In discussing the role of poverty in domestic violence in Lima, Gonzales de Olarte and Gavilano Llosa (1999) find that poverty is one among several factors that contribute to men's violence against women in the home. In addition to poverty, contributing factors include the man's age, employment status, and the length of the relationship. Factors such as poverty and unemployment may influence but not determine the incidence of domestic violence (Gonzales de Olarte and Gavilano Llosa 1999). Even within one city, then, "it [is] clear that there is no one-size-fits-all explanation for domestic violence" (Sokoloff and Dupont 2005:50), underscoring the need to be cautious in pinpointing single causes and culprits in our search for explanations to the widespread phenomenon of domestic violence.

Taken together, women's creative and courageous forms of everyday resistance and the limits of these forms of resistance in permanently ending violence in women's lives and those of their children underscore that Peru's history of discrimination and oppression based on gender, geography, culture, and race affects even the most intimate aspects of women's lives. Without changes in the underlying structural conditions that have created a social context in which various forms of racism and sexism can thrive, it is unlikely that violence will significantly decrease (Breines, Connell, and Eide 2000; Buvinic, Morrison, and Shifter 1999; Sokoloff and Dupont 2005).

Cross-cultural research on violence against women points to several structural conditions that contribute to women's experiences of violence. In the United States, domestic violence is most prevalent "in those states where structural inequality in economic, educational, political, and legal institutions is greatest" (Yllö and Straus 1990:397). Worldwide, societies in which gender roles are strictly enforced and in which it is socially acceptable to punish women for transgressing those roles exhibit higher rates of domestic violence than more egalitarian societies (Heise 1998).

In his examination of data on physical domestic violence from ninety societies throughout the globe, Levinson (1989) concluded that "most people in the world have at some time been a perpetrator of, the victim of, or a witness to violence between family members" (9). More specifically, in discussing factors that contribute to high levels of violence against women, Levinson found economic inequality between men and women, violent resolution of conflicts within and outside the home, family isolation, a history of domestic violence intergenerationally, low rates of intervention by kin and neighbors in cases of domestic violence, and unequal gender roles to be predictors of domestic violence against women. The experiences of Daisy, Jimena,

Virginia, Racquel, and the other women whose lives I discuss in this book suggest that the conditions identified by Levinson contributed to women's increased vulnerability to intimate violence in Lima.

Just as findings from outside of Peru are relevant to the cases discussed in this book, so findings from analyses of women's lives in Lima may have broader implications for research outside Peru. For example, the interrelations among interpersonal, institutional, and structural violence in women's lives in Lima caution us against treating domestic violence as a separate, isolated phenomenon. The women's experiences suggest that intimate partner violence is linked to broader forms of violence, including institutional and political violence, and may be exacerbated by these other forms of violence. Although there is ample research focusing on specific forms of violence against women, research on the interconnections among different forms of violence in women's lives has received less attention. The scarcity in studies on the interrelations between different forms of violence has been a missed opportunity to expose and challenge the normalization of a continuum of violence against women.

Other findings for Lima that could be taken into consideration in studies in other settings include the linking of women's negative treatment at police stations and by unsupportive family members to women's entrapment in abusive relationships, noting how police and family indifference and hostility hampers women's efforts to leave their abusive partners and rebuild their lives; how conciliation, whether required or encouraged, can further victimize women; how women's everyday resistance is varied and may include secretly using birth control, undergoing sterilization, denying a husband's demands for sex, or teaching children about male privilege and the unacceptability of violence, among other things, all of which may be initially invisible in analyses of women's actions and experiences in situations of domestic violence.

The discussion of domestic violence in Lima also suggests that structural factors such as racism may also play a role in some women's experiences of violence. While there is widespread research on how rural-to-urban migrants are denied access to resources that facilitate upward mobility, positions of power, and even to basic services throughout Latin America, research on the role of race and racism within abusive intimate relationships is sorely lacking for Latin America as well as for other parts of the globe. The Lima case underscores that women migrants from the highlands and other parts of Peru who arrive in Lima to build a more promising future for themselves and their children encounter persistent hierarchical structures and ideologies based largely on geography and race and that structural forms of discrimination permeate even the most intimate aspects of their lives. Racism may also play a role in men's violence against women in other settings.

### Looking Back, Looking Forward

In this book, women's resistance takes place in a setting of poverty and discrimination. Because of this, I do not present an unequivocally optimistic picture of the options available to very poor women who have little or no family support and little or no institutional support in their efforts to rebuild their lives. I have, however, attempted to present a realistic picture of the difficulties women face and of the creativity and strength women exhibit in attempting to survive, leave, or rebuild their lives after an abusive relationship. Rather than romanticize women's actions within difficult and constrained circumstances, I analyze them in their context. While not offering a particularly cheerful picture, it is also not completely bleak.

The absence of resources for—and widespread prejudices against—poor women in abusive relationships have restricted and silenced their actions, yet the analysis of their resistance offers a way to understand their experiences, strength, needs, and demands. Once we have analyzed their experiences and the contexts in which these take place, a possible next step is to explore ways to challenge personally the structural conditions that maintain or facilitate violence, through academic research, through activism, or through a better understanding of on-the-ground experiences.

# Notes

All translations of Spanish-language sources are by the author, unless otherwise noted.

*Acknowledgments*

1  The Centro de la Mujer Peruana Flora Tristán is the Flora Tristan Center of the Peruvian Woman; the Liga Internacional de Mujeres pro Paz y Libertad is the Women's International League for Peace and Freedom (WILPF).

*Introduction*

1  According to Adams (1995), other forms of invisible violence with which men intimidate and control women include destruction of property and harming family pets. Men may also force a woman to have sex with an animal as a way to humiliate and control her. In the United States, some women do not leave because of fear of what would happen to their pets (60). In Lima, among women I interviewed, none spoke of violence against family pets or of being forced to have sex with an animal. However, it is possible that concern for pets may pose an additional obstacle to women escaping violent relationships since shelters do not allow women and children to bring pets. Additionally, I did not ask women questions specifically about their partner's violence against family pets.

2  I use the Spanish term *conviviente* in the sense in which it is popularly used in Peru. Although the term *conviviente* could be loosely translated as "live-in partner," "lover," "boyfriend/girlfriend," "concubine," or "common-law spouse," none of the preceding terms capture the exact meaning or connotations of *conviviente*. A *conviviente* can be either a man or a woman. A woman could use the term *conviviente* to refer to someone with whom she has lived anywhere from a few weeks to a few months to several years. *Convivientes* may or may not have children, but it is most often the case that children follow soon after the couple begins to live together. In addition, although it is becoming more common for middle-class and upper-class couples to live together without marrying, the term *conviviente* is used almost exclusively by and to refer to relationships among working-class and poor people. *Convivientes, convivencia*, and the implementation of Peru's family violence law in cases of *convivencia* are further discussed in Chapter 4.

3  The three Peruvian newspapers I regularly consulted were *El Comercio, La República*, and *Liberación. El Comercio* is the most influential and old-

225

est daily newspaper in Peru. It has print and online versions and it appeals mostly to middle- and upper-class Peruvians in Lima. *La República*, also a leading newspaper with print and online versions, is somewhat more liberal than *El Comercio* and appeals to a slightly smaller audience. *Liberación* had a smaller audience than *La República* but was also a popular newspaper in Lima in 2001–2002. I also perused "chicha" (tabloid-style sensationalist) newspapers to find stories on domestic violence.

4  When the women agreed to speak with me, it was also in the hope that more people would find out about their experiences and that this would lead to greater awareness and action by others to prevent future violence against women. In translating our conversations into text, this book aims to facilitate greater awareness of women's experiences.

5  The journal *Latin American Perspectives* dedicated an entire issue to the controversy in 1999, titled "If Truth Be Told: A Forum on David Stoll's *Rigoberta Menchú and the Story of All Poor Guatemalans*" (volume 26, no. 6).

6  In Menchú's transcribed, translated, and edited words, "I'd like to stress that it's not only my life, it's also the testimony of my people. It's hard for me to remember everything that's happened to me in my life since there have been many very bad times but, yes, moments of joy as well. The important thing is that what has happened to me has happened to many other people too: My story is the story of all poor Guatemalans. My personal experience is the reality of a whole people" (Burgos 1983:1).

7  Additionally, while the short excerpts of women's stories in this book cannot be compared to the book-length narrative presented in *I, Rigoberta*, unlike Burgos, to more clearly represent women's identities I include excerpts that illustrate women's ways of speaking even when these ways of speaking may appear to be excessively repetitive to some. In Chapter 2, for example, Virginia's description of how her sister forced her to live with her first *conviviente* contains several repetitive phrases.

8  One of the first books to approach domestic violence from an ethnographic perspective was Counts, Brown, and Campbell's edited volume, *To Have and to Hit: Cultural Perspectives on Wife Beating* (1999). Full-length ethnographies on domestic violence are a very recent phenomenon and include Hautzinger 2007; Lazarus-Black 2007; McClusky 2001; Merry 2006; Plesset 2006; and Van Vleet 2008.

9  My focus on domestic violence among heterosexual couples does not imply that in Lima domestic violence among same-sex couples does not occur. While I did not encounter or seek out experiences of same-sex domestic violence during my research, I am hopeful that other researchers will tackle this important issue in the context of Lima. In the shelters with which I worked, however, I only met heterosexual women during my research period.

10  FV approaches have used large-scale surveys to investigate domestic violence and have resulted in the faulty assumption that women assault men just as much as men assault women. Straus, one of the most prominent and earliest advocates of the FV approach to domestic violence, argues

that "to end 'wife beating,' it is essential for women also to end the seemingly 'harmless' pattern of slapping, kicking, or throwing things at male partners who persist in some outrageous behavior and 'won't listen to reason'" (1993:67). At the same time, Straus fails to offer alternatives through which women could defend themselves from their partners' violence. If, as Straus suggests, women stop protesting violence by defending themselves through what they perceive as their only forms of immediate defense, available alternatives would include simply accepting the violence or hoping the next assault will not be as or more severe than the one just suffered.

11 Within the literature on domestic violence, the FV and VAW schools of thought are complemented by more specific theories that seek to explain the causes of domestic violence. These more specific theories are informed by psychological, sociological, and feminist perspectives. Some of the most prominent theories emphasize pathology, expressive tension, instrumental power, and the social system. According to the pathology approach, violence against one's spouse is abnormal and should be treated as the symptom of an underlying pathology. This theory calls for the treatment and cure of the underlying pathology or mental illness to end the violence. The expressive tension theory suggests that men who beat their spouses are the subject of powerful forces from within and that they express tension and stress through violence. According to this approach, men must be taught to express their stress and tension in alternative ways to stop them from beating their partners. The instrumental power approach views violence as a means to an end. Unlike the previous two theories, this theory treats abusive men as rational beings who are goal-oriented and capable of controlling their actions. It holds that violence allows men to get what they want effectively, since, in general, men can be violent toward their wives or girlfriends without being punished. Feminists studying domestic violence have used this approach to argue that intimate partner violence is a controlling behavior used to create and maintain male dominance. Social system theory views male abusers as relatively passive agents trapped in the logic of their cultural heritage while also granting them a certain amount of agency. It points out that society socializes men to be violent and women to be passive. According to the social system theory, the way to change men's behavior is by modifying the norms within society.

12 One recent celebrity case that received media attention was the Aguirre-Meier case. In 2007, actress Marisol Aguirre filed for divorce from her husband, actor and singer Christian Meier, after twelve years of marriage. Aguirre filed a domestic violence complaint, citing physical and psychological abuse, not long before she filed for divorce.

13 The emphasis placed on physical violence is evident in one of the few anthropological compilations on domestic violence, Counts, Brown, and Campbell 1999. Their exclusive focus on physical violence poses numerous limitations to the study of violence against women, given how intertwined physical violence is with other forms of violence. Similarly, a

more recent book on domestic violence in Belize (McClusky 2001) also
privileges physical violence over other forms of violence.

14 The exception is my 2005 interview with fifteen-year-old Yonatan, the
son of one of the women I originally interviewed. I interviewed him to
understand better the impact of violence on different members of his
family—a family I have become increasingly personally close to and involved with over the last seven years.

Men's perspectives on their violence against women is a relatively new
topic of feminist research (Anderson and Umberson 2001:359). Since my
original fieldwork in Lima, my research agenda has expanded to include
men's perspectives on violence and nonviolence. Since 2007, I have been
engaged in a project on violent and nonviolent discourses of Latino masculinities in the United States.

15 In Europe, the United States, and Australia, men are responsible for between 80 percent and 90 percent of all violent crimes (Breines, Connell,
and Eide 2000:15). In the United States, approximately 26 percent of
women report being abused by their intimate male partners (Tjaden and
Thoennes 2000).

16 Movimiento Manuela Ramos is the Manuela Ramos Movement, at times
referred to simply as "Manuela Ramos."

17 "Intersectionality" was originally coined to address the experiences of
women of color that mainstream feminist discourses fell short of addressing in the United States. Although it continues to be most often associated with black feminist theory, the concept has been applied to the
analysis of women's lives in a variety of settings.

18 Among the disagreements over the meanings attributed to "resistance"
is whether or not an action should be conscious, successful, collective,
individual, or overt to be considered resistance.

*Chapter 1*

1 Leinaweaver provides the following insightful definition: "*Superarse* is a
technical device urging poor Peruvians to get ahead, survive, scrape by,
but there is something more at stake. . . . it is not wholly a self-centered
act" because it is done on behalf of the family, and commonly requires
a painful separation from the family to migrate to a city or country with
greater opportunities for work and upward mobility (2008a:129). Women
in Lima sought to *superarse* not only for themselves but, more importantly, for their children.

2 In other parts of Latin America, similar settlements are known as *favelas*
(Brazil), *colonias* (Mexico), *ranchos* (Venezuela), and *campamentos* (Chile).

3 Homosexual Movement of Lima.

4 I am grateful to an anonymous manuscript reviewer for Vanderbilt University Press for reminding me that beyond my original discussion of
the term *cholo* as a positive descriptor during the Toledo presidency, the
fact that *cholo* was also applied to Toledo negatively also deserved more
attention.

5 In 1780, José Gabriel Condorcanqui took the name Túpac Amaru II, after the Inca Túpac Amaru I, whom he claimed as an ancestor, and led an army of tens of thousands of largely indigenous peoples against peninsular Spaniards to restore a mythic version of Inca rule. Although the rebellion was ultimately defeated and Túpac Amaru captured and publicly executed, it left Spaniards and Creoles with a sense of distrust and fear of future expressions of indigenous resistance (Méndez 1996:222).

6 Sendero typically recruited young members through local universities and high schools as well as from shantytowns and nearby rural communities.

7 I have limited my discussion of what shelters experienced during the period when Sendero dominated a number of shantytowns in the capital to general descriptions, and omitted names to protect informants who gave me more detailed information in confidence.

8 According to Virginia Vargas, Sendero Luminoso denounced the feminist NGO she headed for several years, Centro de la Mujer Peruana Flora Tristán, for being made up of "bourgeois feminists that attempt to prevent women from the popular classes from having children to support the revolution" (1996:127).

9 Moyano was killed during a fundraising event for Vaso de Leche. The day before she was assassinated, she gave a speech in which she stated, "We do not support those who assassinate popular leaders and massacre leaders of the soup kitchens and Vaso de Leche" (cited in Poole and Rénique 1992:92). The Vaso de Leche program distributes milk to committees made up of women who in turn distribute a glass of milk daily to each child in their neighborhoods, thus ensuring that the children consume at least a minimal amount of milk each day.

10 Acknowledging that women's violence against their partners is also a reality in some relationships does not change the fact that the majority of partner violence is men's violence against women.

11 Temporary Income Support Program.

12 "In Peru Protest, Women Urge Action on Food Prices," *New York Times*, May 1, 2008.

13 Although Fujimori's self-coup was criticized by the international community, Peruvians praised Fujimori for taking such a strong position in the midst of a worsening economic crisis and escalating Sendero Luminoso violence (Ewig 2006:639).

14 Latin American and Caribbean Committee for the Defense of Women's Rights. Feminist NGOs in Peru were initially slow to criticize the family planning program in part due to their "fear of losing the little ground that women had gained in birth control issues" (Ewig 2006:651).

15 "Peruvians Tire of Toledo, but Worry About Ousting Him," *New York Times*, August 5, 2004.

16 *Comedores populares* were initially created in the late 1970s; the *Vaso de Leche* program began in 1984. Although both of these assisted families in meeting their basic needs, neither initiative was initially supported by male *dirigentes* (Córdova Cayo 1996:71). Today, both programs continue to be run and staffed by women.

17   In particular, Ana Güezmes of Flora Tristán drew my attention to women's experiences of domestic violence as a possible research topic during a pre-fieldwork research trip.

18   On one occasion, through family connections to a wealthy private school, I assisted in setting up visits by students from the school to the shelter at which I volunteered. Students provided temporary tutoring for children in the shelter and worked to organize additional donations to the shelter.

*Chapter 2*

1   The first two times we met, there were several instances in which she did not understand what I was asking her and I did not understand what she was telling me due to our different uses of Spanish. Although I had taken Quechua lessons, my level of understanding, particularly considering the vocabulary needed to hold a conversation about violence, was not sufficient to attempt to interview Virginia in Quechua. More importantly, Virginia did not want to speak in Quechua.

2   For detailed information on laws protecting domestic workers in Peru, I refer readers to Law 27986. The full text of the law is available at *www.cajpe.org.pe*. Although the law grants domestic workers the right to fifteen days of vacation annually, among other things, it does not grant them the right to minimum wage.

3   Twenty-eight percent of domestic workers in Peru have been sexually assaulted in their workplace (MIMDES 2007:46).

4   Fuller's finding among working-class men in Lima that "in spite of being conscious that they [the men] are discriminated against for racial motives, they declare that they prefer a woman with lighter skin" (2001:371) because it is a way to improve their social status also provides a possible explanation for Virginia's husband's abandonment of Virginia for a lighter-skinned urban woman. By beginning a relationship with a lighter-skinned woman, her husband may have sought to improve his status.

5   In expressing an interest in permanently returning to her community of origin and in visiting her community of origin almost annually, Virginia was unlike many of the women I interviewed. Many other women— including Racquel, whose experiences I discuss later in this chapter—did not want to return permanently to their communities of origin.

6   Writing on the performance of femininity and class in the United States, Anyon describes a case parallel to that of Virginia's public accommodation and private resistance, that of "the working-class woman who submits in various (demeaning) ways to the demands of her boss, in order to survive in an oppressive job situation, and who thus accommodates to the role of submissive female. However, if she resists this public degradation psychologically (that is, privately) by holding on to her own value, and 'dreams' of a better life, where such submission is not necessary, she is manifesting public/private discrepancy which is part of her simultaneous accommodation and resistance to her own exploitation" (1983:24).

7 Feminist scholars of the Andes (Weismantel 1998) and elsewhere (Bordo 1993; Gremillion 2003; Narayan 1997) observe that food is synchronous with prestige and social power. As suggested by Bordo, in associating women's worth with food production and consumption, women's bodies become sites of social anxiety and "if woman *is* the body, then women are that negativity, whatever it may be" (1993:5). In Inés's case, that negativity is the lower value attributed to the *sierra*.

8 As discussed in the Introduction, according to a recent study on masculinity in three Peruvian cities, the majority of lower-class men interviewed for the study preferred women with lighter skin. At the same time, the gender hierarchies that place men as superior to women can problematize a man's preference for lighter women, because a lighter woman from a higher class may also threaten his status as the dominant and superior individual in the relationship (Fuller 2001:371).

9 In reinforcing gendered uses of violence in her sons' upbringing, Virginia's case does not exemplify the teaching of more egalitarian gender roles I referred to earlier in the chapter.

10 Virginia's sons are not the only ones prepared to react to their father's violence against their mother by attempting to protect her through physical violence. For example, Inés recounted how her youngest son reacted to his father's violence against her: "They cried by themselves, out of fear. My youngest son at five, six years old, placed a knife beneath his pillow. When I asked him why he did that, he responded, 'In case my father hits you, I'll kill him.'"

## Chapter 3

1 The Truth and Reconciliation Committee found widespread sexual violence against women between 1980 and 2000. The army and police were responsible for the vast majority of the rapes (83 percent), and Sendero Luminoso was responsible for approximately 11 percent of the rapes.

2 Women who have been raped by their partners, as many of the women in Lima had been, have two options if they wish to report the rape: they can either file a psychological abuse complaint under the Family Violence Law or file a standard criminal rape complaint. Unlike women who file physical or psychological violence complaints, women who file rape complaints must pay for their forensic examination (Human Rights Watch 2000). For those women who wish to report rape, the cost of the forensic exam constitutes an important barrier to seeking justice and serves to silence women's experiences of sexual violence.

3 Women did use the term "rape" (*violar*) to refer to similar episodes of sexual violence in other women's lives, particularly those they heard about in the news.

4 According to Gagnon and Parker, "Changes in patterns of negotiation [over sex] often depend on distal effects—the level of education of women in the society, the rights of women to leave the home without a man's permission or the availability of contraception. At the proximate level,

men's responsibility for children, whether they are employed, whether they drink in groups, and so on, have profound effects on how the sexual encounter is managed" (1995:14).

5   Maria's first two children died on the same day as toddlers as a result of being poisoned. Maria never discovered how they were poisoned but suspects they accidentally ingested the poison (possibly powdered rat poison commonly found on the streets) while playing on the street and being watched by a friend while Maria worked.

6   Although her children attended public schools, which are free, supplies and uniforms had to be purchased for each of her six children, because these are not provided by the schools. Purchasing these items proved to be a hardship for many of the women I interviewed.

7   Most studies of abuse among pregnant women have been hospital or clinic-based, and the Perales et al. study (2009) is no exception. In general, hospital-based studies find a higher prevalence of violence than population-based studies. This limitation notwithstanding, given that no other studies on pregnancy and domestic violence exist for Lima, the Perales et al. study provides a valuable window into abuse among pregnant women in Lima.

8   Based on her analysis of *autodiagnósticos* in Huancavelica, Boesten suggests that "male anxieties about women's use of modern contraceptives are reinforced by their exclusion from the family planning process" (2007:16) and proposes the incorporation of men into family planning education and programs as part of the solution.

9   Sterilization usually takes two forms, hysterectomy or tubal ligation. Hysterectomy is the surgical removal of the uterus. Tubal ligation, the procedure to which most women I interviewed referred, involves the blocking of the fallopian tubes. The tubes are hardened either chemically or by injection of silicone rubber. In both cases, sterilization is considered an irreversible form of birth control.

10  Similar connections between women's economic dependency on men and sex have been made by women elsewhere. For example, in her study on the sex lives of Mexican women in the United States, Gonzalez-Lopez was told by one of the women she interviewed that in the United States, "I work and support myself so I don't have to have sex with my husband if I don't feel like it," unlike when the woman lived in Mexico and gave in to her husband's demands for sex because she depended on him financially (2005:18).

*Chapter 4*

1   More specifically, while work on the role of in-laws in women's experiences of domestic violence has received significant attention in South Asian contexts (for example, see Abraham 2000; Raj et al. 2006), the role of in-laws has not been an area of significant interest among Andeanists (but see Harvey 1995; Van Vleet 2008).

2   In anthropology, the family was initially described as a primarily nurtur-

ing and universal institution (for a critical discussion of this, see Collier, Rosaldo, and Yanagisako 1997). Since Malinowski's time, anthropologists have further developed ideas regarding the composition of the family, noting the existence of female-headed households among other types of families and households, yet they did not challenge the idea of the primary function of the family to be nurturance for children. As anthropologists began to delve into family dynamics and conflicts in diverse societies, they found varying and often competing voices regarding gender roles and family dynamics within the same culture, challenging traditional functionalist views of the family.

3   The existence of contrasting and sometimes contradictory family ideals and realities is also evident when we consider violence against women, violence against children, and much less often violence against husbands, as well as divorce, state intervention in women's use of birth control, abandonment of children, homelessness, new reproductive technologies, single-parent homes, and same-sex unions.

4   "Women's Harmony House" is a pseudonym for one of the shelters in Lima.

5   Of all the women who filed domestic violence complaints in Emergency Centers for Women in Lima in 1999, 44 percent were *convivientes* and 33 percent were married (PROMUDEH 2000).

6   *Convivencia* also facilitates separation without high legal costs, given that divorce procedures can be costly and lengthy.

7   The distinction between motherhood and mothering has been pivotal to feminist understandings of motherhood not only as oppressive, as originally suggested by early second-wave feminists, but also as positive and potentially empowering and liberating.

8   Studies on child abuse emphasize that most severe forms of child abuse are perpetrated by men (Edleson 1999; Pecora et al. 1992).

9   Three of the five districts included in Yon's study of adolescents were those in which many of the women I interviewed grew up.

10  Through his long-term work with abusive men in Lima, Ramos (2006) found that men had been taught to expect complete obedience from their wives. Men's use of violence constituted an effective way both to discipline women when men believed women's behaviors threatened male control and to prevent women from engaging in behaviors that could potentially threaten men's power and control over them. When men failed to accomplish their goals through emotional violence, they engaged in physical violence. Thus, one interpretation of men's insistence that children witness men's violence against their mother and of cases in which men forced women to witness men's abuse of children, as reported by women, could be that men sought to heighten their power by controlling women by threatening a role women had been taught to highly value: motherhood.

11  Throughout the colonial and early republican period, men's testimonies in cases involving marital conflict upheld the idea that men's violence against women was a private matter that did not concern the state, and

that women should serve, obey, and submit to their husbands in all matters (Chambers 1999; Hunefeldt 1999).

12   On one occasion, Jimena's father intervened in one of their arguments. Juan's reaction was to attempt to hit Jimena's father and to tell him that "she is my wife and I can do what I want [with her]."

13   The women described a clear connection between their partners' abuse as children and abusive behavior later in life. At the same time, many of the women who made these connections were hesitant to make the same connections between the abuse their sons witnessed—and sometimes experienced firsthand—and the possibility that their sons could become abusive toward women as adults. According to a recent study in Lima, children are witnesses to physical violence against their mothers in 59 percent of cases examined (Güezmes, Palomino, and Ramos 2002:83).

*Chapter 5*

1   Today there are thirty-four Women's Emergency Centers spread throughout Peru, with the largest number in Lima. The number of women who visit these centers is likely to increase as more women spread the news of a more woman-friendly center.

2   Overall, the other women I interviewed described being treated fairly and in a helpful manner at the PROMUDEH.

3   National Family Welfare Institution. INABIF was founded in 1981 and is the main state institution in charge of abandoned children, children in the process of being adopted, teenage mothers, and street children, as well as other at-risk children.

4   In 2005, according to a study carried out in three Lima districts (Villa Maria del Triunfo, Villa El Salvador, and San Juan de Miraflores) by Movimiento Manuela Ramos, most medical examinations took place the day after the complaint was placed. However, in 12 percent of the cases, the medical examination was not performed until three to thirty days after the complaint was placed (Movimiento Manuela Ramos 2007:29).

5   My experience trying to gain access to the main women's police station does not parallel the experiences of a woman seeking to file a complaint. However, I discuss it because it provides a glimpse of the long and complicated bureaucratic procedures that one may encounter in seeking information and assistance from the police.

6   I have not been able to locate the newspaper story Ramirez referred to in our conversations.

7   After leaving the main women's police station, I made my way to the main police headquarters. Once inside the compound, I spent two hours trying to find out whom I needed to speak with about getting clearance for interviews in the main women's police station. No one appeared to know of the specific protocol for clearance to interview a police officer for research purposes. According to one officer, it would take two to three days to get clearance. According to another officer, it would take at least fifteen to twenty days to speak with someone about getting clearance. I filled

out and turned in all the paperwork I was ultimately handed at the head-quarters. Each time I visited to check on the progress of my paperwork, depending on the person with whom I spoke, I was told that my papers had gotten temporarily lost or that the clearance simply wasn't ready yet. I continued to visit the women's police station over the next month and a half, and I spoke with the psychologist and Officer Ramirez during each of my visits.

8    In India and Brazil, two pioneering countries in the realm of women's police stations, these stations "tend to be understaffed and unpopular among women police officers" because they do not facilitate professional upward mobility (Merry 2007:142). My informal conversations with police officers suggest that women officers in Lima face a similar situation.

9    Another possible interpretation, suggested by an anonymous reviewer of an earlier version of this book manuscript, is that sexual violence claims are treated as psychological violence because officers do not consider rape in marriage to exist.

10   The DEMUNA is the Family Municipal Defense Center.

11   Similar to what I found in Lima, workshops organized by Movimiento Manuela Ramos in rural areas found that "the police prefer to not get involved in cases of violence against women, as they are [considered by the police as] 'private problems' or 'customs of long standing'" (Movimiento Manuela Ramos 2003: 41).

12   As a volunteer at the shelter, I became involved in its daily functioning and was consulted on major decisions for the shelter in the same way other shelter workers were consulted. During the coordinator's maternity leave, the staff asked if I could cover two of the days for which there was no one else available and I agreed. During the two months I covered those two extra days, I was often the only staff member at the shelter for hours. This period proved beneficial to my research, as I developed a more profound understanding of what a typical day at the shelter entailed.

13   Nationally, there are shelters in Lima, Trujillo, Huancayo, and Moquegua.

14   The Red Nacional de Casas de Refugio para Mujeres y Niñez Victimas de Violencia Familiar y Sexual is the National Network of Shelters for Women and Child Victims of Family and Sexual Violence.

15   During the presidential campaign, Karp gave several speeches in Quechua, and this also appealed to the indigenous Quechua-speaking populations in rural Peru who had traditionally been ignored during presidential campaigns. In speeches, Karp emphasized that Toledo's election would help the country end the oppression that had historically characterized the lives of indigenous Peruvians.

16   Until 2008, Shelter 1 functioned largely through funding from an international nonprofit women and human rights organization. After losing its funding that year, the shelter was forced to eliminate the positions of assistant coordinator and nocturnal assistant and change its policy to admit only women who had jobs and could therefore buy their own food while at the shelter. My discussion of Shelter 1 is therefore limited to pre-2008 events.

17  In English, DEMUS stands for "Research for the Defense of Women's Rights."

18  This information comes from a meeting with lawyer Gina Yañez at Manuela Ramos in March 2001. Yañez also noted that most women who request legal counsel on issues of domestic violence are in their forties and fifties because, to allow their children to grow up in a two-parent household, they waited until their children were adults to escape their violent partners.

19  After working with shelters for a few months, it became clear to me that some tensions existed between some feminist organizations and shelter workers. Sometimes there were misunderstandings within shelters about how the more powerful feminist organizations used funds for research on domestic violence issues; other times shelters felt they were "used" for research purposes by members of these organizations but did not directly benefit from the funding these organizations received as a result of the research. While my research initially carried similar suspicions among shelter workers, I chose to distance myself a bit from prominent feminist organizations to present myself as an independent researcher to shelters and avoid the extra baggage the history of relationships between specific feminist organizations and shelters carried. In spite of existing tensions between feminist and women's organizations and shelters, however, the overall relationship among these groups is positive as both groups recognize common goals and work together to achieve these goals, particularly in the realms of human and women's rights. For a broader discussion of tensions between grassroots organizations and feminist NGOs in Lima, I recommend Moser 2004.

*Chapter 6*

1  In the late 1990s, over half of the Peruvian population lived below the poverty line.

2  Pine found that rather than resemble what she had become accustomed to define as friendships in the United States, the relationships she developed in Honduras "hovered between patron-client and U.S.-style friendship" (2008:8).

3  One significant difference, however, is that while I write about Daisy's experiences, she does not write about, and is not interested in making public, intimate aspects of my life. Throughout our relationship, I have supplied Daisy with copies of publications that discuss her experiences.

4  As mentioned in other chapters, my use of the phrases "forced to have sex" and "forced sex" instead of the word "rape" is a reflection of the women's own descriptions and word choices. I do, however, view the episodes of forced sex the women described to be rape.

5  In addition to having family in Cuzco, the lower living costs there influenced Daisy's decision. She hoped to make enough money in Lima, where there are generally more employment opportunities than in Cuzco, to meet her sons' lower living expenses in Cuzco.

6    Although property transactions between residents in newer shantytowns may be recognized within the neighborhood, these transactions, if they do not include an official land title, will not be legally recognized by the state.

7    According to Daisy, her *conviviente* sniffed glue and used cocaine.

8    Daisy wanted to place her children in one of the children's homes set up by the INABIF.

9    As Scheper-Hughes notes in her account of a northeastern Brazil shantytown, "Staying alive in the shantytown demands a certain 'selfishness' that pits individuals against each other and rewards those who take advantage of those even weaker" (1992:473). Daisy knew that as newcomers, her family was potentially vulnerable to gang violence and burglaries.

10   For example, although being a single parent may signify a marked improvement over the violence lived as a traditional nuclear family, the negative connotations associated with being a single mother bring new obstacles. In Peru, it is often the case that "the individual is worth little outside of kinship ties and is only fully realized when he is part of a relationship which produces a nuclear family" (Yanaylle 1996:74). For a woman, having a male partner is understood as being protected and having (indirect) power through male protection from outside violence. For some women, the fear of being a single parent pushes them to remain in an abusive relationship longer. Karen, a twenty-four-year-old woman with a three-year-old son, explained her fears to me. Going from calm to nervous to crying within a few minutes, she told me she was very afraid of being a single mother. Like Amada, she was afraid that her son would some day reproach her for "throwing out" his father and for his growing up without a father. She also dreaded being talked about by neighbors and others. Although not mentioned by Karen, lack of money to support children is another major worry many women share. Yet, in spite of women's real fears about life as a single parent, women do become single parents due to their own decisions or to other events they are unable to control, such as abandonment by or death of a partner.

11   Other women also commented on the worker's behavior, and this led to the dismissal of the worker soon after Daisy and her sons left the shelter.

*Conclusion*

1    The experiences of Racquel and other women I interviewed in Lima cannot be generalized to apply to all of Latin America. At the same time, when considered together, Peru's colonial past and its contemporary dominant ideologies regarding gender, race, and space, and women's experiences today suggest that when a pattern and rate of urbanization similar to that of Lima is combined with ideologies of race, gender, space, and class developed over hundreds of years of Spanish colonial rule, the experiences of women who are poor, nonwhite, and experience intimate partner violence may be similar to the experiences of the women I interviewed.

# References

Abercrombie, Thomas. 1998. *Pathways of Memory and Power: Ethnography and History among an Andean People*. Madison: University of Wisconsin Press.

Abraham, Margaret. 2000. *Speaking the Unspeakable: Marital Violence Among South Asian Immigrants in the United States*. Piscataway: Rutgers University Press.

Abu-Lughod, Lila. 1990. "The Romance of Resistance: Tracing Transformation of Power Through Bedouin Women." *American Ethnologist* 17 (1): 41–55.

———. 1986. *Veiled Sentiments: Honor and Poetry in a Bedouin Society*. Berkeley: University of California Press.

Adams, Carol. 2000 [1990]. *The Sexual Politics of Meat: A Feminist-Vegetarian Critical Theory*. New York: Continuum.

———. 1995. "Woman-Battering and Harm to Animals." In *Animals and Women: Feminist Theoretical Explorations*, ed. Carol J. Adams and Josephine Donovan, 55–84. Durham: Duke University Press.

Adelman, Madelaine. 1997. "Gender, Law, and Nation: The Politics of Domestic Violence in Israel." PhD dissertation, Duke University.

Agar, Michael. 1996. *The Professional Stranger*. St. Louis: Academic Press.

Aggarwal, Ravina. 2000. "Traversing Lines of Control: Feminist Anthropology Today." *Annals of the American Academy of Political and Social Science* 571:14–30.

Alat, Zeynep. 2006. "News Coverage of Violence Against Women: The Turkish Case." *Feminist Media Studies* 6 (3): 295–314.

Alcalde, M. Cristina. 2009. "Ripped from the Headlines: Newspaper Depictions of Battered Women in Peru." In *Local Violence, Global Media: Feminist Analyses of Gendered Representations*, ed. Lisa Cuklanz and Sujata Moorti, 46–64. New York: Peter Lang Publishing.

———. 2007. "Going Home: A Feminist Anthropologist's Reflections on Dilemmas of Power and Positionality in the Field." *Meridians: Feminism, Race, Transnationalism* 7 (2): 143–62.

———. 1999. "Dominant Discourses, Everyday Lives: Gender, Ethnicity, and Reproductive Health Abuses in late Twentieth Century Peru." MA thesis, Indiana University.

Alcántara de Samaniego, Elsa. 1999. *Salud reproductiva, pobreza y condiciones de vida en el Perú*. Lima: INEI.

Alcoff, Linda. 2004. "Identities: Modern and Postmodern." In *Identities*, ed. Linda Alcoff and Eduardo Mendieta, 1–8. Williston: Blackwell Publishers.

Allen, Catherine. 1998. *The Hold Life Has: Coca and Cultural Identity in an Andean Community*. Washington: Smithsonian Institution Press.

Alvarado, Elvia. 1987. *"Don't Be Afraid, Gringo": A Honduran Woman Speaks from the Heart*. New York: Harper Perennial.

Anderson, Kristin, and Debra Umberson. 2001. "Gendering Violence: Masculinity and Power in Men's Accounts of Domestic Violence." *Gender and Society* 15 (3): 358–80.

Anderson, Michael, Paulette Gillig, Marilyn Sitaker, Kathy McCloskey, Kathleen Malloy, and Nancy Grigsby. 2003. "'Why Doesn't She Just Leave?': A Descriptive Study of Victim Reported Impediments to Her Safety." *Journal of Family Violence* 18 (3): 151–55.

Andreas, Carol. 1985. *When Women Rebel: The Rise of Popular Feminism in Peru.* New York: Lawrence Hill Books.

Anglin, Mary. 1998. "Feminist Perspectives on Structural Violence." *Identities: Global Studies in Culture and Power* (5) 2: 145–52.

Anyon, Jean. 1983. "Intersections of Gender and Class: Accommodation and Resistance by Working-Class Females to Contradictory Sex-Role Ideologies." In *Gender, Class, and Education*, ed. Stephen Walker and Len Barton, 19–37. New York: Falmer Press.

Babb, Florence. 1989. *Between Field and Cooking Pot.* Austin: University of Texas Press.

Bacigalupo, Ana Mariella. 2007. *Shamans of the Foye Tree: Gender, Power, and Healing Among Chilean Mapuche.* Austin: University of Texas Press.

Balbuena, Laura. 2007. "Violencia y agencia femenina: Puede el terror empoderar a la mujer?" In Barrig 2007, 325–40.

Barrig, Maruja, ed. 2007. *Fronteras interiores: Identidad, diferencia y protagonismo de las mujeres.* Lima: Instituto de Estudios Peruanos.

———. 1982. *Convivir: La pareja en la pobreza.* Lima: Mosca Azul Editores.

Barrios de Chungara, Domitila, with Moema Viezzer. 1978. *Let Me Speak!* Translated by Victoria Ortiz. New York: Monthly Review Press.

Behar, Ruth. 1993. *Translated Woman.* Boston: Beacon Press.

Behar, Ruth, and Deborah Gordon, eds. 1996. *Women Writing Culture.* Berkeley: University of California Press.

Bejarano, Cynthia. 2002. "Las Supermadres de Latino America: Transforming Motherhood by Challenging Violence in Mexico, Argentina, and El Salvador." *Frontiers* 23 (1): 126–50.

Bennice, Jennifer, and Patricia Resick. 2003. "Marital Rape: History, Research, and Practice." *Trauma, Violence, & Abuse* 4 (3): 228–46.

Boesten, Jelke. 2007. "Free Choice or Poverty Alleviation? Population Politics in Peru under Alberto Fujimori." *European Review of Latin American and Caribbean Studies* 82:3–20.

———. 2006. "Pushing Back the Boundaries: Social Policy, Domestic Violence, and Women's Organizations in Peru." *Journal of Latin American Studies* 38:355–78.

Bordo, Susan. 1993. *Unbearable Weight: Feminism, Western Culture, and the Body.* Berkeley: University of California Press.

Boric, Rada, and Mica Mladineo Desnica. 1996. "Croatia: Three Years After." In *Women in a Violent World*, ed. Chris Corrin, 133–52. Edinburgh: Edinburgh University Press.

Bossio, Enrique. 1995. "Interview with a Gay Activist." In *The Peru Reader*, ed. Orin Starn, Carlos Iván Degregori, and Robin Kirk, 477–81. Durham: Duke University Press.

Breines, Ingeborg, Robert Connell, and Ingrid Eide, eds. 2000. *Male Roles, Masculinities, and Violence: A Culture of Peace Perspective.* Paris: UNESCO.

Brown, Karen McCarthy. 1991. *Mama Lola: A Vodou Priestess in Brooklyn.* Berkeley: University of California Press.

Brown, Michael. 1996. "On Resisting Resistance." *American Anthropologist* 98 (4): 729–35.

Burgos, Elisabeth. 1983. *I, Rigoberta Menchú: An Indian Woman in Guatemala.* London: Verso.

Butler, Judith. 1990. *Gender Trouble: Feminism and the Subversion of Identity.* New York: Routledge.

Buvinic, Mayra. 1996. "Promoting Employment Among the Urban Poor in Latin America and the Caribbean: A Gender Analysis." Development and Technical Cooperation Department, International Labour Office. Discussion Paper 12. Geneva: Issues in Development.

Buvinic, Mayra, Andrew Morrison, and Michael Shifter. 1999. "Violence in Latin America and the Caribbean: A Framework for Action." In Morrison and Biehl 1999, 3–34.

Callirgos, Juan Carlos. 1996. *Sobre heroes y batallas: Los caminos de la identidad masculina.* Lima: Escuela para el Desarrollo.

Campbell, Jacquelyne C. 1999. "Wife-Battering: Cultural Contexts versus Social Sciences." In Counts, Brown, and Campbell 1999.

Canadian International Development Agency. 2002. "Gender Profile in Peru (January 2002)." Available at *www.acdi-cida.gc.ca.*

Canessa, Andrew. 2007. "Commentary on 'Why Would you Marry a Serrana?'" *Journal of Latin American and Caribbean Anthropology* 12 (1): 33–36.

———, ed. 2005. *Natives Making Nation: Gender, Indigeneity, and the State in the Andes.* Tucson: University of Arizona Press.

———. 2005a. "Introduction: Making the Nation on the Margins." In Canessa 2005, 3–31.

———. 2005b. "The Indian Within, the Indian Without: Citizenship, Race, and Sex in a Bolivian Hamlet." In Canessa 2005, 131–55.

Castro, Roberto, Corinne Peek-Asa, and Agustin Ruiz. 2003. "Violence against Women in Mexico: A Study of Abuse Before and During Pregnancy." *American Journal of Public Health* 93 (7): 1110–6.

Chaney, Elsa, and Mary García Castro, eds. 1989. *Muchachas No More: Household Workers in Latin America and the Caribbean.* Philadelphia: Temple University Press.

Chambers, Sarah. 1999. *From Subjects to Citizens: Honor, Gender, and Politics in Arequipa, Peru 1780–1854.* University Park: Penn State University Press.

Chant, Sylvia, with Nikki Craske. 2003. *Gender in Latin America.* New Brunswick: Rutgers University Press.

CLADEM. 1998. *Silencio y complicidad: Violencia contra las mujeres en los servicios públicos de salud en el Perú.* Lima: Comité Latinoamericano y del Caribe para la Defensa de los Derechos de la Mujer.

Collier, Jane, Michelle Z. Rosaldo, and Sylvia Yanagisako. 1997. "Is There a Family? New Anthropological Views." In Lancaster and di Leonardo 1997, 71–81.

Colson, Elizabeth. 1995. "War and Domestic Violence." *Cultural Survival Quarterly* 19 (1): 35–38.

Connell, Robert W. 2000. "Arms and the Man: Using the New Research on Masculinity to Understand Violence and Promote Peace in the Contemporary World." In Breines, Connell, and Eide 2000, 21–33.

———. 1987. *Gender and Power.* Stanford: Stanford University Press.

Córdova Cayo, Patricia. 1996. *Liderazgo femenino en Lima.* Lima: Fundación Friedrich Ebert.

Counts, Dorothy Ayers, Judith K. Brown, and Jacquelyn C. Campbell, eds. 1999. *To Have and to Hit: Cultural Perspectives on Wife Beating*. Champaign: University of Illinois Press.

Crain, Mary. 1996. "The Gendering of Ethnicity in the Ecuadorian Andes: Native Women's Self-Fashioning in the Urban Marketplace." In *Machos, Mistresses, and Madonnas: Contesting the Power of Latin American Gender Imagery*, ed. Marit Melhuus, 134–58. London: Verso.

Crenshaw, Kimberlé Williams. 1991. "Mapping the Margins: Intersectionality, Identity Politics, and Violence Against Women of Color." *Stanford Law Review* 43 (6): 1241–99.

Cubitt, Tessa. 1995. *Latin American Society*. Essex: Longman Group.

D'Alisera, Joann. 1999. "Field of Dreams: The Anthropologist Far Away at Home." *Anthropology and Humanism* 24 (1): 5–19.

Daniel, E. Valentine. 1996. *Charred Lullabies: Chapters in An Anthropology of Violence*. Princeton: Princeton University Press.

Das Dasgupta, Shamita. 2007. *Body Evidence: Intimate Violence against South Asian Women in America*. Piscataway: Rutgers University Press.

Degregori, Carlos Iván. 1998. "Movimientos etnicos, democracia y nación en Peru y Bolivia." In *La construcción de la nación y la representación ciudadana en Mexico, Guatemala, Perú, Ecuador, y Bolivia*, ed. Claudia Dary, 159–226. Guatemala: FLACSO.

———. 1990. *Qué difícil es ser Dios: Ideología y violencia politica en Sendero Luminoso*. Lima: El Zorro de Abajo.

DeKeseredy, Walter, and Carolyn Joseph. 2006. "Separation and/or Divorce Sexual Assault in Rural Ohio: Preliminary Results of an Exploratory Study." *Violence Against Women* 12:301–11.

de la Cadena, Marisol. 2000. *Indigenous Mestizos: The Politics of Race and Culture in Cuzco, Peru, 1919–1991*. Durham: Duke University Press.

———. 1991. "Las mujeres son más indias: Etnicidad y género en una comunidad del Cusco." *Revista Andina* 9 (1): 7–30.

Denegri, Francesca. 2000. *Soy Señora: Testimonio de Irene Jara*. Lima: Flora Tristán.

Dobash, Russell, and Rebecca Emerson Dobash. 1992. *Women, Violence, and Social Change*. New York: Routledge.

———. 1979. *Violence Against Wives: A Case against Patriarchy*. New York: Free Press.

Doughty, Paul. 1968. *Huaylas: An Andean District in Search of Progress*. Ithaca: Cornell University Press.

Driant, Jean-Claude. 1991. *Las barriadas de Lima: Historia e interpretación*. Lima: DESCO.

Edleson, Jeffrey. 1999. "The Overlap Between Child Maltreatment and Woman Battering." *Violence Against Women* 5 (2): 134–54.

Ellsberg, Mary, Lori Heise, Rodolfo Pena, Sonia Agurto, and Anna Winkvist. 2001. "Researching Domestic Violence against Women: Methodological and Ethical Considerations." *Studies in Family Planning* 32 (1): 1–16.

Enloe, Cynthia. 2000. *Maneuvers: The International Politics of Militarizing Women's Lives*. Berkeley: University of California Press.

———. 1987. "Feminist Thinking about War, Militarism and Peace." In *Analyzing Gender: A Handbook of Social Science Research*, ed. Beth B. Hess and Myra Marx Ferree, 526–48. Newbury Park: Sage.

Estremadoyro, Julieta. 2001. "Domestic Violence in Andean Communities of

Peru." *Law, Social Justice and Global Development* 1. Available at www2
.warwick.ac.uk.

Ewig, Christina. 2006. "Hijacking Global Feminism: Feminists, the Catholic
Church, and the Family Planning Debacle in Peru." *Feminist Studies* 32 (3):
633–59.

Farmer, Paul. 2004. "An Anthropology of Structural Violence." *Current
Anthropology* 45:305–25.

Farmer, Paul, Margaret Connors, and Jane Simmons, eds. 1996. *Women, Poverty
and AIDS: Sex, Drugs and Structural Violence.* Monroe: Common Courage
Press.

Femenías, Blenda. 2005. *Gender and the Boundaries of Dress in Contemporary
Peru.* Austin: University of Texas Press.

Fernández, Graciela, and Richard Webb. 2002. *Perú en números 2002.* Lima:
Instituto Cuánto.

Ferraro, Kathleen J. 1996. "The Dance of Dependency: A Genealogy of Domestic
Violence Discourse." *Hypatia* 11 (4): 77–91.

Finkelhor, David, Gerald Hotaling, and Kersti Yllö. 1988. *Stopping Family
Violence: Research Priorities for the Coming Decade.* Newbury Park: Sage.

Foucault, Michel. 1978. *Discipline and Punish.* New York: Vintage Books.

Freire, Paulo. 1973. *Education for Critical Consciousness.* New York: Seabury.

Frye, David. 1996. *Indians into Mexicans: History and Identity in a Mexican Town.*
Austin: University of Texas Press.

Fuller, Norma. 2003. "The Social Constitution of Gender among Peruvian Males."
In Gutmann 2003, 134–152.

———. 2001. *Masculinidades: Cambios y permanencias.* Lima: Fondo Editorial de la
Pontificia Universidad Católica del Perú.

———. 1996. "Los estudios sobre masculinidad en el Perú." In Ruiz-Bravo 1996,
39–56.

Gagnon, John H., and Richard G. Parker. 1995. *Conceiving Sexuality: Approaches
to Sex Research in a Postmodern World.* London: Routledge.

Galtung, Johan. 1969. "Violence, Peace, and Peace Research." *Journal of Peace
Research* 6 (3): 167–91.

García, María Elena. 2005. *Making Indigenous Citizens: Identity, Development, and
Multicultural Activism in Peru.* Stanford: Stanford University Press.

———. 2000. "Ethnographic Responsibility and the Anthropological Endeavor:
Beyond Identity Discourse." *Anthropological Quarterly* 73 (2): 89–101.

García Ríos, José Maria, and Giulia Tamayo. 1990. *Mujer y varón: Vida cotidiana,
violencia, y justicia: Tres miradas desde El Agustino, 1977–1984–1990.* Lima:
Ediciones Raíces y Alas.

Gelles, Richard J., and Donileen R. Loseke, eds. 1993. *Current Controversies on
Family Violence.* Newbury Park: Sage.

Gill, Lesley. 2004. *The School of the Americas.* Durham: Duke University Press.

Ginsburg, Faye. 1989. *Contested Lives: The Abortion Debate in an American
Community.* Berkeley: University of California Press.

Ginsburg, Faye, and Rayna Rapp. 1995. *Conceiving the New World Order: The
Global Politics of Reproduction.* Berkeley: University of California Press.

Glenn, D. M., J. C. Beckham, M. E. Feldman, A. C. Kirby, M. Á. Hertzberg, and S.
D. Moore. 2002. "Violence and Hostility among Families of Vietnam Veterans
with Combat-Related Posttraumatic Stress Disorder." *Violence and Victims*
17:473–89.

Glissant, Édouard. 1989. *Caribbean Discourse: Selected Essays*. Translated by Michael Dash. Charlottesville: University Press of Virginia.

Gluck, Sherna Berger, and Daphne Patai. 1991. *Women's Words: The Feminist Practice of Oral History*. New York: Routledge.

Goldstein, Daniel. 2004. *The Spectacular City: Violence and Performance in Urban Bolivia*. Durham: Duke University Press.

Goldstein, Donna. 2003. *Laughter Out of Place: Race, Class, Sexuality, and Violence in a Rio Shantytown*. Berkeley: University of California Press.

Gonzales de Olarte, Efrain, and Pilar Gavilano Llosa.1999. "Does Poverty Cause Domestic Violence? Some Answers from Lima?" In Morrison and Biehl 1999, 35–50.

Gonzalez-Lopez, Gloria. 2005. *Erotic Journeys: Mexican Immigrants and their Sex Lives*. Berkeley: University of California Press.

Gordon, Linda. 1988. *Heroes of Their Own Lives: The Politics and History of Family Violence*. New York: Viking.

Gow, Peter, and Penelope Harvey, eds. 1994. *Sex and Violence*. New York: Routledge.

Gould, Jeffrey. 1990. *To Lead as Equals: Rural Protest and Political Consciousness in Chinandega, Nicaragua, 1912–1979*. Chapel Hill: University of North Carolina Press.

Graham-Bermann, Sandra, and Alytia Levendosky. 1998. "Traumatic Stress Symptoms in Children of Battered Women." *Journal of Interpersonal Violence* 13 (1): 111–28.

Green, Linda. 1994. "Fear as a Way of Life." *Cultural Anthropology* 9 (2): 227–56.

Greene, Shane. 2007. "Entre lo indio, lo negro, y lo incaico: The Spatial Hierarchies of Difference in Multicultural Peru." *Journal of Latin American and Caribbean Anthropology* 12 (2): 441–74.

Gremillion, Helen. 2003. *Feeding Anorexia: Gender and Power at a Treatment Center*. Durham: Duke University Press.

Griffiths, Sue. 2000. "Women, Anger, and Domestic Violence: The Implications for Legal Defences to Murder." In Hanmer and Itzin 2000, 133–52.

Güezmes, Ana, Nancy Palomino, and Miguel Ramos. 2002. *Violencia sexual y física contra las mujeres en el Perú*. Lima: Flora Tristán.

Gutmann, Matthew. 2007. *Fixing Men: Sex, Birth Control, and AIDS in Mexico*. Berkeley: University of California Press.

———, ed. 2003. *Changing Men and Masculinities in Latin America*. Durham: Duke University Press.

———. 1996. *The Meanings of Macho: Being a Man in Mexico City*. Berkeley: University of California Press.

Guzmán, Virginia, and Patricia Portocarrero. 1992. *Construyendo diferencias*. Lima: Flora Tristán.

Hanmer, Jalna, and Catherine Itzin, eds. 2000. *Home Truths about Domestic Violence: Feminist Influences on Policy and Practice*. New York: Routledge.

Harris, Olivia. 1994. "Condor and Bull: The Ambiguities of Masculinity in Northern Potosí." In Gow and Harvey 1994, 40–65.

Hart, Gillian. 1991. "Engendering Everyday Resistance: Gender, Patronage, and Production Politics in Rural Malaysia." *Journal of Peasant Studies* 19 (1): 93–121.

Harvey, Penelope. 1994. "Domestic Violence in the Peruvian Andes." In Gow and Harvey, 68–89.

Hautzinger, Sarah. 2007. *Violence in the City of Women: Police and Batterers in Bahia, Brazil*. Berkeley: University of California Press.

Heise, Lori. 1998. "Violence against Women: An Integrated, Ecological Framework." *Violence Against Women* 4 (3): 262–90.

———. 1997. "Violence, Sexuality, and Women's Lives." In Lancaster and di Leonardo, 411–33.

Heise, Lori, Mary Ellsberg, and Megan Gottemoeller. 1999. *Ending Violence Against Women. Population Reports, Series L, No. 11*. Baltimore: Johns Hopkins University School of Public Health, Population Information Program.

Henríquez, Narda. 1996. "Las señoras dirigentes, experiencias de ciudadanía en barrios populares." In Ruiz-Bravo 1996, 145–61.

Hinton, Alexander Laban. 2002. *Annihilating Difference: The Anthropology of Genocide*. Berkeley: University of California Press.

Hijar, Martha. 1992. "Violencia y lesiones." *Salud Pública* 15:15–23.

Hoff, Lee Ann. 1990. *Battered Women as Survivors*. New York: Routledge.

Hollander, Jocelyn, and Rachel Einwohner. 2004. "Conceptualizing Resistance." *Sociological Forum* 19 (4): 533–54.

hooks, bell. 1989. *Talking Back: Thinking Feminist, Thinking Black*. Cambridge: South End Press.

Human Rights Watch. 2000. "Peru: Law of Protection from Family Violence." Memorandum, March 31. New York: Human Rights Watch.

Hunefeldt, Christine. 2000. *Liberalism in the Bedroom: Quarreling Spouses in Nineteenth Century Lima*. University Park: Penn State University Press.

ICRW. 2003. *How to Make the Law Work? Budgetary Implications of Domestic Violence Policies in Latin America*. Washington, DC: International Center for Research on Women.

Isbell, Billie Jean. 1978. *To Defend Ourselves: Ecology and Ritual in an Andean Village*. Austin: University of Texas Press.

Itzin, Catherine. 2000. "Gendering Domestic Violence: The Influence of Feminism on Policy and Practice." In Hanmer, and Itzin, 356–80.

Jackson, Jean. 1995. "Culture, Genuine and Spurious: The Politics of Indianness in Vaupés, Colombia." *American Ethnologist* 22 (1): 3–27.

Jelin, Elizabeth, and Ana Rita Diaz-Muñoz. 2003. "Major Trends affecting Families: South America in Perspective." New York: United Nations Department of Economic and Social Affairs Division for Social Policy and Development Programme on the Family. Available at *www.un.org*.

Kabeer, Naila. 1999. "Resources, Agency, Achievements: Reflections on the Measurement of Women's Empowerment." *Development and Change* 30 (3): 435–65.

Kelly, Liz. 2000. "Wars Against Women: Sexual Violence, Sexual Politics, and the Militarised State." In *States of Conflict: Gender Violence and Resistance*, ed. Susie Jacobs, Ruth Jacobson, and Jennifer Marchbank, 45–65. London: Zed Books.

Kimmel, Michael. 2000. "Reducing Men's Violence: The Personal Meets the Political." In Breines, Connell, and Eide 2000, 239–47.

Kirk, Robin. 1993. *Grabado en piedra: Las mujeres de Sendero Luminoso*. Lima: Instituto de Estudios Peruanos.

Kokotovic, Misha. 2007. *The Colonial Divide in Peruvian Narrative: Social Conflict and Transculturation*. Portland: Sussex Academic Press.

Kondo, Dorinne. 1990. *Crafting Selves: Power, Gender and Discourses of Identity in a Japanese Workplace*. Chicago: University of Chicago Press.

Kuumba, M. Bahati, and Femi Ajanaku. 1998. "Dreadlocks: The Hair Aesthetics of Cultural Resistance and Collective Identity Formation." *Mobilization* 3:227–43.

Lamphere, Louise, Helena Ragoné, and Patricia Zavella, eds. 1997. *Situated Lives: Gender and Culture in Everyday Life*. New York: Routledge.

Lancaster, Roger N., and Micaela di Leonardo, eds. 1997. *The Gender/Sexuality Reader: Culture, History, Political Economy*. New York: Routledge.

Larson, Brooke. 2004. *Trials of Nation-Making: Liberalism, Race, and Ethnicity in the Andes 1810–1910*. Cambridge: Cambridge University Press.

Lather, Patti, and Chris Smithies. 1997. *Troubling the Angels: Women Living with HIV/AIDS*. Boulder: Westview Press.

Lavrin, Asunción, ed. 1989. *Sexuality and Marriage in Colonial Latin America*. Lincoln: University of Nebraska Press.

Lazarus-Black, Mindie. 2007. *Everyday Harm: Domestic Violence, Court Rites, and Cultures of Reconciliation*. Urbana: University of Illinois Press.

Leinaweaver, Jessaca. 2008a. *The Circulation of Children: Kinship, Adoption, and Morality in Andean Peru*. Durham: Duke University Press.

———. 2008b. "Improving Oneself: Young People Getting Ahead in the Peruvian Andes." *Latin American Perspectives* 35 (4): 65–78.

Levinson, David. 1989. *Family Violence in Cross-Cultural Perspective*. Thousand Oaks: Sage.

Lewin, Ellen. 1993. *Lesbian Mothers: Accounts of Gender in American Culture*. Ithaca: Cornell University Press.

López, Iris. 1994. "The Social Construction of Reproductive 'Choice': An Ethnographic Study of Puerto Rican Women and Sterilization in New York City." In *Gender and Puerto Rican Women*, ed. Alice Colon. Rio Piedras: CERES, CIS, and the Universidad de Puerto Rico.

Malkki, Liisa. 1995. *Purity and Exile: Violence, Memory, and National Cosmology among Hutu Refugees in Tanzania*. Chicago: University of Chicago Press.

MacLeod, Arlene. 1993. *Accommodating Protest*. New York: Columbia University Press.

———. 1992. "Hegemonic Relations and Gender Resistance: The New Veiling as Accommodating Protest in Cairo." *Signs* 17 (3): 533–57.

Mahoney, Maureen, and Barbara Yngvesson. 1992. "The Construction of Subjectivity and the Paradox of Resistance: Reintegrating Feminist Anthropology and Psychology." *Signs* 18 (1): 44–73.

Mallon, Florencia. 2002. *When a Flower is Reborn: The Life and Times of a Mapuche Feminist, Rosa Isolde Reuque Paillalef*. Durham: Duke University Press.

Martin, Del. 1976. *Battered Wives*. New York: Pocket Books.

Martin, Emily. 1987. *The Woman in the Body: A Cultural Analysis of Reproduction*. Boston: Beacon Press.

Marzal, Manuel. 1995. *Historia de la antropología indigenista: México y Perú*. Lima: Fondo Editorial de la Pontificia Universidad Católica del Perú.

Matos Mar, José. 1984. *Desborde popular y crisis del Estado*. Lima: Instituto de Estudios Peruanos.

McClintock, Cynthia. 2001. "Peru's Sendero Luminoso Rebellion: Origins and Trajectory." In *Power and Popular Protest: Latin American Social Movements*, ed. Susan Eckstein, 61–101. Berkeley: University of California Press.

McClusky, Laura. 2001. *"Here Our Culture is Hard": Stories of Domestic Violence from a Mayan Community in Belize*. Austin: University of Texas Press.

McWhirter, Paula. 1999. "La violencia privada: Domestic Violence in Chile." *American Psychologist* 54:37–40.

Méndez G., Cecilia. 1996. "Incas Sí, Indios No: Notes on Peruvian Creole Nationalism and Its Contemporary Crisis." *Journal of Latin American Studies* 28 (1): 197–225.

Merino, Beatriz. 1997. *Matrimonio y violación: El debate del Artículo 178 del Código Penal*. Lima: Movimiento Manuela Ramos.

Merry, Sally Engle. 2006. *Human Rights and Gender Violence: Translating International Law into Local Justice*. Chicago: University of Chicago Press.

Miller, Susan. 2005. *Victims as Offenders: The Paradox of Women's Violence in Relationships*. New Brunswick: Rutgers University Press.

Miloslavich Tupac, Diana, and Maria Elena Moyano. 2000. *The Autobiography of Maria Elena Moyano: The Life and Death of a Peruvian Activist*. Gainesville: University Press of Florida.

MIMDES. 2007. *Detrás del mandil*. Lima: Ministerio de la Mujer y Desarrollo Social.

Mirandé, Alfredo. 1997. *Hombres y Machos: Masculinity and Latino Culture*. Boulder: Westview Press.

Mires, Fernando. 1991 *El discurso de la indianidad*. San José, Costa Rica: DEI.

Mitchell, William. 2006. *Voices from the Global Margin: Confronting Poverty and Inventing New Lives in the Andes*. Austin: University of Texas Press.

Mohanty, Chandra. 1991. "Under Western Eyes: Feminist Scholarship and Colonial Discourses." In *Third World Women and the Politics of Feminism*, ed. Chandra Mohanty, Ann Russo, and Lourdes Torres, 51–80. Bloomington: Indiana University Press.

Mooney, Jayne. 2000. *Gender, Violence, and the Social Order*. New York: St. Martin's Press.

Moore, Henrietta. 1994. *A Passion for Difference: Essays in Anthropology and Gender*. Oxford: Polity Press.

Morrison, Andrew R., and María Loreto Biehl, eds. 1999. *Too Close to Home: Domestic Violence in the Latin America*. Washington, DC: Inter-American Development Bank.

Moser, Annalise. 2004. "Happy Heterogeneity? Feminism, Development, and the Grassroots Women's Movement in Peru." *Feminist Studies* 30 (1): 211–37.

Movimiento Manuela Ramos. 2007. *Evaluacion de la ruta critica del sistema policial-judicial en los casos de violencia familiar en los distritos de San Juan de Miraflores, Villa El Salvador, y Villa Maria del Triunfo*. Lima: Movimiento Manuela Ramos.

———. 2003. *Opening Our Eyes: A Work Experience with Men on Gender Issues and Sexual and Reproductive Health*. Lima: Movimiento Manuela Ramos.

———. 1998. *La violencia contra la mujer*. Lima: Movimiento Manuela Ramos.

Murrell, Amy, Karen Christoff, and Kris Henning. 2007. "Characteristics of Domestic Violence Offenders: Associations with Childhood Exposure to Violence." *Journal of Family Violence* 22:523–32.

Myerhoff, Barbara. 1978. *Number Our Days*. New York: Dutton.

Narayan, Kirin. 1993. "How 'Native' is a 'Native' Anthropologist?" *American Anthropologist* 95 (3): 671–86.

Narayan, Uma. 1997. *Dislocating Cultures: Identities, Traditions, and Third World Feminism*. New York: Routledge.

Nelson, Sara. 1996. "Constructing and Negotiating Gender in Women's Police Stations in Brazil." *Latin American Perspectives* 88:131–48.

Nencel, Lorraine. 2000. *Mujeres que se prostituyen: Género, identidad y pobreza.* Lima: Flora Tristán.

Nordstrom, Carolyn, and Antonius C. G. M. Robben. 1995. *Fieldwork Under Fire: Contemporary Studies of Violence and Survival.* Berkeley: University of California Press.

Nugent, José Guillermo. 1992. *El laberinto de la choledad.* Lima: Fundación Friedrich Ebert.

Oboler, Suzanne. 2005. "The Foreignness of Racism: Pride and Prejudice among Peru's Limeños in the 1990s." In *Neither Enemies nor Friends: Latinos, Blacks, Afro-Latinos,* ed. Anani Dzidzienyo and Suzanne Oboler, 75–100. New York: Palgrave Macmillan.

Olmedo, Irma. 2003. "Accommodation and Resistance: Latinas Struggle for Their Children's Education." *Anthropology and Education Quarterly* 34 (4): 373–95.

Olson, Karen, and Linda Shopes. 1991. "Crossing Boundaries, Building Bridges: Doing Oral History with Working-Class Women." In Gluck and Patai 1991, 189–204.

Ong, Aihwa. 1987. *Spirits of Resistance and Capitalist Discipline.* Albany: State University of New York Press.

O'Reilly, Andrea. 2006. *Rocking the Cradle: Thoughts on Motherhood, Feminism and the Possibility of Empowered Mothering.* Toronto: Demeter Press.

———, ed. 2004. *Mother Outlaws: Theories and Practices of Empowered Mothering.* Toronto: Women's Press.

Orlove, Benjamin. 1993. "Putting Race in Its Place: Order in Colonial and Post-Colonial Peruvian Geography." *Social Research* 60 (2): 301–36.

Ortner, Sherry B. 1996. "Resistance and the Problem of Ethnographic Refusal." In *The Historic Turn in the Human Sciences,* ed. Terrence J. McDonald, 281–304. Ann Arbor: University of Michigan Press.

Ossio, Juan. 1994. *Las paradojas del Perú oficial: Indigenismo, democracia y crisis structural.* Lima: Fondo Editorial de la Pontificia Universidad Católica del Peru.

Palmer, David Scott. 1992. *Shining Path of Peru.* New York: Palgrave Macmillan.

Panourgiá, Neni. 1994. "A Native Narrative." *Anthropology and Humanism* 19 (1): 40–51.

Patai, Daphne. 1991. "U.S. Academics and Third World Women: Is Ethical Research Possible?" In Gluck and Patai 1991, 137–54.

Paulson, Susan. 1996. "Familias que no 'conyugan' e identidades que no conjugan: La vida en Mizque desafía nuestras categorías." In *Ser mujer indígena, chola, birlocha en la Bolivia postcolonial de los años 90,* ed. Silvia Rivera Cusicanqui, 85–161. La Paz: Subsecretaría de Asuntos de Género.

Paz, Octavio. 1959 [1950]. *El laberinto de la soledad.* Mexico City: Fondo de Cultura Económica.

Pecora, Peter, James Whittaker, and Anthony Maluccio, with Richard Barth and Robert Plotnick. 1992. *The Child Welfare Challenge: Policy, Practice, and Research.* New York: Aldine Transaction.

Perales, Maria Teresa, Swee May Cripe, Nelly Lam, Sixto Sanchez, Elena Sanchez, and Michelle Williams. 2009. "Prevalence, Types, and Pattern of Intimate Partner Violence Among Pregnant Women in Lima, Peru." *Violence Against Women* 15 (2): 224–50.

Physicians for Human Rights. 2007. *Deadly Delays: Maternal Mortality in Peru.* Cambridge: Physicians for Human Rights.

Pine, Adrienne. 2008. *Working Hard, Drinking Hard: On Violence and Survival in Honduras*. Berkeley: University of California Press.

Pleck, Elizabeth H. 2004. *Domestic Tyranny: The Making of American Social Policy Against Family Violence From Colonial Times to the Present*. Champaign: University of Illinois Press.

Plesset, Sonja. 2006. *Sheltering Women: Negotiating Gender and Violence in Northern Italy*. Stanford: Stanford University Press.

Ponce, Ana. 2007. "'Padre y madre para mis hijos': Las familias dirigidas por mujeres." In Barrig 2007, 95–120.

Poole, Deborah, and Gerardo Rénique. 1992. *Peru: Time of Fear*. London: Latin America Bureau.

———. 1991. "The New Chroniclers of Peru: U.S. Scholars and their 'Shining Path' of Rebellion." *Bulletin of Latin American Research* 10 (2): 193–221.

Portocarrero, Gonzalo. 2007. *Racismo y mestizaje*. Lima: Ediciones del Congreso del Perú.

PROMUDEH. 2000. *Manual de legislación para la prevención y atención de la violencia familiar*. Lima: Ministerio de Promoción de la Mujer y Desarrollo Humano.

Quijano, Aníbal. 1980. *Dominación y cultura: lo cholo y el conflicto cultural en el Perú*. Lima: Mosca Azul.

Radcliffe, Sarah, and Sallie Westwood. 1996. *Remaking the Nation: Place, Identity and Politics in Latin America*. New York: Routledge.

Raj, Anita, Kai Livramento, M. Christina Santana, Jhumka Gupta, and Jay Silverman. 2006. "Victims of Intimate Partner Violence More Likely to Report Abuse From In-Laws." *Violence Against Women* 12 (10): 936–49.

Ramos, Miguel Ángel. 2006. *Masculinidades y violencia conyugal: Experiencias de vida de hombres de sectores populares de Lima y Cusco*. Lima: Universidad Peruana Cayetano Heredia.

Reidner, Ellen. 2004. "Using Freirean Empowerment for Health Education With Adolescents in Primary, Secondary, and Tertiary Psychiatric Settings." *Journal of Child and Adolescent Psychiatric Nursing* 17 (2): 78–84.

Rich, Adrienne. 1986. *Of Woman Born: Motherhood as Experience and Institution*. New York: W.W. Norton.

Rivera Cusicanqui, Silvia. 1996. "Trabajo de mujeres: explotación capitalista y opresión colonial entre las migrantes aymaras de La Paz y El Alto, Bolivia." In *Ser mujer indígena, chola, o birlocha en la Bolivia postcolonial de los años 90*, ed. Silvia Rivera Cusicanqui, 163–300. La Paz: Subsecretaría de Asuntos de Género.

Robben, Antonius C. G. M. 1996. "Ethnographic Seduction, Transference, and Resistance in Dialogues about Terror and Violence in Argentina." *Ethos* 24 (1): 71–106.

Robben, Antonius C. G. M., and Marcelo Suarez-Orozco. 2000. *Cultures Under Siege: Collective Violence and Trauma*. Cambridge: Cambridge University Press.

Rodriguez, Lilia. 1994. "Barrio Women: Between the Urban and the Feminist Movement." *Latin American Perpectives* 21 (3): 32–48.

Ruiz-Bravo, Patricia. 2001. *Sub-versiones masculinas: Imágenes del varón en la narrativa joven*. Lima: Flora Tristán.

———, ed. 1996. *Detrás de la puerta: Hombres y mujeres en el Perú de hoy*. Lima: Pontificia Universidad Católica del Perú.

Saavedra, Jaime, Maximo Torero, and Hugo Ñopo. 2002. *Social Exclusion in Peru: An Invisible Wall*. Lima: Grupo de Análisis para el Desarrollo.

Sagaria, Mary Ann D. 2000. "Constructions of Feminism in Unequal Relationships: A Personal Account from a North American in a Cross-Cultural Household." *NWSA Journal* 12 (1): 100–118.

Salazar, Claudia. 1991. "A Third World Woman's Text: Between the Politics of Criticism and Cultural Politics." Gluck and Patai, 1991, 93–106.

Santos, Cecilia MacDowell. 2005. *Women's Police Stations: Gender, Violence, and Justice in São Paulo, Brazil*. New York: Palgrave Macmillan.

Sawicki, Jana. 1991. *Disciplining Foucault: Feminism, Power, and the Body*. New York: Routledge.

Scheper-Hughes, Nancy. 1995. "The Primacy of the Ethical: Propositions for a Militant Anthropology." *Current Anthropology* 36 (3): 409–40.

———. 1992. *Death Without Weeping: The Violence of Everyday Life in Brazil*. Berkeley: University of California Press.

Scheper-Hughes, Nancy, and Philippe Bourgois, eds. 2004. *Violence in War and Peace: An Anthology*. Malden: Blackwell Publishing.

Schmidt, Bettina, and Ingo Schroeder, eds. 2001. *Anthropology of Violence and Conflict*. New York: Routledge.

Schneider, Elizabeth M. 2000. *Battered Women and Feminist Lawmaking*. New Haven: Yale University Press.

Scott, Alison MacEwen. 1994. *Divisions and Solidarities: Gender, Class, and Employment in Latin America*. New York: Routledge.

Scott, James. 1985. *Weapons of the Weak: Everyday Forms of Peasant Resistance*. New Haven: Yale University Press.

Seidler, Victor. 2005. *Transforming Masculinities: Men, Cultures, Bodies, Power, Sex and Love*. New York: Routledge.

Seligmann, Linda J. 2004. *Peruvian Street Lives: Culture, Power, and Economy among Market Women of Cuzco*. Champaign: University of Illinois Press.

Sivaramakrishnan, K. 2005. "Some Intellectual Genealogies for the Concept of Everyday Resistance." *American Anthropologist* 107 (3): 346–55.

Sluka, Jeffrey, ed. 1999. *Death Squad: The Anthropology of State Terror*. Philadelphia: University of Pennsylvania Press.

Snajdr, Edward. 2005. "Gender, Power, and the Performance of Justice: Muslim Women's Responses to Domestic Violence in Kazakhstan." *American Anthropologist* 32 (2): 294–311.

Sokoloff, Natalie, and Ida Dupont. 2005. "Domestic Violence at the Intersections of Race, Class, and Gender." *Violence Against Women* 11 (1): 38–64.

Solomon, Zahavi. 1988. "The Effect of Combat-Related Posttraumatic Stress Disorder on the Family." *Psychiatry* 51:323–29.

Sommer, Doris. 1994. "Resistant Texts and Incompetent Readers." *Poetics Today* 15 (4): 523–51.

Spitta, Silvia. 2007. "Lima the Horrible: The Cultural Politics of Theft." *PMLA* 122 (1): 294–300.

Starn, Orin. 1999. *Nightwatch: The Politics of Protest in the Andes*. Durham: Duke University Press.

———. 1995. "Maoism in the Andes: The Communist Party of Peru–Shining Path and the Refusal of History." *Journal of Latin American Studies* 27 (2): 399–421.

Stanko, Elizabeth. 1985. *Intimate Intrusions: Women's Experience of Male Violence*. New York: Routledge.

Stephen, Lynn. 1997. *Women and Social Movements in Latin America: Power from Below*. Austin: University of Texas Press.

Stephenson, Marcia. 1999. *Gender and Modernity in Andean Bolivia*. Austin: University of Texas Press.

Stern, Steve, ed. 1998. *Shining and Other Paths: War and Society in Peru, 1980–1995*. Durham: Duke University Press.

Sternbach, Nancy S. 1991. "Re-membering the Dead: Latin American Women's Testimonial Discourse." *Latin American Perspectives* 18 (3): 91–102.

Stokes, Susan. 1995. *Cultures in Conflicts: Social Movements and the State in Peru*. Berkeley: University of California Press.

Stoll, David. 1998. *Rigoberta Menchú and the Story of All Poor Guatemalans*. Boulder: Westview Press.

Strathern, Andrew, Pamela Stewart, and Neil Whitehead, eds. 2005. *Terror and Violence: Imagination and the Unimaginable*. London: Pluto Press.

Straus, Murray A. 1993. "Women's Violence Toward Men is a Serious Social Problem." In Gelles and Loseke 1993, 55–78.

Straus, Murray A., and Richard J. Gelles, eds. 1990. *Physical Violence in American Families: Risk Factors and Adaptations to Violence in 8,145 Families*. New Brunswick: Transactions.

———. 1988. *Intimate Violence*. New York: Simon and Schuster.

Straus, Murray A., and Michael Kantor. 1987. "The Drunken Bum Theory of Wife Beating." *Social Problems* (34): 213–30.

Swanson, Kate. 2007. "'Bad Mothers' and 'Delinquent Children': Unraveling Anti-Begging Rhetoric in the Ecuadorian Andes." *Gender, Place, and Culture* 14 (6): 703–20.

Tam, Son-Yum, and Yan Tang. 2005. "Comparing Wife Abuse Perceptions Between Chinese Police Officers and Social Workers." *Journal of Family Violence* 20:29–38.

Theidon, Kimberly. 2004. *Entre prójimos: El conflict armado interno y la política de la reconciliación en el Perú*. Lima: Instituto de Estudios Peruanos.

Tishkov, Valery. 2004. *Chechnya: Life in a War-Torn Society*. Berkeley: University of California Press.

Tjaden, Patricia, and Nancy Thoennes. 2000. *Extent, Nature, and Consequences of Intimate Partner Violence: A Research Report*. Washington, DC: National Institute of Justice and the Centers for Disease Control and Prevention.

Tula, Maria Teresa. 1994. *Hear My Testimony: Maria Teresa Tula, Human Rights Activist*. Boston: South End Press.

Truth and Reconciliation Committee. 2003. *Informe final*. Lima: Comisión de la Verdad y Reconciliación.

UNICEF. 2001. "Mexico: Violencia y maltrato." Available at *www.unicef.org*.

Usta, Jinan, Jo Ann M. Farver, and Lama Zein. 2008. "Women, War, and Violence: Surviving the Experience." *Journal of Women's Health* 17 (5): 793–804.

Valcárcel, Luis. 1972 [1927]. *Tempestad en los Andes*. Lima: Editora Amauta.

Valderrama, Ricardo, and Carmen Escalante. 1996. *Andean Lives: Gregorio Condori Mamani and Asunta Quispe Huamán*. Austin: University of Austin Press.

Vallenas, Sandra. 2007. "De las AQV a las AOE: Diez años de políticas en salud sexual y reproductiva." In Barrig 2007, 279–304.

Van Vleet, Krista. 2008. *Performing Kinship Narrative, Gender, and the Intimacies of Power in the Andes*. Austin: University of Texas Press.

Vargas, Virginia. 1996. "Las actuales vertientes del movimiento de mujeres." In Ruiz-Bravo 1996, 105–43.

Vega-Centeno, Imelda. 2000. *Imaginario femenino? Cultura, historia, política y poder*. Lima: Escuela para el Desarrollo.

Vigier, Maria Elena. 1986. *El Impacto del PAIT en el Empleo y los Ingresos: Lima Metropolitana 1986*. Lima: Proyecto Planificacion del Mercado Laboral, Organizacion Internacional del Trabajo (OIT).

Visweswaran, Kamala. 1994. *Fictions of Feminist Ethnography*. Minneapolis: University of Minnesota Press.

Viveros, Mara. 2003. "Contemporary Latin American Perspectives on Masculinity." In Gutmann 2003, 27–60.

Wade, Peter. 1993. *Blackness and Race Mixture: The Dynamics of Racial Identity in Colombia*. Baltimore: Johns Hopkins University Press.

Wallace, James M. 1984 "Urban Anthropology in Lima: An Overview." *Latin American Research Review* 19 (3): 57–85.

Warwick, Nancy. 1997. "Patterns of Diversity and Forms of Interpretation: A Cultural Analysis of Immigrant Mexican Women who have been Battered." PhD dissertation, UCLA.

Weismantel, Mary. 2001. *Cholas and Pishtacos: Stories of Race and Sex in the Andes*. Chicago: University of Chicago Press.

———. 1998. *Food, Gender, and Poverty in the Ecuadorian Andes*. Long Grove: Waveland Press.

Wheaton, Belinda, and Ann Tomlinson. 1998. "The Changing Gender Order in Sport? The Case of Windsurfing." *Journal of Sport and Social Issues* 22:252–74.

Wolf, Marsha, Ly Uyen, Margaret Hobart, and Mary Kernic. 2003. "Barriers to Seeking Police Help for Intimate Partner Violence." *Journal of Family Violence* 18:121–29.

WHO. 2001. *Putting Women's Safety First: Ethical and Safety Recommendations for Research on Domestic Violence Against Women*. Geneva: World Heath Organization.

Yanaylle, Maria Elena. 1996. "Tiene ventiocho años y aún es virgen: femineidad y estereotipo de la mujer sin pareja." In Ruiz-Bravo 1996, 73–90.

Yllö, Kersti. 1993. "Through A Feminist Lens: Gender, Power and Violence." In Gelles and Loseke 1993, 47–62.

Yllö, Kersti, and Murray A. Straus. 1990. "Patriarchy and Violence against Wives: The Impact of Structural and Normative Factors." In Straus and Gelles 1990, 383–99.

Yon, Carmen. 1998. *Género y sexualidad: Una mirada de los y las adolescentes de cinco barrios de Lima*. Lima: Movimiento Manuela Ramos.

Zamudio, Delia. 1995. *Piel de Mujer*. Lima: Fomento de la Vida.

Zavella, Patricia. 1997. "Feminist Insider Dilemmas: Constructing Ethnic Identity with Chicana Informants." In Lamphere, Ragoné, and Zavella 1997, 42–61.

# Index

*Page numbers in bold indicate illustrations.*